WELFARE IN NEWLY-INDUSTRIALISED SOCIETY

To Kwan

Welfare in Newly-Industrialised Society

The Construction of the Welfare State in Hong Kong

RAYMOND K. H. CHAN
Department of Applied Social Studies
City University of Hong Kong

Avebury
Aldershot • Brookfield USA • Hong Kong • Singapore • Sydney

Published by
Avebury
Ashgate Publishing Limited
Gower House
Croft Road
Aldershot
Hants GU11 3HR
England

Ashgate Publishing Company
Old Post Road
Brookfield
Vermont 05036
USA

British Library Cataloguing in Publication Data

Chan, Raymond
Welfare in newly industrialised society : the construction of the welfare state in Hong Kong
1. Welfare state 2. Hong Kong - Social policy
I. Title
361.6 ' 5 ' 095125

ISBN 1 85972 464 7

Library of Congress Catalog Card Number: 96-86167

Printed and bound by Athenaeum Press, Ltd., Gateshead, Tyne & Wear.

Contents

Figures and Tables

Foreword

In recent years there has been a significant shift away from largely descriptive, and frequently prescriptive analyses of the welfare state to accounts which combine empirical and historical work with theoretical frameworks derived, in the main, from sociology and political science. These efforts have resulted in an immense improvement in our understanding of how and why welfare states have become an indispensable component of all advanced industrial countries, and of the dynamics of their development.

However, most of this pioneering work has focused on a relatively limited range of welfare states, especially those of Western Europe, North America and a few others. Much less attention has been paid to welfare states elsewhere, and yet the growth of social expenditure and welfare state institutions is a central feature of a far wider range of nations than these studies consider, or than their theories can necessarily encompass. The situation in the newly industrialising countries of the Far East and South East Asia is of particular interest, both from a theoretical perspective and because of the distinctively different relationships between economic and welfare state development that some of them exhibit.

Raymond Chan's study of the development of Hong Kong's welfare state is one of the very few examples so far of research which applies the new theoretical insights developed by recent welfare state research to the situation of a non-western advanced industrial (or 'post-industrial') society. As he notes, previous studies of the remarkable growth of Hong Kong's system of publicly funded housing, health, education and social services provision have lacked any adequate theoretical framework, being largely descriptive rather than analytical, and frequently as concerned to sustain what are basically political and normative as social scientific concerns.

His book provides us with a clear and persuasive analysis of the forces and factors which have driven the expansion of Hong Kong's welfare state in recent decades, based on detailed case studies of housing, health and education. One serious disadvantage of many Western academics' attempts to understand non-western welfare states is, of course, the relatively limited access that most of them have had, for linguistic and other reasons, to the full range of statistical, documentary and other sources of information about the developments that they are attempting to analyse. All too frequently what results is thinly descriptive accounts, based on limited and official sources, which lack any analytical or critical cutting edge.

By contrast, Chan's study is based on a rich and previously unexploited array of empirical material - statistics, official reports and debates, the media and, most notably, a unique series of interviews with many of the key actors in the development of Hong Kong's welfare state over the past three decades - leading government officials, politicians, business and community leaders, and so on. This effort has enabled him to produce the most authoritative account so far available of the economic, political, social and cultural factors which have moulded the development of Hong Kong's fascinating blend of a dynamic, market-based economy and large scale welfare expenditure and institutional development. He is able to provide a rigorous examination of different theories of the welfare state in the course of this account, comparing and contrasting their ability to explain the reasons for this distinctively constructed welfare capitalist regime.

A further important aspect of Chan's study is his attention to the shifting basis, over time, of the motive forces behind Hong Kong's welfare state growth, the links between this development and the changing economic basis of the society, the emergence of democratic mechanisms and movements, the rise and decline of social classes and economic elites, the changing position and power of the government bureaucracy, and so on. Unlike most of the western welfare states, where the class structure, political systems and economies change at a relatively slow pace, this has not been the case in the newly industrialising societies such as Hong Kong. There is, therefore, a particular interest in studying welfare states in societies where the pace of change has been much more rapid, and of testing the ability of the existing theoretical frameworks to account for such situations.

By the time this book is published Hong Kong will be within a few months of experiencing the most dramatic transition in its circumstances since the imposition of British rule in 1841, as the colonial power gives way to the city state's incorporation into the People's Republic of China. Considerable uncertainty surrounds the future development of the welfare services in Hong Kong, as much else besides. However, there do seem to be powerful economic and political reasons why the new rulers of this territory should be content to largely maintain and develop the institutions and provision that they are inheriting, rather than seeking to tear them down and attempt a radical reconstruction. Economically there is a symbiotic relationship between Hong Kong's economic success and its welfare system, as Chan clearly demonstrates. The withdrawal or termination of social rights and provision would be likely to have adverse effects on the political and social stability that has underlain this economic success, apart from any more direct impact on the quality and supply of labour power.

So, whatever the future holds for Hong Kong's welfare state, most likely it will continue to exhibit many of the characteristics which Raymond Chan's study so incisively describes and analyses. His book is a pathbreaking contribution to the analysis of non-western welfare states and deserves to attract the attention of all those who have an engagement, whether from policy oriented or theoretical concerns, with the role of and prospects for welfare provision in western and non-western states alike.

Michael Harloe
Pro-Vice-Chancellor (Academic & Research)
University of Essex
April 1996

Acknowledgements

The current publication originated from my doctoral research conducted at Essex University and I am grateful to those who gave me academic guidance and support during this period. I am particularly grateful for the excellent advice of Professor Michael Harloe. Thanks are also due to Professor Dennis Marsden, Professor Ray Forrest, Dr Colin Samson, Dr Rod Stones and Professor Glenn Drover for their invaluable comments on the manuscript.

During the past years, I have been fortunate to have many friends and colleagues sharing in the difficulties and pressure in pursuing such a study. They are Brenda Corti, Mary Girling, Edward, Lorna, Alvin, Connie, Sik-ying, Petrus, Jimmy, Chak, Lyndon and Brenda. Also, I would like to thank my colleagues at the City University of Hong Kong, Joseph, Cecilia, Pearl, Elaine and especially the Head of our Department, Mr Wing-tai Chan, for their kind support.

I would also like to thank those persons who kindly consented to be interviewed by me, offering information and insightful comments to the research questions. Among them, I am particular grateful to Lord Murray Crawford MacLehose of Beoch and Lord David Clive Wilson of Tillyorn who helped me to locate suitable interviewees. The Fuller Memorial Fund of the Department of Sociology at the University of Essex has sponsored part of my research expenses, which enabled me to travel for interviews and afford the costs of obtaining research materials.

Finally, I would like to thanks my wife, Kwan, whose patience and tolerance in allowing me to be away for a whole year made the study possible. Mere words cannot fully convey what she has done to my life. It is to her that this book is dedicated.

List of abbreviations

AC	Area Committee
AGNS	Association of Government Nursing Staff
CDC	City District Committee
CDO	City District Office
CS	Chief Secretary
CSD	Census & Statistics Department
DB	District Board
DoE	Director of Education
DoH	Director of Housing
DoSW	Director of Social Welfare
EC	Education Commission
ED	Education Department
ExCo	Executive Council
FS	Financial Secretary
FTU	Federation of Trade Unions
GDA	Government Doctors' Association
GDP	Gross Domestic Products
GNP	Gross National Products
HA(HKHA)	Hong Kong Housing Authority
HB	Housing Branch
HD	Housing Department
HeD	Health Department
HK	Hong Kong
HKAR	Hong Kong Annual Report
HKG	Hong Kong Government
HKPA-CSA	Hong Kong Private Anglo-Chinese Schools Association
HKPCPHP	Hong Kong People's Council on Public Housing Policy
HKS	Hong Kong Standard
HPLS	Home Purchase Loan Scheme

HoA	Hospital Authority
HOS	Home Ownership Scheme
HS	Housing Society
HSD	Hospital Service Department
HWB	Health and Welfare Branch
ICSW	International Council on Social Welfare
IHA	Independent Hospital Authority
LegCo	Legislative Council
LTHS	Long Term Housing Strategy
MAC	Mutual Aid Committee
MDAC	Medical Development Advisory Committee
MHD	Medical & Health Department
MP	Ming Pao
MPs	Members of Parliament (UK)
NCNA	New China News Agency (*Xinhua News Agency*)
NGO	Non-governmental Organisation
NYFCEP	Nine Years Free and Compulsory Education Policy
OECD	Organisations of Economic Co-operation and Development
OMELCO	Office of Members of Executive and Legislative Council
PHoA	Provisional Hospital Authority
PRC	People's Republic of China
PRH	Public Rental Housing
PSPS	Private Sector Participation Scheme
PTU	Professional Teachers' Union
PWD	Public Works Department
RC	Regional Council
RD	Resettlement Department
SAR	Special Administrative Region
SCMP	South China Morning Post
SCOPG	Standing Committee on Pressure Group
SecEM	Secretary for Education & Manpower
SecH	Secretary for Housing
SecHW	Secretary for Health & Welfare
STJP	Sing Tao Jih Pao (*Sing Tao Daily News*)
SWD	Social Welfare Department
TUC	Trade Union Council
TYHCP	Ten Years Housing Construction Programme
UC	Urban Council
UK	United Kingdom (used synonymous with Britain)
UMELCO	Office of Unofficial Members of Executive & Legislative Council

Exchange rate

Year	Exchange rate (for reference only) (Pound : HK $)	(US $: HK $)
1946	1 : 16.00	1 : 5.65
1959	1 : 16.00	1 : 5.65
1967	1 : 14.55	1 : 5.65
1971	1 : 14.55	1 : 5.65
1972	1 : 13.40	1 : 5.65
1973	1 : 11.80	1 : 5.09
1974	1 : 11.53	1 : 4.91
1975	1 : 10.21	1 : 4.92
1976	1 : 7.95	1 : 4.68
1977	1 : 8.87	1 : 4.62
1978	1 : 9.82	1 : 4.80
1979	1 : 10.98	1 : 4.93
1980	1 : 12.27	1 : 5.10
1981	1 : 10.88	1 : 5.70
1982	1 : 10.58	1 : 6.50
1983	1 : 11.32	1 : 7.80
1984	1 : 9.11	1 : 7.82
1985	1 : 11.27	1 : 7.81
1986	1 : 11.48	1 : 7.80
1987	1 : 14.52	1 : 7.76
1988	1 : 14.17	1 : 7.81
1989	1 : 12.60	1 : 7.81
1990	1 : 14.95	1 : 7.80
1991	1 : 14.53	1 : 7.78
1992	1 : 11.77	1 : 7.74

Sources: *HKAR, various years*

Part One
THEORETICAL FRAMEWORK
&
RESEARCH METHODOLOGY

1 Introduction

Domain of welfare state theory

This study investigates and evaluates various factors which have contributed to the emergence and development of social services in Hong Kong from 1971 to 1992. The research topic falls within the domain of 'welfare state theory'. As elaborated by Quadagno, this involves the investigation and explanation of the factors which contribute to the emergence and development of the welfare state (Quadagno, 1987; Therborn, 1983).

Within this block of work, several theoretical perspectives have gradually emerged as of major significance. These explanations are mainly derived from the analytical perspectives of the disciplines of sociology, economics, political science and cultural studies based on socio-economic data and/or qualitative historical research. The growth of these different explanations provides a range of convincing arguments and examples for explaining the welfare state but at the same time, also makes the emergence of a unified and general theory problematic.

The difficulties are two-fold: the extremely complicated tasks of taking account of all the independent variables, and the definition and selection of the dependent variables. By independent variable, we refer to the factors which contribute to the emergence and development of welfare states. The list of variables offered by different disciplines is often too 'lengthy' to be fully considered in any one piece of research. By dependent variable, we refer to the definition of the welfare state in the various studies. This is an even more problematic issue. The welfare state is so difficult to define that Titmuss once described it as an 'indefinable abstraction' (1968, p.2).

Given the complexity of the contemporary welfare state and its different formats in different nations, it is not surprising that different and even contradictory explanations of its emergence and development have been provided by different researchers. Some studies focus primarily on public expenditure on social programmes while others put greater emphasis on social insurance, social legislation and social provision of services. Given such differences, it is not surprising that the results of different studies vary. One lesson is that researchers have to pay close attention to the definition of variables and in the research design and also be aware of the applicability of the findings in their own analyses and conclusion.

Background and constraints of the study

The subject of the welfare state has not received adequate attention in Hong Kong, a newly industrialised society, as in comparison with the West. Possible reasons include the pragmatic and predominant emphasis on the 'applied' side of social policy analysis in Hong Kong. Researchers, officials and the general public are more interested in analysing social problems and their implications, finding suitable solutions to these and implementation. Although there are a few quality studies, overall, there are still no systematic and critical studies in this area with very few exceptions (Jones, 1990; Chow, 1990). Most analyses are rather narrowly confined to one specific policy area or issue or only cover a limited span of time which inevitably limits their explanatory power. Hence, it is rather difficult to generate a theory of the welfare state relevant to Hong Kong's welfare development.

This allows the existence of blind-spots in the understanding of Hong Kong's history of social services. Such blind-spots reproduce further inadequate and inaccurate explanations of the Hong Kong welfare state and reinforce views which are based on unwarranted claims and a distorted construction of history. The decision to change the situation explains the origin of this study.

The study covers the period of 1971 to 1992. Generally speaking, in the 1970s, we will notice a general improvement in virtually every aspect of social provision. It has been perceived as the 'golden age', though not the period of origin, of Hong Kong's social services. In the 1980s, we will observe a gradual change of direction from expansion to marketisation of social services especially in housing, health and education. Thus, the 1970s and 1980s were very different but together they were the most significant phases of social services development in Hong Kong (Cheung, 1987, p.56).

The study is both exploratory and explanatory in its nature. The study does not, and cannot, provide an all-embracing theoretical explanation of all social services in Hong Kong as different factors operated at different levels and in different areas of policy. Any such research would generate an over-general explanation for individual cases or be swamped in a mass of detail. Instead, this study will mainly provide an explanation explaining the major characteristics (not the minute daily operations) of the selected welfare services within the period of study.

Yet, the study still suffers from inadequate data, especially with respect to the interpretation of the views and actions of officials and persons who were responsible for policy-making. Some of them have passed away, migrated or returned to their home countries before their opinions could be documented,. Moreover, though there are an increasing amount of official information available for analysis, the research still suffers from limited access to government documents, such as the Executive Council's minutes. Another major difficulty is the problem of exploring the latent and implicit impact of various factors on the development of welfare state. These limitations will be further discussed later.

Plan of Book

The first part of the book explains the theoretical framework and research methodology. Chapter 1 introduces the field of 'welfare state theory', the aim and objectives of the study and the plan of the book. Chapter 2 gives definitions to the terms, welfare state' and 'marketisation'. As noted in the first chapter, the definition of the dependent variable, the welfare state, is one of the explanations for the divergence of research findings. It is both wise and necessary to derive a clear definition of the term at an early stage. Also, as there is a tendency in Hong Kong to deny the use of the term 'welfare state', the effort to find a definition is also necessary to defend the application of this term in local context. The author will explain the reasons for this, clarify the myths, misunderstandings and discourses involved, and try to justify the application of the term. 'Welfare state', defined as a system of provision meeting human need through social services. It has basic functions and objectives which are defined as poverty relief and redistribution. Different types and models of welfare state are in fact, the realisation of different extended functions of welfare systems. 'Privatisation' also describes a form of welfare system though with contrasting features to those models before. However, privatisation, as a catch-all phrase, cannot describe the explicit changes in Hong Kong in the 1980s. It is argued that 'marketisation' is a more suitable and relevant description than privatisation.

Chapter 3 describes the contemporary theories of the welfare state and the debate among them. After showing the differences, similarities and limitations of each of these explanations, the author argues that the differences are more often apparent than real. A more general model will be presented. On this basis, it is argued that several theoretical perspectives are worth drawing on in the following analysis. These are the 'state-centered' thesis, elitist models, Neo-Marxist notions of legitimation and accumulation, socio-economic explanations of industrialisation and resource factors, and certain elements of the diffusion and convergence theses. Efforts will also be made to outline the current explanations of welfare state development in Hong Kong and their limitations.

Chapter 4 explains the research design and methodology of the study. Two types of methodology, quantitative and qualitative, will be outlined in this chapter. Considering the nature of the research topic and the practical constraints, the writer argues for adopting a historical qualitative approach based on case studies. There are four cases selected for detailed examination. These are the Ten Year Housing Construction Programme (TYHCP), the Nine Year Free and Compulsory Education Policy (NYFCEP), the Hospital Authority (HoA) and the related fee-charging policy, and the Long Term Housing Strategy (LTHS). A short explanation of the data collection methods will also be provided in this chapter.

Part 2 of the book describes the context of the welfare state in Hong Kong. Based on the different theoretical perspectives which are incorporated in the general model, chapter 5 will describe and analyse the foundations of the welfare state which were laid before 1970s. Political, social, economic and cultural factors will be discussed. All these factors form the overall context for the welfare state though different factors played different roles and had different degrees of influence. Much emphasis is placed on state power and governing ideology and the relative dominance of the state officials and the business interests in the policy process.

Chapter 6 provides a short historical account of the welfare state development before 1971 to give the reader a basic understanding of the 'starting point' of the development in 1970s. In fact, historical development is a process of evolution and one cannot completely separate the later development from the previous history. Hence, there will be a brief discussion of the impact on later social services development. It is argued that this early development until the edge provided a sound basis for further expansion. Evaluating the applicability of the various welfare state theories, it is argued that several socio-economic factors contributed to the shaping of objective social conditions but the impact on the policy decisions were mediated and interpreted by the officials and the business interests in the policy process. The relative powerlessness of other interests explains, partially, the relative dominance of the state and the business interests.

Part 3 focuses on the development of the welfare state from 1971 to 1981. Chapter 7 describes the context in this period. While part of the previous context remained intact, changes also occurred in various factors. The riots which occurred in 1960s set a new agenda for the social services. Together with such changes, new requirements emerged, such as the further development of the economy, the increasing youth population, the intensification of social activism, the coming of a new Governor, the modification of the power distribution and administrative structure. All these served to modify the policy context.

Chapter 8 describes the general development of various social services within this period. The overall characteristic of this period is expansion. The major focus of expansion was on housing and education, followed by medical and social welfare services. Detailed examination will be given to the two selected cases of TYHCP and NYFCEP. It is found that the policies were generally supported by all sectors of the community and within the government itself (though internal disagreement was also found) for different reasons. Comparatively speaking, the residents of public rental housing (PRH) as the consumers and the professional unions, such as Professional Teachers' Union (PTU) were most actively involved in the housing and education services respectively.

Chapter 9 argues for a theories of the welfare state for that period. As observed in the previous chapters, though changing needs of the economy and the overall economic situation did have an impact on the overall expansion of services, mere socio-economic explanations cannot explain the detailed development of the services. The participation of the social action groups served to monitor the state's policies but was unable to direct the agenda. The state's interests, legitimation, accumulation and a paternalistic caring ideology, seem to be more able to explain the expansionist policy in the 1970s. In deciding the course of action, the state included the traditional elite from the business sectors, and the professionals and middle class in the policy process. However, influence from China was not a significant factor in this period. But there was possibly some influence from overseas countries (trading counterparts) and Britain on local policies, especially in the case of education policy.

Part 4 focuses on the development of the welfare state from 1982 to 1992. Chapter 10 establishes the policy context for that period. The context of welfare state development kept changing, in a more drastic manner, in the 1980s. These changes were centred on the rising social consciousness, expectations and participation of the public in government. Social problems such as migration, an aging population, and economic problems formed a new context for the state to react to. There were further changes in the power relationship between the state, the traditional elite, professionals and middle class, and the mass public and such changes were reflected in the changes in the formal structure and in various policy debates.

Chapter 11 describes the general development of various social services within this period. Detailed examinations are made of the establishment of HoA and the fee-charging policy for hospital services, and the LTHS. The overall characteristic of this period is marketisation. Such reforms occurred in various services, especially in public sector housing and hospital services. Similar reforms in education and social welfare services were implemented on a smaller scale.

Chapter 12 constructs a theories of the welfare state for that period. Based on the previous analysis, it is argued that socio-economic factors could serve to provide an explanation for the emergence of new needs and problems that deserved attention and action from the public sector. However, the details of the policies and their implementation still very much depended on the outcome of negotiation and bargaining between different interests in the policy process. The state's power and authority was gradually diminished and more power shifted to the fragmented business sectors, and the parties which were led by professionals and the middle class, with the support from the mass public through voting. However, due to various factors, the state still maintained a certain degree of autonomy in the sphere of social services policy. The influence from China was more imminent but her direct control on local policies in this period was rare. The influence from Britain was restricted to other policy areas and local social services policies were more exposed to international experience.

Part 5 suggests a model of theory of the welfare state for Hong Kong for the period from 1971 to 1992. In the concluding chapter, a theory of Hong Kong's welfare state development will be outlined. It is argued that different factors had differential impacts and roles in this process. Among them, the role of Hong Kong as a place for conducting business was an abiding and fundamental concern for the state. This structure also set an implicit and subtle boundary for policy formation. The specific socio-economic-political context formed at different stages had engendered different problems and needs for the state to deal with. However the transmission of demands and needs to the policy process, the interpretation of them, their priority and the details of the corresponding actions very much depended on the relative power (and the respective orientations) among the traditional elite, the business sectors, the state officials, the professionals and middle class and the public (represented by social action groups or parties).

2 Welfare state and marketisation

When evaluating theories of welfare state, Uusitalo argues that the inconsistencies among different explanations are 'more often apparent than real' (1984, p.404). He argues that the differences are due to the selection of methodology and the data employed. The definition of the dependent variables, as well as the independent variables, often has significant impact on the findings. Hence, the definition of the 'welfare state' within the studies can generate different conclusion which can, subsequently, verify or falsify different theories (ibid).

Therefore, it is wise to start by defining the dependent variable, the 'welfare state', before proceeding with this study. In the following paragraphs, the writer will elaborate the definition of welfare state adopted in the study. Also, marketisation, as a specific form of privatisation, is argued to be one form of welfare state system.

Definition of 'welfare state'

Similar to many social science terminologies, the term 'welfare state' has a highly abstract and ambiguous meaning. Different people, in different periods have given different meanings to the term. Moreover, it is not only used to describe the objective phenomenon but has been employed as a label for political debate which signifies an ideal society. The term is, undoubtedly value-laden in the sense that people can impose their own values in the formulation of the definition of 'welfare state'. However, as described above, the definition problem of this 'dependent variable' is at the heart of the debate about welfare state theory and will certainly affect the research construction and findings. Hence, we now focus on clarifying and deriving a working definition of the term and examine its application in Hong Kong's context.

The origin of the word 'welfare state' has itself engendered debates. If judged by the existence of the programmes of the welfare state, such as social security, then it originated from the social insurance programmes in late nineteenth century in Germany. However, the term was explicitly used over years later in June 1932 by the German Chancellor von Papen in criticising the Weimer Republic 'Wohlfahrtstaat' for inducing the 'moral exhaustion' of the German by 'creating a kind of welfare state' (Flora & Heidenheimer, 1981, p.19). The term 'welfare state' was also applied to Britain during the Second World War (Johnson, 1987, p.3; Skocpol & Ikenberry, 1983, p.90).[1] The wide public usage of the term came closer with the 1942 Beveridge Report's proposals (Peterson, 1985, p.601). Marshall argued that the term then began to take shape and evolved as the antithesis to the old poor law institutions (Flora & Heidenheimer, 1981, p.20).

So we can argue that both some of the programmes and some concepts of the 'welfare state' existed before the formal adoption of the term 'welfare state' around World War II. After the war, the term was used as a rather 'convenient shorthand way of referring to the social and economic policy changes then taking place' (Johnson, 1987, p.3). Generally speaking, the 'welfare state' definition was gradually shifted from a social insurance dominated concept to include other forms of state intervention via social provision and legislation.

A quick summary of the various definitions of welfare state suggests that there are two general ways to define it: 1) by objectives or functions (desired outcome) and 2) by scope of programmes (output). From the first perspective, people tend to relate it to objectives such as maintaining national minimum standards (Mishra, 1990, p.34; Bryson, 1992, p.36; Wilensky, 1975, p.1); full employment (Mishra, 1990, p.34; Parry, 1985, p.289); preventing or relieving poverty (Mishra, 1990, p.34; Walker, 1983, p.131; Parry, 1985, p.289); achieving equality and justice (Flora & Heidenheimer, 1981, p.25; Robertson, 1988), social solidarity (Esping-Andersen, 1982; Baldwin, 1990), societal integration and inclusion (Bendix et al, 1987, p.23; Robertson, 1988); de-commodification (Furniss & Tilton, 1979; Esping-Andersen, 1982; 1990); redistribution and modification of the market system (Walker, 1983, p.131; Wilensky, 1975, ch.5; Esping-Anderson, 1982).

From the second perspective, people tend to relate it to the taxation policies (Walker, 1983; Titmuss, 1968; Bryson, 1992), entitlement and benefits under the mainstream programmes of income security, medical and education (Mishra, 1990, p.33), housing (Wilensky, 1975) etc.. Some have derived certain classifications for this seemingly never-ending list, such as direct payments and transfer payments, direct provision of services (Flora & Heidenheimer, 1981, p.25; Peterson, 1985) and the famous notion of social division of welfare of Titmuss, i.e. fiscal welfare, occupational welfare and social welfare. Some further divide these programmes into core and peripheral types. Wilensky has argued that 'the essence of the welfare state is government-protected minimum standards of income, nutrition, health, housing and education, assured to every citizen as a political right, not charity' and so, the core of the welfare state is a nation's health and welfare effort (Wilensky, 1975, p.6-7).[2] There are frequent references to principles for access to these provisions based on universality, on citizenship and social rights, instead of charity (Marshall, 1963) or market criteria of distribution.

These different foci and definitions of the welfare state engender different definitions and operationalisations of it in welfare state research. Such diversified understanding of the term adds difficulty to theorising the topic. We cannot find a dominant discourse of the definition of welfare state across both perspectives. There seems to be no strong and valid ground to reject any ideas or items suggested above as they are describing different aspects of the welfare state. One way to unify this diversification is to draw a 'definition' which embraces all the features described above and certainly, such a definition can have a greater generalising power. Another approach is to derive a core or 'irreducible element' in the definition and without this core, any set of programmes cannot amount to a welfare state. Different additional characteristics serve to define different categories or types of welfare state.

An overview of the development of the welfare state shows that it has encompassed more and more programmes, and engendered further internal complexity and divergence. From this rather confusing maze, however, we find that poverty relief (so as to meet national minima) and redistribution are the two most commonly included desired objectives or functions of different types of welfare programmes. The extent of redistribution is judged by its outcome, i.e. whether it has achieved a level of minimum national standard of living for all or more than this.[3] Hence, these two functions could be set as the basic objectives of welfare state.

This is not to say that other objectives are irrelevant but, instead, they are rather 'specific' to different models of the welfare state and the expanded effects based on these two objectives.[4] It seems that the moralistic and idealistic objectives, such as equality, justice and solidarity, are full of passion and romanticism of reform and revolution. These were 'added' to the welfare state during the process when the liberal social security metaphor of the welfare state was transformed to a rather socialist comprehensive metaphor during the post-war period. In fact, these values are more related to the ideal of a 'welfare society' in which they are assumed as an 'organic part of everyday life' (Robertson, 1988, p.222).

Another clarification is that the welfare state is different from social policy. In this sense, we agree with Walker's argument that social policy has a wider domain than the welfare state (1983).[5] Welfare state programmes are directly related to the state in the forms of either provision or regulation (by means of policies, rules and legislation etc.) by it. This narrower definition excludes that part of the social services provided by voluntary (the part which is not subsidised by the state), private (market) and informal sector bodies.[6] Together these four sectors can be seen to provide the 'total welfare' of a society (Rose, 1983, p.294; Barrs & Hills, 1990, p.26). Thus, the welfare state primarily refers to the institutionalised system of services provided collectively through the state (Bryson, 1992, p.36; Offe, 1987, p.13). This definition adopted here, is a 'narrower' and 'limited' one but more concrete and viable in this limited study.

On such a basis, different writers derive different categories of welfare states. Generally speaking, there are four approaches to defining these categories:

1 Expenditure Approach:
This is probably the 'simplest' and most widely adopted methodology in defining the types of welfare state. The method is to calculate the expenditure on the programmes (output) and classify the different states as, for example, welfare states and non-welfare states, and developed, developing and under-developed welfare states. Thus a leaders and laggers league table can be derived (Wilensky, 1975).

2 Ideal Type/Programme Approach:
This approach tries to derive different attributes and characteristics of programmes (output) and group these into different categories. Then, it seeks to classify different types of existing programmes into categories such as Furniss & Tilton's division of social security states and social welfare states (1979), or residual welfare states and institutional welfare states[7] (Wilensky & Lebeaux, 1958, pp.138-140). This approach is rather crude in its methodology.

3 Structural Approach:
This approach tries to define the welfare state programme's according to their relationship with wider social structure and society. Examples are the categories of differential welfare state and integrated welfare state

derived by Mishra (1986) and the *welfare* capitalism and welfare *capitalism* derived by Jones (1985a).

4 Integrative Approach:
This approach categorises different types of welfare state by a combination of the efforts (output) and outcomes of the welfare states. This is made possible by the existence of detailed data other than welfare expenditure. Examples are the Esping-Anderson's classification of liberal, conservative and socialist welfare states (1990) and Castles & Mitchell's addition of the fourth type of radical welfare state (1992).

The first and the second approach are based on the size and nature (output) of the welfare state. The third approach focuses on its location in wider structural context. The last one categorises it by both the output and outcome of the programmes.

Application of the 'welfare state' to Hong Kong

A cursory review of the literature on Hong Kong shows that there is a consensus that Hong Kong is not a welfare state. In contrast, the western countries, such as United Kingdom, United States of America and the Scandinavian countries are all perceived as typical examples of welfare states. This proposition results from the politics of welfare state discourse among different groups and misinterpretation of its meaning in academic studies. The following paragraphs will seek to examine the development and re-assess the discourse of the welfare state in Hong Kong and argue for the application of the term to Hong Kong.

The development of Hong Kong's social services reached a significant scale of provision before the 1970s, and received tremendous government support from the 1970s when Sir Murray MacLehose began his governorship. By 1971, Hong Kong provided six years of free and compulsory education, a primitive social security system, a large scale public rental housing programme, public health and hospital systems with nominal charges. However, the welfare state was not at the centre of social services discourse. Neither the government nor the Non-Governmental Organisations (NGO) mentioned this concept vigorously. The focus of debate was on expanding the provision of the individual services.

During MacLehose's office as Governor from 1971 to 1982, there were massive and remarkable developments in every aspect of social services. In 1978, there came the Nine Years Free and Compulsory Education (NYFCEP). Hospital beds were also significantly increased in this decade[8] and medical charges were maintained at a very low level. Although the Ten Years Housing Construction Programme (TYHCP) could not eventually reach its target of housing 1.8 million people, the number of person living in public sector housing increased by 24.8 per cent. Moreover, the Home Ownership Scheme (HOS) started in the mid-1970s also received very favourable response. There were remarkable improvements in terms of the welfare output. These policies not only improved the standard of living of Hong Kong's people but also stimulated the welfare debate and the people's desire for further improvement of the welfare system.

We can observe that MacLehose's policies and speeches were always perceived as full of 'socialist' meaning. In 1973, he suggested that housing, education, medical and social welfare services were the 'Four Pillars' of Hong Kong society.[9] In 1976, when he mentioned the concept of 'Community Building', he pointed out that the government's objective was to build up a mutually caring society. In his speech, he said 'our aim must be to build a society in which there is mutual care and responsibility. Our social programmes are of course relevant because people will not care for a society which does not care for them'.[10] However, MacLehose's socialist attitude did not permeate every aspect of the government. The government repeatedly denied it was pursuing a 'welfare state' policy in Hong Kong or that Hong Kong was approaching to a 'welfare state'. In the annual report of 'Hong Kong 1975', the government stated very clearly that Hong Kong was not a welfare state and citizens were expected to be self-reliant. All these social services policies had to be considered in terms of their implications for the economy. This belief was strongly advocated by the powerful Finance Secretary (FS), Sir Philip Haddon-Cave, in particular (Hodge, 1981, pp.10-11; Chow, 1985b, p.145). This is why Chow argues that Hong Kong, in this period, was still far from the ideal of a welfare state (Chow, 1980, p.9).

In the 1980s, the government still had little interest in the welfare state terminology, as in the 1970s. Its discourse was concentrated on the pursuit of privatisation policy and phrases such as 'those who can pay should pay'; 'those who use it should pay for it'; 'better utilisation of resources' and 'sharing of responsibility of financing the services' were everywhere in government documents.

Also in the 1980s, the government's effort in expanding the social services aroused more and more debates among the public. There was a heated debate on the welfare state in the mid-1980s caused by the further development of representative government. Those who rejected further democratisation of the government had referred to the adverse experience of the Western welfare states from the 1970s and tried to prove that welfare state development would only lead to 'free lunches'. These critics mainly came from a business background. The opposite camp argued that Hong Kong was still far from being a welfare state and hence, they supported the positive function of social services and more services to meet social needs (Chow, 1990, pp.12-13). While the politicians were heavily engaged in the debate, the notion of 'welfare state' had never been a popular ideology among the ordinary people though they, in principle, supported more welfare.

Apart from the political groups, the academics also had more discussion about the 'welfare state'. In their discourse, the definition was heavily influenced by the Fabian tradition which emphasised social rights, the government's responsibility to meet social needs and that the scope of welfare state was 'from cradle to grave' (Chow, 1980, p.8). It seems that there was a general consensus, that Hong Kong was not a welfare state (Chow, 1984b, 1985a; Chiu, 1985, 1987; Ngan, 1987). Of course, there were several scholars who held a different standpoint, who pointed out that Hong Kong's system was comparable to that of a welfare state and the problem was the reluctance to label it as a 'welfare state'. For example, Jones argues that, judging from the extent of public sector involvement (output), Hong Kong was certainly an example of a welfare state. Though it does not have a social insurance scheme, the overall welfare effort was not significantly decreased by this (Jones, 1990, p.257; Chow, 1984a, p.178). So, Jones terms it as a model of welfare *capitalism*. Some others denied that Hong Kong was an institutional welfare state with comprehensive service provision, but proposed that it was a residual type of welfare state (McLaughlin, 1993).

In these academic studies, two criteria were adopted to help to make such judgments:

1 Output (Expenditure, Programme Approach):
This corresponds to the previously stated expenditure and ideal programme approach. The reason why Hong Kong is not a welfare state, mainly, is that its services provision cannot reach the standard of 'from cradle to grave', that many social needs have not been fulfilled and there is no social insurance scheme nor compulsory retirement protection plan.[11]

2 Objective/Function (Ideal Type Approach):
This corresponds to the previously stated ideal type approach. From their arguments, it is obvious that they perceive a welfare state as a state of society which reflects values of fairness, equality, equity, justice and human worthiness. Welfare is not an activity of pure charity but is more

a right of being a citizen of Hong Kong society (Chow, 1984b, p.14; Chan, 1987; Yeung, 1985, 1987). It is expected that through redistributive mechanisms and policies, we can achieve that state of society. According to these propositions, the size of the social services is rather small and therefore, the redistributive effect must be very limited. It is impossible for this limited redistributive effect to achieve the kind of society that they are looking for. They argue that welfare rights have never been formally recognised and the recent privatisation policies have further marginalised the poor and the under class.

These attempts at definition have their weaknesses. They tended to adopt a 'negative definition approach'. That is, they define Hong Kong as a non-welfare state because 'it is not so and so'. Though they point out the inadequacy of the welfare system, they seldom draw a clear picture of what a welfare state should be. No one has made the idea of 'from cradle to grave' clear enough to be an accurate yardstick to measure the welfare system. They still rely very much, and perhaps too much, on the expenditure approach in their argument.

Yet, even if we measure the welfare effort in terms of expenditure and output, Hong Kong did see a tremendous improvement in the 1970s and 1980s. Of course, there still were plenty of social needs yet to be fulfilled: the waiting list for public housing services was very long, the redistribution effect was limited and the gap between the poor and the rich widened in the past 10 years. The Gini Coefficient has widened from 0.43 in 1971 to 0.48 in 1991 (Tang, 1992, p.296). Nevertheless, it is clear that the provision of social services has moved from the minimal standard of protection and poverty relief to achieving human and social development. The overall living standard and per capita income have been improved, the numbers in absolute poverty has been reduced to an insignificant level.[12] The educational attainment of the Hong Kong people has improved.[13] The health indicators, such as crude death rate, infant mortality rate and life expectancy rate have all improved.[14] Currently, about half the population live in various types of subsidised housing.[15] The existence of service shortfalls and failures to meet certain needs cannot serve as a strong argument to deny the welfare achievement, in terms of expenditure, output and outcome. Housing, medical, educational and social welfare services have been gradually integrated with the larger social system and became a vital part of the Hong Kong society.

The fact is that the government is pursuing a welfare state policy and is moving closer to the Western welfare state while continuing to reject employing this term to describe their policies. It is because in their view, the welfare state denotes an institutional type with comprehensive services to meet every citizen's need. Such a policy direction is certainly against their tradition and ideology and they are extremely reluctant to put the government under such heavy burden.

If we strictly follow the ideal of 'from cradle to grave', Hong Kong is not a welfare state. However, if we take both the output and outcome of welfare provision into consideration, Hong Kong has certainly become a welfare state. At least, it has met the basic criteria of poverty relief and protection of national minima. The remaining question concerns what type of the welfare state it is. For example, using Esping-Andersen's classification (1990), Hong Kong is probably a mixture of conservative and liberal welfare states. On one hand, a significant part of the welfare services is primarily based on the market (occupational welfare) and individuals to deliver care and welfare. Apart from this, the family has been given a very important role in caring for its members. On the other hand, civil servants have, traditionally, enjoyed better welfare than employees of the private market. This is, as described by Esping-Andersen, to protect and secure the loyalty of this group of people as servants of the 'rulers'. Yet, it must be stressed that the welfare state cannot be fully described by such a simple dualistic or crude categorical division.

Hong, Kong's welfare state's provision, has reached a scale that can be compared to that of the Western welfare states. The debate on the applicability of the term certainly rests on an inappropriate understanding of the meaning of the term. Here, we are not aiming at providing a simple categorisation of Hong Kong's welfare state but are seeking to explain the reasons that contribute to the specific formation of the policy direction and significant changes in the period of study.

Privatisation or marketisation?

Privatisation, though perceived as an innovation in the 1980s, is not so. Walker has argued that 'the importance of market principles in the public social services - privatism - has a long history and some elements of a free market of welfare were built into the original framework of services, for example in the provision for voluntary insurance in the social security system' in Beveridge Report (Walker, 1987, p.185). The debate on the role of private and public sectors occurred even in the heyday of the welfare state. Such ideas, in the form of policy proposals, were suggested by Peter Drucker in 1968 and, in a more comprehensive way, by the Rand Corporation in 1972 and during the economic crisis which followed

(Donahue, 1989, p.4). Thus, it seems invalid to argue that privatisation is a brand new product of the new socio-economic-political context from the mid-1970s. Instead, 'what is relatively new is the social and economic strategy ... which is designed to radically shift the balance between public and private welfare much further in favour of the latter than at any previous period in the history of the Welfare State' (Walker, 1987, p.185).

Privatisation, in its widest meaning, describes a range of policy initiatives designed to alter the balance between the public and private sectors (Cook & Kirkpatrick, 1988, p.3). Kielland argues that it signifies the 'change from public action or property to private' and Hanke describes the transferal as including 'public assets, infrastructure and service functions to the private sector' (Lundqvist, 1986, p.5). Veljanovski argues that 'to privatize is to render private or to bring into the private sector' (1988, p.1). Donahue refers to privatisation as the 'practice of delegating public duties to private organizations' (1989, p.3) and such idea is also supported by Starr (1987, 1989). In a similar way, Pulkingham suggests that privatisation 'is an umbrella term encompassing an array of policies designed, in the Government's views, to re-establish the primacy of so-called market principles in the provision of public services' (1989, p.387). This suggests that privatisation involves a change in the operating principles of the public services. Different people have suggested different interpretations along these lines.

Generally speaking, privatisation can be defined from two perspectives: structure and policy. Concerning the structural aspect, we can say that privatisation occurs when the state reorganises itself and gives up or shares its responsibility for producing and providing services with non-public sectors. The changes are from the public (state) sector to the private (market), informal (family) and voluntary sectors (Leat, 1986). Withdrawal from provision of services involves reducing or retreating from, primarily, the ownership of the services. Accompanying this, the duties of policy-making, planning, financing and subsidising, operating and administering are also withdrawn (Kolderie, 1986, 1987). Common strategies includes selling off assets to private ownership (denationalisation) or setting up of non-governmental organisations, to manage the public services (if they are not to be totally owned by the private sector). In this case, the new owners take responsibility for organising and providing the services (Saunders & Harris, 1990, pp.59-60). Nevertheless, such structural change may not lead to a change in the nature of the service.

More important than structural change are changes in policy. This perspective focuses more on the operation of the services and suggests that privatisation takes place when market principles, such as the advocacy of efficiency, competition, fee charging, profit-maximising, intrude in the public sector which has been assumed to be free from market influence. As argued by Walker, 'privatisation may be said to take place when ... market criteria, such as profit or ability to pay are used to ration or distribute benefits and services' (1984, p.25). Privatisation, in these aspects, involves changes in the values, principles of operation, management and delivery of services and hence, a contrasting welfare system with the one before. The creation of a quasi-market within the services, and contracted-out services are examples of such changes. The mode of consumption and production, such as the change of status from client to customers, will be changed and customers will assume greater responsibility in 'buying' (paying) for the services.

Harloe has adopted the term 'recommodification' to describe changes in housing policy which include the growing domination of the housing market by individualised owner occupation, accompanied by the retreat from socialised (or semi-socialised) subsidised, 'non-profit' or council housing (1981).[16] Ramanadham suggests that privatisation is the 're-marketisation' of the public sector (1990, p.3).

Privatisation and socialisation are the two ends of a continuum (Lundqvist, 1986). Any change away from socialisation along this continuum can be described as privatisation. It is difficult to say when or which form represents 'total privatisation'[17] but it is easier to identify the 'trend' and 'type' of privatisation by analysing the strategies adopted.

Privatisation is not restricted to welfare policies but also extends to economic policy, such as selling off or de-nationalisation of the national enterprises in United Kingdom and currently in Eastern Europe, the former Soviet Union and China. Even confined to the welfare state, it has wider implications than just expenditure cuts. Not only services output and expenditure may be cut or restricted to a very modest rate of growth, the principle of citizenship has also been attacked. Provision is switched from universal to selective services (King, 1987a; Mishra, 1990), and individualism and the familial (especially female's role) responsibility for self and mutual care have been promoted as an alternative to the bureaucratic public system (Samson, 1994; Vettenrant, 1986, p.257). Professional power in managing services has been challenged and taken over by business-type operations and administration. Market provision has been promoted as superior to public services in terms of the quality of services, accountability, consumer control and efficiency. Privatisation has been perceived as a hegemonic project, 'selling' to the public and promoting various structural changes in policy and, especially, value changes (such as ownership as human instinct, enterprise culture) (Samson, 1994).

All in all, privatisation is used as a catch-all phrase to describe the general policy trend 'from public to private'. However, to use such phrase without referring to the specific form of privatisation may oversimplify the phenomenon.[18] Therefore, the step that researchers have to attempt is to clarify the specific forms of privatisation that specific countries adopt. There are two general aspects of change: structural change which refers to denationalisation (changes of ownership and management) and policy change which primarily refers to marketisation (or commodification).[19] In such changes, market-type relationships and allocation procedures will penetrate into the social welfare arena (Millard, 1988, p.1; Salamon, 1993, p.17). It is argued here that changes in the second aspect will have greater impacts on the 'privatisation' of social services.

Application of marketisation in Hong Kong

Generally speaking, privatisation has had greater impacts on the 'liberal' welfare states such as Britain and America but relatively speaking, lesser effects on the 'conservative' welfare states such as Germany (formerly West Germany), 'socialist' welfare states such as Sweden and the 'radical' welfare states such as Australia (Esping-Andersen, 1990; Castles & Mitchell, 1992). Its effect on Hong Kong, comparatively speaking, is more moderate and gradual as compared to that on Britain. For several major services, such as education and health, there has been no cut-back in their overall expenditure, instead, the growth of the services has slowed pace and there are changes in their financing. Of course, one of the reasons is that the welfare state's size in Hong Kong is relatively small and a great part of the services are, in fact, produced and provided by the voluntary sector and market, though maybe regulated or subsidised by the government,[20] and an even greater portion by the informal sector. However the definitions in the above, there are still considerable changes in the services in both their structural and policy aspects. However, the changes in the latter aspect are more significant.

Structural changes include the reconstitution of the public housing and public and subsidised hospitals operated by the voluntary organisations, and then placing under the management of new Authorities in 1987[21] and 1991[22] respectively. In education, the government implemented a scheme of Direct Subsidy for secondary schools to provide a way for them to opt out of the control of the Education Department (ED).[23] All these changes signified the government's attempt to shift the responsibility for administering, planning and management from the state to semi-statal or non-public sectors.

However, such reforms are not equivalent to denationalisation. On one hand, the government is still responsible for the majority of the expenses of these services. Although their operation all rests in the hands of the Authorities, the government still retains its overall policy control. The Authorities are semi-statal organisations whose members and chairman are appointed by the Governor though they enjoyed greater autonomy than before.

The reforms in the operation of policy reflect the trend of privatisation more explicitly. Generally speaking, the strategy is two-fold. The first is to change the financing method of the services through the increase of charges to recover a greater proportion or even the whole of the production costs. The second is to encourage the private provision of the services. In the first aspect, the government has announced scheme to increase drastically the charges for public health services and higher education.[24] The rent level of public housing has increased from around 10 per cent of the public housing household's median income in 1986 to 18 per cent in 1992. Also, the Authority has cut-back its assistance to the so-called 'better-off' sitting tenants. The sale of the HOS and Private Sector Participation Scheme's (PSPS) flats has already generated huge profits for the Authority. In these two services, those who can afford to pay more can receive better services than those who can only barely afford to pay or even rely on the social security. The latest proposal is to sell rental units to prospective and current tenants.

On the other hand, due to the modest growth of subsidies for various services, the voluntary or the subsidised sector has to find alternative sources of finance such as imposing higher charges on users, appealing to private charity for donations or forming partnerships with private organisations. The joint-venture model, with child care centres as the forerunners was praised by the Secretary of Health & Welfare (SecHW) as the model for the voluntary sector to follow.

Concerning the private provision of welfare, the elderly residential care services are already dominated by the private sector partly due to the huge service gap left by very limited growth in the public sector planned by the government. Such scale of growth was a result of both the government's failure to provide adequate residential places and the provision for sending the clients to these homes and paying for their fees through social security, if they are eligible. Due to the limited level of provision of the social security benefit, the under-developed occupational welfare and pension scheme for the majority of the working population and the foreseeable increase of medical charges, the private insurance market has gained more profit from the increasing number of customers who want to pay for certain kinds of protection themselves (i.e. individual care) instead of solely relying on public services. Such private services and insurance schemes, together with the privatised hospital and housing services show the intrusion of the market sector and forces into the public services. All these changes signified the 'marketisation' of the social services in Hong Kong in the 1980s.

Of course, this does not mean that the Hong Kong government aims to dismantle the welfare state. The welfare state's scale has not been significantly trimmed down or restricted. It still maintains its financial commitment to the services. Education services, except pre-primary education, are still heavily financed by the government. The Hospital Authority still relies on the government for most of its income, though with an increasing share from the service users. Land provision continues to be the major government subsidy to the Housing Authority. The majority of the social welfare services are still receiving subsidies from the government. When necessary, the government will still be the last resort for finance to the public services. The changes are not on a dramatic scale and the denationalisation of the social services has never been attempted in Hong Kong.

At present, we cannot conclude that Hong Kong's welfare state is in crisis, as (perhaps it is) in the West. If marketisation is a form of privatised welfare provision and is one of the formats of the welfare state, such changes signifying the changing of the welfare state, mainly in terms of its operation, policies and values and hence, in its outputs and outcomes, not its abolition.

Summary

In this chapter, we have clarified the definition of welfare state and privatisation and established a working definition of both terms in this study. Though it is not widely accepted to use the term of 'welfare state' to describe the Hong Kong's system, the writer argues that such position is due to misconceptions, or alternative perceptions, of the meaning of the term. It is valid to use the term welfare state in Hong Kong. 'Welfare state' is here conceived in a narrower sense, taking a structural and organisational perspective, which includes the formal services, policies and regulations provided and managed by the government. It also includes those rules and legislation which serve to regulate those services provided by the market, voluntary and informal sector and the subsidised services.

Privatisation is an alternative form of welfare state arrangement, though, it is significantly different from the ideal-type institutional welfare state and less redistributive. Compared with the conventional welfare state construct, such new arrangements differs in their values, operations and structural arrangements. They give greater shares to the private sector and lesser controls on it. As described in the above paragraphs, the changes in Hong Kong in the 1980s are typical examples of privatisation policies. To be more exact, the changes involve the 'marketisation' of social services rather more than structural changes. The setting up of various Authorities was to smooth the way for the introduction of 'marketisation' policies. A detailed description of the expansion and marketisation of the welfare state in Hong Kong in the period of study will be provided in the following chapters.

Notes

1 Archbishop Temple, a clergyman, has 'coined the phrase in an attempt to characterise a polar contrast to the 'power' and 'warfare' sate of the Nazis'. See Flora & Heidenheimer, 1981, p.19.
2 Wilensky does not clearly spell out the scope of the peripheral programmes though he has argued for the scope of core programmes.
3 This is judged by the individual national standard of living and expectation.
4 We can argue that through poverty relief and redistribution, certain degree of equality and justice can be achieved, and thus promote integration and inclusion (instead of marginalisation and alienation). Or in another perspective, reproduction of capitalism and social relationship is possible and government's legitimacy guaranteed.
5 Some writers will propose a boarder definition for welfare state which 'equals to' social policy. See for example, Ginsburg, 1992.
6 Though the services may be regulated by policies and legislation, the subject of study is the regulatory framework instead of the services themselves.
7 In that category, other approaches are also used but the primary focus is the size of provision.
8 The number of public hospital beds increased for 55.4 per cent from 1971 to 1981 and the number of subsidised hospital beds increased for 14.2 per cent at the same period. For details, please refer to chapter 6.
9 In Governor's Speech to Legislative Council, 1973.
10 In Governor's Speech to Legislative Council, 1976.

11 Though the government and some large companies have provided pension schemes to their employees and some companies, such as the social welfare agencies, have joined a central transferable provident fund scheme, the majority of the labour force have not been protected.
12 The concern is on the extent of relative poverty and deprivation.
13 For example, only 74.8 per cent of those youth can receive secondary education (including those studied in private school) in 1971 and currently, secondary education has been made compulsory and free. See also chapter 8 and chapter 11.
14 In view of the population increase by 56 per cent from 1967 to 1992, the number of hospital bed per person has been increased from 3.79 to 4.47 and the infant mortality rate has been decreased from 17.7 in 1971 to 6.4 in 1991. Life expectancy rate has been increased from 67.8 and 75.3 for male and female respectively in 1971 to 75.1 and 80.6 for male and female respectively in 1991. See also chapter 8 and chapter 11.
15 In 1993, the figure is approximately 3 million and the total provision of public and subsidised units has been increased from 260,000 in 1971 to 691,000 in 1991. See also chapter 8 and chapter 11.
16 Saunders and Harris also use the term 'commodification' to describe the sale of council housing to those who previously consumed them in United Kingdom (1990, p.60).
17 It is very often that though the government has withdrawn from its responsibility in provision or subsidisation of the services, the privatised services are still under a legal framework established by relevant laws, rules and regulations enforced by bureaucracy or organisations entrusted. Therefore, direct provision and subsidisation are substituted by regulation.
18 Several scholars in Hong Kong researching in 'privatisation' have agreed that it is only a general term applied to describe the overall trend. They have suggested various terms, such as 'marketisation' (Chiu, 1988), commercialisation (Chow, 1988), commodification (ibid; Lee, 1988) to refer to the specific form within the general trend.
19 In such 'market' situation, services are treated as a 'commodity' sold to the customers with a price-tag on it.
20 For example, overwhelming majority of the child care, youth centre, outreaching and counselling services, primary schools and secondary schools are run by the NGOs. A considerable percentage of hospital beds and doctors are privately run.
21 The Housing Authority was set up the government in 1973 and it took up all the previous duties in housing policy from the government in 1987. See chapter 8.

22 The idea of management by an Authority evolved in mid-1980s. The provisional Authority was set up in 1989 and the formal one set up in 1992. The delay was due, mainly, to arguments over arrangements, terms of employment and job benefits of transferal of civil servants in hospital to the new Authority which meant the loss of their civil servant status. See chapter 11.

23 Yet, the scheme received a very poor response from subsidised schools.

24 The proposal to increase the hospital charge was strongly objected to by the Legislative Council did not receive a favourable response from the public and, has been held up for years. The proposal for increasing the post-secondary tuition fee was endorsed in 1990. The amount for 1990/1991 academic year was HK$8,700 (9.4 per cent of the cost per place) rising to HK$ 24,000 in 1994/1995 (15.6 per cent of the cost per place). Please refer to chapter 11.

3 Theories of welfare state

Welfare state theory does not have a distinguished history. This is understandable because the welfare state had hardly formed before the Second World War in most Western countries and it only developed on a significant scale after the War. This also partly explains why the main theoretical bases for welfare state theorizing were originally derived from political science, sociology and economics, and continue to be so even today (Therborn, 1986, pp.132-133; Mishra, 1987, p.69). From the 1960s a group of sociologists, historians and political scientists tried to establish more sophisticated analyses of the state, welfare and capitalism. The following paragraphs will explain the development of the various strands of thought, their development, major propositions and arguments, and strengths and weaknesses.

Socio-economic explanations

Functionalism, industrialism, diffusion and convergence theses

There have been two theoretical foundations for the socio-economic analysis of the welfare state, namely structural functionalism and the "logic of industrialism". The philosophical roots of functionalism can be traced back to Comte, Spencer and Durkheim. Spencer and Comte were concerned with organicism and an evolutionary view of development, and Durkheim concentrated on establishing the general theoretical orientation of modern functionalism. While Durkheim did not focus specifically on the analysis of welfare. He did suggest the functional division, specialisation and increasing complexity of modern society required a corresponding scale of coordination and regulation,

> A multitude of functions which were diffuse become concentrated. The care of educating the young, of protecting public health, of presiding over the ways of administering public aid, of administering the means of transport and communication, little by little move into the sphere of the central organ (1964, p.221).

Thus Durkheim perceived social service growth as a normal evolutionary development which could serve to maintain harmony in the interdependence among systems in the course of specialisation, and the common solidarity of society (Durkheim, 1964, p.197, p.227; Mishra, 1987, ch.4; Waters, 1994, pp.135-136). However, Durkheim was against reliance on the state and argued for occupational and professional guilds to regulate individual desires and actions, working alongside with the state (1964, pp.24-28).

Parsons perceived society from a systems view and different forms of societies represented different forms of structural arrangement of systems. For any society to survive, the system has to fulfill four functions: pattern maintenance (tension management), goal attainment, integration and adaptation. Pattern maintenance refers to the upkeep of the overall structure of the system. Goal attainment refers to the establishment of a common goal which the system has to follow. Integration refers to the maintenance of solidarity and to ensure a smooth and orderly relationship among the subsystems. Finally, adaptation refers to the adjustment of the systems in line with the external environment. Any change in one subsystem requires necessary changes from others accordingly. Also, the system will undergo modernisation, which was the basic developmental process of contemporary Western societies.

In the course of modernisation, specialisation and functional differentiation occurred. During the course, disequilibria might occur and the survival of the social system and subsystem, could be threatened, although a certain degree of disequilibrium was possible. Parsons regarded adaptation as a mean by which disequilibria were responded to:

> If differentiation is to yield a balanced, more evolved system, each newly differentiated sub-structure ... must have increased adaptive capacity for performing its primary function, as compared with the performance of that function in the previous, more diffused structure (1966, p.22).[1]

Another functionalist, Smelser, has explained the functional differentiation and growth of the new system of capitalism in the nineteenth century, as well as new social welfare provision. According to him, the separation of production from familial and kinship systems in the Industrial Revolution engendered integrative problems.

> How is information concerning employment opportunities to be conveyed to work people? How are the interests of families to be integrated with the interests of firms? How are families to be protected from market fluctuation? Whereas such integrative exigencies were faced by kinsmen, neighbours, and local largesse in pre-modern settings, development gives birth to dozens of institutions and organisations geared to these new integrative problems - labour recruitment agencies and exchanges, labour unions, government regulation of labour allocation, welfare and relief arrangements, co-operation societies, and saving institutions (1964, p.268).

From this theoretical perspective, social welfare is seen as a system which accompanied the process of modernisation, specialisation and differentiation and which is primarily concerned with the integration of systems and maintaining solidarity. The second theoretical source for socio-economic explanations was industrialisation. According to the industrialism thesis, industrial and economic development are the central forces of change of modern societies and the social system is arranged around this process. The thesis tries to explain the 'nature and development of social institutions of industrial societies in terms of the "pull" and "push" of an industrial technology and economy' (Mishra, 1987, p.39). The 'pull' factors refer to the requirements and functional necessities of an industrialized and modernized society. The 'push' factors refer to the consequences of industrialisation and modernisation.

Early analysis using this perspective can be found in Kerr et al (1973 [1964]). In his analysis, Kerr described the development of industrialised societies and suggested that new social groups[2] emerged in the early stages of industrialisation. These groups' varying positions of dominance in various nations resulted in different systems of welfare (1973, pp.61-73). Kerr and his colleagues focus on developments in the later stage of industrialisation. As societies become more advanced industrially, there is a narrowing of differences among nations, they assert. There is convergence on a system which lies between the two extremes of totalitarian state control and laissez-faire (ibid, p.270). Social services, either provided by governments or by enterprises perform the function of integration in this complex society (ibid, p.186). As summarised by Quadagno,

> The core argument of this thesis, sometimes termed 'the logic of industrialism', is that all industrializing nations, regardless of their historical and cultural traditions or present political and economic structures, become similar through an evolutionary process resulting from the impact of economic and technological growth on the occupational system. As industrialization proceeds, it creates new needs for public spending by reducing the functions of the traditional family and by dislocating certain categories of individuals whose labor becomes surplus -- the very young, the old, the sick, and the disabled. Because the traditional societal institutions are unable to meet the needs of these vulnerable individuals, the state expands more or less automatically (1987, p.112).

Wilensky and Lebeaux adopt the functionalist/industrialism account to explain the emergence of social welfare in America (1965). According to their account, industrialisation has served to transform work and occupation patterns from agriculture peasants and wage labour. The emergence of the factory system entailed new forms of discipline, job insecurity, work specialisation, class and social mobility. They argue that 'specialization based on mechanization in the early years of industrial development can mean robotization for some workers, technological unemployment for others. Both have a drastic impact on life in the family and community' (ibid, pp.62-63). Some of the results are unemployment and alienation in the workplace.

Concerning the family, they note that 'production has been removed from home, and extended kin sheared away; family size has been reduced, and at the same time a great deal of family sentiment has probably been fostered and directed toward the few persons left' (ibid, p.72). They also noticed the changing status of children and women which resulted in new family structures, new family conflicts and problems, declining status of the aged and the breakup of family systems in terms of increasing divorce rates (ibid, pp.72-81). Continuing industrialisation engendered the rise of white-collar and professional classes, changes within the composition of the white-collar population, an increase of scale of the factory system, companies and other types of organization resulting from competition and domination, and a fairer distribution of income (ibid, ch.4).

In this industrialized society, accompanied by urbanisation, new social problems emerged. Wilensky and Lebeaux suggest that,

> ... problems of fitting in of newcomers, of urban growth, of overcrowding of slums, of unemployment and injuries, of mental illness and medical

care, of delinquency and crime, of the inequalities of opportunity for minorities, and more. Other problems intensify: leisure time use, worker retraining, the older worker, suburban sprawl, the journey to work, preserving a creative culture despite mass education. And the uneven development of industrialization means different problems in different places (ibid, p.133).

The major argument of Wilensky and Lebeaux is 'that the technological changes of industrialism lead to changes in the structure of society' and these 'produce and intensify concern about social problems, which creates a demand for welfare services' (ibid, p.181; chart D). These demands have led to the supply of services by social agencies (public and private) manned by professional workers. They use studies of family problems and juvenile delinquency to illustrate their arguments (ibid, ch.8 & 9).

All these theoretical constructs and observations have been developed and empirically tested by various researchers. Cutright discovered that the coverage of social security programmes correlated with the level of economic development of countries (1965).[3] In later research, he also found a correlation between GNP per capita and social security expenditures using from data of 40 countries (1967). Aaron concluded that income per capita was the most important determinant of social security expense per capita (1967).[4] Pryor found that though age of the system is the most important predictor of social spending, economic level is the underlying cause of this (1968).[5] Wilensky, in a comparative study , argues that welfare effort varied in different countries according to their level of economic development. He finds a strong correlation between economic level and social security effort.[6] The development of social services is also perceived as a natural development in changing capitalist society and as response to the new needs of the population in this process of change, such as unemployment and ageing (Pampel & Williamson, 1989; Wilensky, 1975). All these researches support the argument that economic development and accompanying social phenomena resulting from industrialisation and modernisation are the major determinants of social service development.

Concerning the convergence thesis, the research conducted by Cutright (1965), Pryor (1968) and Wilensky (1975) offered evidence and proof of convergence. Wilensky argues that 'economic growth makes countries with contrasting cultural and political traditions more alike in their strategy for constructing the floor below which no one sinks' (1975, p.27) and furthermore, 'once the programs were established they matured, everywhere moving toward wider coverage and higher benefits' (ibid, p.47).

A parallel notion to the convergence thesis is the idea of diffusion. The diffusion thesis perceived 'social policy initiatives primarily as the outcome of processes of imitation, whereby nations copy the efforts of welfare-state pioneers' (Wilensky et al, 1987, p.389; Flora & Alber, 1981). Therefore, the diffusion thesis considers that the development of social services arise from external factors, i.e. influences from outside the nation. Diffusion could be through two channels: spatial diffusion and hierarchical diffusion. Spatial diffusion refers to the spillover effort from nearby countries (Taira & Kilby, 1969). Hierarchical diffusion refers to diffusion from the major centres of innovation, usually from the more advanced societies to the marginal countries which are usually the less developed countries in terms of their political, social and economic situations (Collier & Messick, 1975, p.1306). Collier & Messick propose that diffusion could occur through major lines of communication such as colonial rule. MacPherson takes up this idea and argues for the significance of the legacy of colonialism on the development in the third world countries (1985). Furthermore, in their research, Collier and Messick suggest that diffusion could be 'down' as well as 'up' the hierarchy. They use Germany as an example and argue that when this country pioneered social security, it was less advanced as compared with the United Kingdom, yet the latter country was later in adopting a social security system (1975, p.1306).

The diffusion thesis was later linked to the 'world system' thesis, as in the comment from Thomas and Lauderdale:

> A central point in our theory is that differences in adoption, funding and expansion of these programmes are conditioned by interaction at two levels of social order, the internal national level and external world system, which are conceptualized as an institutional environment of the nation state (1988, p.384).

They propose that incorporation into the world system will force a nation to improve its welfare to international standards which are mostly based on the Western welfare states' standards (1988, pp.388-389). Cameron has also argued that the openness of individual nations' economies to the world trade system has explanatory power with respect to the growth of the public expenditure (1978).[7]

These functional/industrialist explanations, were constructed in an age of growth and prosperity. They assumed that there was a value consensus in society over the expansion of social welfare. Yet, such a view is challenged by the new social conditions of recent years. The discovery of new social problems has discredited the consensus view and 'undermined the credibility of a doctrine based on the notions of harmony, equilibrium and value consensus' (Mishra, 1987, p.67). Societies were not consensual nor did the different parts share a common vision or have a harmonious relationships with each other. Therefore, what might be functional for some parts of society might be dysfunctional for others. The social system might only serve sectoral interests instead of the whole, and engender problems instead of solving them. The common belief that social welfare system as a natural tendency evolved as means to cope with the emerging social problems needed to be re-examined, especially its relation to sectoral interests.

Another theoretical weakness of the functionalist account is its problem in differentiating between the causes and the consequences of the system. This created a teleological type of explanation which took the consequences as the causes of the system. (Haralambos, 1990, p.778). The development of social services was seen as a linear and natural development which accompanied the growth of economy and the changing social conditions that resulted. Such a mechanistic and deterministic view neglects the role and conscious thinking of the individual agents who compose the system. A study of the process of social services development needs to consider the role of agency not just the functions that social services perform for society.

This theoretical perspective is also weak when it comes to explaining differential patterns of services across societies which share similar levels of industrialisation and modernisation (Harloe, 1995, p.520). Merton tried to explain such types of difference by the concept of 'functional alternatives', that is different 'manifest' systems which perform, nevertheless, the same function (1968, p.106). Yet, the thesis cannot explain the detail of welfare policy and focuses too much on the analysis of aggregate social welfare expenditure (Alber et al, 1987; Weed, 1979).

Other than the doubts about the theoretical assumptions of this approach, there have been empirical findings which question its explanatory power. Thus Carrier and Kendall argue that the thesis cannot satisfactorily explain the relatively backward development of the welfare state in America and New Zealand which have comparable levels of economic development to those of other developed countries (1973). O'Connor also argues that, comparing the GNP of the OECD countries and their levels of welfare expenditure from 1960 to 1980, there was no clear correlation between the two variables (1988).

Concerning the convergence and diffusion thesis, various researchers have pointed out that the thesis has been disproved by subsequent developments. Wilensky et al, in a later study, modified their earlier argument and state that 'it is less clear below these aggregate levels [in terms of expenditure], programmes have converged'. They further argue that 'to infer convergence from aggregate data may obscure radical differences in the conditions of eligibility, benefit levels, duration of benefits, administrative direction -- and hence, the benefits and services received' (Wilensky et al, 1987, p.388). Concerning the diffusion thesis, they now criticise its inability to 'specify the path of causality running from the appearance of an idea or proposal to its adoption and implementation' (ibid, p.391; Alber et al, 1987, p.460). In this context, Heclo has suggested that the German initiation of social security provided a strong demonstration effect in Sweden but had a lesser impact on Britain (1974). Kuhnle furthers this argument and stresses that the German policy initiative only has a sectoral influence on accident insurance in Finland, old age pensions in Sweden, accident and sickness insurance in Norway and had no influence on Denmark (1981). Even if we can establish the evidence of similarity among countries, it is still difficult to argue that which countries copy which countries' experience (Thomas & Lauderdale, 1987).

All these counter-findings do not entirely reject the socio-economic explanation that is strongly embedded in functionalism and industrialism. While still accepting that the economic factor did have an impact on welfare state development, they suggest that the explanation must incorporate other factors alongside the economic explanation. Apart from differences in demographic structures, individual nation's political and socio-economic situations also shaped their unique welfare systems (Flora & Alber, 1981).

From socio-economic to political explanation: classical Marxism

While socio-economic accounts, based on the notions of functionalism and industrialism, are perceived as holding an unwarranted consensus view of society, political-conflict perspectives abandons this assumption. Their roots can be traced back to Marx. As does the functionalist/industrialism thesis, Marx recognised the impact of industrialisation on society, particularly on the division of power between the capitalists who owned the means of production and the proletariat who worked for the capitalists in exchange for wages. Such an economic structure has a determining influence on the state through the political domination of the capitalists. He argued that the state is the executive of the whole bourgeoisie to suppress and rule society (Ham & Hill, 1984, pp.32-33; Bryson, 1992, p.185) and welfare provision was just one of its strategies. Basically, the capitalist structure is antithetical to any radical form of welfare and welfare 'reform', in such societies cannot change the basic nature of the capitalist system.[8]

Of course, Marx's theory was too simple and deterministic to account for the contemporary situation. From 1950s, there were other theories which focused on the 'parts' of society instead of on the 'macro structure' to explain the state's action. Such theories tend to explain the welfare state as the product of the dynamics (or conflict) between the parts of society, these being based on various divisions, not just class. The welfare state (and the state) was no longer viewed as a 'blind follower' of the capitalism and macro-structural change. The role of politics was introduced into theories of the welfare state.

Political explanation

Pluralism

The first perspective was pluralism which had its heyday in early post-war era (Therborn, 1986, p.131). This theory differed from classical Marxism in its perception of the power distribution in society but was similar to functionalism in terms of its interpretation of modernization as the cause of various new social phenomena (Alford & Friedland, 1985, ch.2). One of the pioneers in this field of study was Dahl. His research on New Haven concludes that power is not monopolised by capitalists, but instead, it is widely distributed among groups. Every group exerts pressure on the decision-making process and different interest groups ally with other groups with similar interests (1961). This is the typical interplay of power in a liberal democratic society. Though, the power distribution among groups may be unequal, even the weakest groups can still voice their opinion, exert a certain degree of influence and, most important of all, no one group can dominate the scene. Tension builds up but it can be resolved by communication and discussion. Political competition is similar to a 'marketplace' where different groups, according to their resources and outputs, bargain with each other. Therefore, Janowitz suggests that the 'welfare state responds to the needs and demands of the increasingly large and specialized social segments, transcending class-based categories' (Pampel & Williamson, 1989, p.42). Welfare is seen as the result of the power interplay among these groups. From such viewpoint, government may be perceived largely as a neutral agent which acts according to the majority views in the process of competition.[9]

This classical pluralist perspective has been criticised for its methodological and theoretical assumptions. The perspective's pre-occupation with the 'first dimension of power' has been criticised by Lukes as it only focuses on manifest behaviour and neglects 'non-decision making' processes and the shaping of orientations, these are the second and third dimensions of power (Lukes, 1981; Marsh, 1983; Richardson & Jordan, 1979).

Marsh has developed an alternative conception, 'elite pluralist theories'. According to this approach, society is still democratic and the political process is one of the compromises between interest groups. However, there is an unequal distribution of power and the theory stresses the stronger influence of the elite groups. Eckstein, in an earlier study of the British Medical Association, illustrated this by showing the positive impact of the Association on the Ministry of Health and its effect on medical policy (1960). Richardson and Jordan, in an analysis of the British government, find that interest groups were, represented by their elite (e.g. union leaders) and groups' influence was differentiated by their proximity to the core of power (i.e. whether they were 'insider' or 'outsider' groups) (1979). All these arguments contribute to undermine the basic assumption of classical pluralism.

Elitism and corporatism

This gap left by classical pluralism is filled by another two explanations of power distribution. They are the elitism and corporatism. The classical version of the elite theory was developed by Pareto and Mosca. Pareto argued that human behaviour was related to types of human personality, the 'foxes' and the 'lions'. The people who are 'lions' tend to be conservative and unimaginative and are the 'ruled' while the 'foxes' are the elite and the 'rulers' (Waters, 1994, p.225; Haralambos, 1990, pp.136-137).[10]

Mosca agreed that certain segments of society would inevitably be 'ruled' by a small elite group. The elite could be found in both autocratic-aristocratic and the liberal-democratic types of society. Mosca suggested that,

> In all societies - from societies that are very meagerly developed and have barely attained the dawnings of civilisation, down to the most advanced and powerful societies - two classes of people appear - a class that rules and a class that is ruled. The first class, always the less numerous, performs all political functions, monopolises power and enjoys the advantages that power brings, whereas the second, the more numerous class, is directed and controlled by the first ... (quoted from Ham & Hill, 1987, p.29).

The elite are authorised by the non-elite to rule through various legitimate means. Pareto argued that the elite might decline and be replaced by another elite (i.e. circulation of elites), Mosca suggested that the vacated positions could be filled by the former non-elite (Haralambos, 1990, p.137). Mills held a similar view, that society and power are dominated by a relatively coherent set of interlinked power elites who occupy key positions in the government, business and the military (1956). These elites are frequently drawn from those who control the economy and in that sense, Mills has similarities with the Marxist tradition of thought.

Another group of theorists has discussed the development of capitalism at an advanced stage and its impact on the organisation and distribution of power. In this advanced stage of capitalism, there is increasing competition among companies which results in an increasing size of corporations and the growth of multi-national companies. Different interests group together to pursue their interests, for example, chambers of commerce, business committees and professional organisations, as well as trade unions. Cawson states that,

> ... in the context of the 1970s, as economic growth faltered and the legitimacy of party government was eroded ... According to liberal theory, the relentless pressure for expansionary social policies, fueled by the ever-increasing demands of a plethora of welfare pressure groups, and the willingness of politicians to trade promises for votes, combined to 'overload' the once robust democratic governments. Democracy, it seemed, was beginning to bite the hand that fed it (1982, p35).

Such an increasing number and power of intermediate organisations and the growing involvement of the state in economic and social affairs bought these two into a closer corporatist relationship which has gradually replaced the discredited democratic parliamentary system. Power has gradually shifted to this interaction either through formal or informal channels and structures (Cawson, 1982; Ham & Hill, 1987, p.37; Lee, 1987, pp.268-269). Schmitter has described the corporatist system as,

> ... a system of interest representation in which the constituent units are organised into a limited number of singular, compulsory, non-competitive, hierarchically ordered and functionally differentiated categories, recognised or licensed (if not created) by the state and granted a deliberate representational monopoly within their respective categories in exchange for observing certain controls on their selection of leaders

and articulation of demand and supports (quoted from Ham & Hill, 1987, p.38).

Schmitter has differentiated two forms of corporatism, namely 'state' and 'societal' corporatism. The first type occurs when an authoritarian and anti-liberal state co-opts groups into the political system while the second type is a better form of corporatism in which there is a true cooperation between the state and the organisations (ibid, p.39; Ham & Hill, 1987, p.38; Lee, 1987, p.268). Corporatism is 'a pattern of articulation between the state and functional interests' in an 'interdependent relationship' (Cawson, 1982, p.41). The relationship among the groups can be competitive in their respective policy sectors.[11] According to corporatism, the key forces behind decision making are 'monopolistic, centralized interest organizations in concentration and bargaining with the state and with each other' (Therborn, 1986, p.141; King, 1986, p.124). Policies will reflect the deals between the organisations and the state. The state can also have an active role in this bargaining process.

Corporatist theories seek to describe policy either as the outcome of a cooperative, peaceful bargaining process or, in some cases, as an arena for 'striving for differentials and for special privileges by small groups or by particular segments, without consideration of broader class and national interests' (Therborn, 1986, p.145). From the second perspective, welfare policies cannot be perceived as a product of cooperation.

Neo-Marxist theories:
instrumentalism, structuralism & contradiction of the welfare state

The Neo-Marxists perspective tries to explain the power distribution and policy making by a modified version of classical Marxism. This stream of thought has been further divided by Therborn into a 'first wave' and a 'second wave' (Therborn, 1986). This perspective shares the Marxist view of class struggle, the capitalist state and production relations but rejects a crude and simplistic deterministic view of these. Theorists include Miliband, Poulantzas, Gough, O'Connor and Offe.[12]

Ralph Miliband represented the stream of instrumentalism in this 'new' wave Marxism. 'Instrumentalist views are those that tend to describe the state as the instrument of a specific social class' (Kasinitz, 1983, p.337). Jessop has suggested that instrumentalism in its least developed form, 'merely involves the claim that the state is not an independent and sovereign political subject but is an instrument of coercion and administration which can be used for various purposes by whatever interests manage to appropriate it' (1982, p.12). This has slightly deviates from the claim of the inevitable and inherent capitalist dominance by classical Marxism. However, the capitalist state still turns out to be just the instrument of the capitalist class. In Miliband's seminal work, 'The State in Capitalist Societies', he analysed the dominant classes in countries such as Britain, USA, France and Germany, and came to the conclusion that the economically dominant class was also dominant in politically (1969).

Miliband has tried to prove this relationship by showing the similarity of background between the capitalist bourgeoisie and the governing elite. He has found that in large part these elites' social origins were in the bourgeoisie, while acted as a pressure group to exert profound influence on the state (1969, pp.119-145; 1977, p.71). Thus, state policy fundamentally serves the capitalist interest as capitalists, either directly manipulates state policies or indirectly exercise its pressure on them. Thus, Miliband concludes that,

> What is wrong with pluralist-democratic theory is not its insistence on the fact of competition but its claim that the major organized 'interests' in these societies, and notably capital and labor, compete on more or less equal terms, and that none of them is therefore able to achieve a decisive and permanent advantage in the process of competition ... In previous chapters it was shown that business, particularly large-scale business, did enjoy such as advantage inside the state system, by virtue of the composition and ideological inclinations of the state elite ... business enjoys a massive superiority outside the state system as well, in terms of immensely stronger pressures which, as compared with labor and any other interest, it is able to exercise in the pursuit of its purpose (ibid, p.146).

Though the bourgeoisie can directly control the state, they generally prefer not to involve themselves in the management of the state directly. Miliband argues that to prevent any fraction of the capitalist class to dominating the state and to create an impartial image of the state, the ruling class prefers not to directly participate in the state apparatus (ibid, p.96).

A further point is that the freedom of state officials is limited by their need to assist capital accumulation, thereby serving the capitalist interest, as economic success is vital to their survival. So even if we disregard the class background of state officials or the pressure exerted on them, the capitalist structure 'has its own rationality to which any government or state must sooner or later submit, and usually sooner' (Miliband, 1977, p.72). Hence, the state will be the instrument serving the long-term interests of capital.

Welfare effort has to be understood as in the capitalist's interest and welfare reform will only, ultimately, serve the capitalist interest instead of the working class's interest.

Miliband's account has been criticised by Poulantzas, who represented the 'structuralist' stream of thought in Neo-Marxism. He disagreed with the instrumentalist's idea that the state can be simply understood as an instrument of the ruling class. He criticised Miliband's approach as putting the 'agent' 'as the genetic principle of the levels of the social whole'.

> This is a problematic of social actors, of individuals as the origin of social action: sociological research thus leads finally, not to the study of the objective co-ordinates that determine the distribution of agents into social classes and the contradictions between these classes, but to the search for finalist explanations founded on the motivations of conduct of the individual actors (1973a, p.295).

He argued that the individual is less significant than structural factors in determining the state's policies. Following Althusser's notion, he argued that class interests are exercised in three fields: economic, political and ideological, and different classes focus their efforts in different fields. The capitalist class focuses its effort on the economy while the working class pays more attention to the political field. Moreover, Poulantzas argued that capitalists are never unified and hence, to prevent any fractional interest dominating the state, it has some autonomy.[13] Moreover, the state has to have power to deal with the pressures and demands from the working class, to make concessions and policies which meet their needs while, at the same time, maintaining a facilitative environment for capital accumulation. Such a situation gives the state some autonomy. However, such autonomy is only 'relative' (1973a; 1973b; Kasinitz, 1983, pp.342-343). The functions of the state are both constrained and limited by the structure of society and the contradictions of capitalism. State actions are the attempts to solve these contradictions, to counter working class unity and capitalist disunity (Gold, Ho & Wright, 1975a, p.36-37).

From this perspective, the driving force of welfare reforms is working class struggle, and the autonomy of state officials to react to these demands to contain the pressure and maintain the conditions for capital accumulation. So, the ultimate rationale still relates to capital accumulation. Both Miliband and Poulantzas shared a similar belief that welfare, ultimately, serves the capitalist and capitalism more than the working class. Their differences concern how this comes about.[14]

Poulantzas's abstract construction of 'relative autonomy' was heavily criticised by Cawson and Saunders as it 'explains everything and nothing' (King, 1986, p.79). Pampel and Williamson also find it difficult to substantiate in their study (1989, ch.7). Yet, Poulantzas's analysis, as well as Miliband's, introduced a relatively systematic investigation to the relationship between economic structure, the ruling class and the state, pointing out the origins and limits of welfare reform in capitalist society (Mishra, 1987, p.77).

Their rather pessimistic view of social welfare in capitalist society (Korpi, 1989, p.309) is shared by other Neo-Marxists. O'Connor, although recognising working class struggle, argued that the inherent nature of the welfare state served the capitalist interest though, it would engender a contradictory situation. The growing demand for state expenditure would eventually lead to a fiscal crisis of the state. This embodies the contradiction between the functions of accumulation and legitimation (1973) and the contradiction between the socialization of costs and the private appropriation of profits (Mishra, 1984, p.70; 1987, p.77).

Gough echoes O'Connor and perceives the welfare state as a 'contradictory unity' within capitalist society, 'the welfare state is a product of the contradictory development of capitalist society and in turn it has generated new contradictions which every day become more apparent' (1979, p.152). Gough argues that 'the working class struggle and influence, the centralisation of the state and the influence of the former over the latter' were the major determinants of the modern welfare state (1979, p.68).

Offe shares a similar analysis with O'Connor and Gough in describing the welfare state as the means for legitimation and accumulation. Due to that contradiction, the state is doomed to fail in forming an alliance between itself and all classes as well as dealing with pressure from classes for their own interests. Particularly in crisis periods, such as in the economic crisis in mid-1970s, the state has to be 'structurally selective', more responsive to the powerful class as its support will be essential to the survival of the state (King, 1986, p.82; Mishra, 1987, p.78).

Thus, although working class struggle has been partially successful in pressing for policies 'against' the capitalist interest and the state's relative autonomy in initiating reforms provide some benefits to the working class, welfare can never truly transform the capitalist system and the dominant class is always the one which benefits from this, ultimately. Any gains are rather superficial and are only temporary solutions to the contradictions of capitalistic society. Apart from this, these Neo-Marxists have pointed out the necessity to disaggregate the working and capitalist class in analysis. All of them argue there are, in fact, fractions and sectoral interests within these two blocs (Wetherly, 1988).

Social democracy

Therborn has suggested that the research that developed out of Neo-Marxism from the 1980s differed from that in the 1960s and 1970s, that is the 'first wave' of Neo-Marxism represented by Miliband, Poulantzas, O'Connor, Offe and others. He recognises that these early studies successfully highlighted the issues of inequality of power in society, and the dynamic relationship between the state and the capitalist economy and contributed to a broader conception of the state. Yet, Therborn argues that these studies, were still predominately theoretical, abstract and without much empirical back-up. The analysis focused more on the state than the welfare state (1986, pp.133-136).

By contrast, he states the 'second wave' of Neo-Marxism has been supported by a vast amount of empirical work focused on the welfare state, particularly on Scandinavian countries, and has advanced a 'new, vigorous, self-confident class theory of politics and state' (1986, p.132). This 'second wave' of Neo-Marxism has been closely linked with the arguments of social democracy, to comment and to analyse the social democratic welfare state, and the role of social democracy in leading welfare state development. The initial attempt of this research was to counteract the once dominant 'logic of industrialism' thesis. The objectives were to 'demonstrate that politics matter and that the party composition of the polity makes a decisive difference' (Esping-Andersen & van Kersbergen, 1992, p.190). In earlier research, Hewitt has suggested a definition of social democracy,

> The term 'social democratic' is used here to describe those movements and parties which avowedly embody socialist ideals or claim to represent the working class or labor interest, and also are committed to the norms of representative democracy. Specifically, social democracy is defined as including those parties which are affiliated to the Socialist International, thereby guaranteeing a certain ideological and programmatic homogeneity to the grouping (1977, p.457).

In later studies of social democracy, more empirical findings have been gathered to develop an in-depth understanding of the variations among advanced capitalist societies (Therborn, 1986, pp.136-137). Large-scale cross-national comparative research as well as historical studies on individual nations have been carried out (Chouinard & Fincher, 1987). The welfare state is perceived as a class issue, it is supported and defended by the working class and organisations which represent their interests. Working class mobilisation, in unions and/or parties, is a determining factor in the development of the welfare state. Shalev has argued that 'growth of reformist labor unions and parties which reflect the class divisions of capitalist society, and in particular the ascension of labor parties to execute power, have been the pre-eminent forces in the initiation and development of public policies for furthering justice and equality between the classes' (1983, p.317).

The major argument of the social democratic thesis has been summarised by Adams,

> ... the state is seen as the vehicle for the achievement of socialist goals. Through the election of social democratic representatives, legislation will be enacted subjecting the capital accumulation process to social control and subordinating markets to politics. The welfare state ... is both an aspect and a mechanism of the transition from capitalism to socialism. The aim, then, is to win governmental power through parliamentary elections and to use the state to control the national economy in the interests of working people, to transform the nation-state into what the Scandinavian social democrats call a 'people's home' (1988, p.29).

The social democratic approach holds a more optimistic view than the previous Neo-Marxist analysis. It expects that the social democratic movement can peacefully transform the capitalism into socialism (Castles, 1978).

A vast amount of research findings have been produced to support such claims. The major independent variables used are working class strength in terms of the rate of unionization, the presence of a strong, centralised and coherent labour movement, and the 'presence and duration of social democratic parties in government' in terms of number of cabinet posts and years of continuous government etc., (Adams, 1988, pp.28-29; Therborn, 1986, p.150; Korpi, 1983, ch.3). In later studies, class mobilisation is not confined to the Left parties or working class unions but extended to the other non-Left parties and Churches etc. A detailed examination of the 'alliances' or 'trade-offs' between social democratic parties and other groups is proposed to widen the scope of analysis (Baldwin, 1990, p.9; Esping-Andersen, 1990; Shalev, 1983, p.337; Skocpol, 1980b; Therborn, 1986).

In the earlier social democratic studies, the dependent variables are rather narrowly focused on the welfare state in terms of overall social expenditure

(Shalev, 1983, pp.323-324). In later studies, the dependent variables representing welfare state, were expanded to include wider aspects of economic and welfare policy, to wider matter such as equality, justice and de-commodification. In terms of economic policy, the variables also include the Keynesian objective of full-employment (Esping-Andersen & van Kersbergen, 1992, p.196).

Hewitt has found that countries which have longer democratic histories and stronger socialist party strength have stronger egalitarian outcomes in income distribution and economic growth (1977).[15] Furniss and Tilton find that the role of social democracy is decisive in the formation and development of welfare states in respective nations (1977).[16] Cameron also argues that, in addition to the degree of openness of the economy to the world system, the power of the social democratic governments helps to explain the growth of public expenditure (1978).

Stephens argues that the extent of socialist party rule is a valid variable to explain the growth of welfare spending, and this together with union strength (measured in terms of centralisation of trade unions) serves to explain the level of income equality (1979). Castles, in an analysis of Western European countries, argues that welfare effort is associated with the political power of the social democratic parties and hence, the higher level of welfare effort in the Scandinavian countries is related to the continuous dominance of a united front of Left parties and a divided Right groups (1978).

Korpi finds countries that have 'highly mobilized working classes and long-term control over governmental power, Sweden and Norway, appear to have less income inequality than most of the other countries' (1983, p.197). These countries also have a smaller proportion of population living in poverty, a higher redistributive effect resulting from taxation policies and government budgetary policies, and a lower unemployment rate (ibid, ch.9).[17] In another study, Korpi also finds that 'as far as the development of social rights in sickness insurance is concerned, left party government participation clearly has been an important factor during both the prewar and the postwar periods' (1989, p.323).[18]

Esping-Andersen, in his effort to classify welfare state regimes, argues that class mobilisation is one of the important factors to be explored in shaping the various types of regimes (1989, p.27; 1990, p.29). He urges a more comprehensive understanding of the causes of welfare state which must incorporate non-working class mobilisations, such as those of farmers, the new middle class and their coalition with the working class, as well as the 'historical legacy of regime institutionalisation' (ibid). 'There are many factors that conspire to make it virtually impossible to assume that any labor, or left, party will ever be capable, single-handedly, of structuring a welfare state' (1989, p.28). Such a cautious stand in appraising the contribution of social democracy is also held by Shalev,

> ... the first generation of studies in the mould of the social democratic model demonstrates that in fact the welfare state emerges and grows in advanced capitalist societies with or without a strong and coherent social democratic labor movement. But its emergence is hastened, its growth is speeded, and its consequences for the class distribution of resources and opportunities are arguably greater under social democracy (1983, p.331).

Shalev and Esping-Andersen have both argued for a more sophisticated understanding of the relationship between social democracy and the welfare state and the interaction or coalition among parties and classes (Shalev, 1983, p.322, p.337; Esping-Andersen & Kersbergen, 1992).

The weaknesses of the social democratic model have also been discovered by other researchers. Flora and Alber have noted that the initiation of social security in Germany was by conservative rulers instead of by the working class or any form of working class mobilisation (1981). Wilensky, in a comparative study, finds that Left party strength has little effect on the level of social security spending while Catholic party strength has a stronger impact (1981).

Weir and Skocpol suggest that the origin of the Swedish welfare state lay neither solely nor mainly with the Social Democrats but rather, from the joint interests of the working class and the farmers, as well as the influence of state experts (1983).[19] Baldwin also finds that the agrarian class, as well as middle class, had a stronger impact on the Scandinavian model of welfare state (1990). He argues that,

> ... such an account formulated in terms of the working class's strength and organisation is but one instance of a broader logic of social interest behind the welfare state and its development. Workers were often that group most concerned with social policy but they have not been the only one. Nor, in a broader comparative analysis, have their interest been more than a single factor, amongst many competing ones (1990, pp.8-9).

In general, the social democratic model is heavily grounded on and seems to be more applicable to the Scandinavian countries, and has been criticised as being only applicable in this particular region, having less explanatory power in other countries (Esping-Andersen & Kersbergen, 1992, p.202).

Nevertheless, the impact of the Left or working class mobilisation has to be considered, as one of the factors, in the analysis of welfare state development. It has provided a more contemporary interpretation of the Marxist and Neo-Marxist thesis of class action in a democratic society. The enriched understanding of social democratic movements, in terms of their coalitions with other parties, classes and contribution to the social basis of the welfare state policy (Therborn, 1984), together with the emphasis on historical legacies is valuable (Esping-Andersen, 1990; Skocpol, 1979; Skocpol & Ikenberry, 1983). These arguments are backed up by empirical studies not just theoretical and abstract speculation. Nevertheless, the explanation is still a class-based one, stressing the inequality of power among classes within the capitalist economy and its consequence for welfare state development.

State-centered explanation

According to the previous perspectives, the major forces behind the origin and development of the welfare state are external to the state. This perspective has been termed 'society-centered' thesis in which, the role of state is considered as secondary or totally irrelevant (Skocpol, 1992, p.4). Of course, the role of state is mentioned and discussed sometimes. Thus Gough stresses the effect of the state structure in shaping policy (1979). Various Neo-Marxists, Miliband, Poulantzas and Offe, have argued for a more detailed understanding of the role and impact of the state in policy making. Offe has argued that welfare programmes are, in fact, a crisis management project of the state and the state has an internal structure which selectively accepts or screens out issues (Saunders, 1979, pp.173-178; Gold, Lo & Wright, 1975b, pp.37-39).[20]

Yet, in these theories the role of the state is still captured within the broader structure. It is no more than an instrument of the ruling class in classical Marxism and the instrumentalism of Miliband and is at best, 'relatively autonomous' in Poulantzas's thesis. In the pluralist and corporatist traditions, the state is given a more active role and an important status in mediating conflicts. Yet, the dominating forces are the external pressure groups. In the functionalist/industrialist thesis, the state's action is a response to the changing social conditions resulting from modernisation and industrialisation. The second wave of Neo-Marxism and the enriched social democratic thesis just considers the state as one of the many potential factors affecting welfare state development.

In sharp contrast, the arguments of the 'state-centered thesis' are 'bringing the state back in' (Skocpol, 1992). As observed by Baldwin,

> The state as an independent actor, not merely the club-wielder for the strongest battalion, has recaptured a certain Hegelian or Hintzian autonomy, a role of its own. Social policy evolution has been analyzed as an outcome of the state's ability to perceive and solve problems, formulating responses that do not simply mirror the demands of a particular group (1990, p.45).

This tradition, with its emphasis on the impact of the state on policy, can be traced back to Weber's study of bureaucracy. Weber had argued that bureaucracy was the modern form of organisation and was an inevitable and most important aspect of modernisation and rationalisation in the modern world. Bureaucrats were those appointed to office with authority to administer public affairs (Albrow, 1970, pp.40-44). Bureaucracy can gain control of the state through its formal organisation, impersonal rules and administration, and its technocratic superiority (Haralambos, 1990, pp.409-410). Michels argued that in a large and bureaucratised organisation, power would be concentrated in the hands of a few in high positions, that is an 'oligarchy'. In his study, he found out that the government and the political parties (even the Social Democratic Party[21]), were all controlled by their top officials (Giddens, 1989, pp.280-281). Weber and Michels made it clear that the bureaucrats that filled the state's offices, have to be given a more detailed examination in studies of policy formulation. The passive, reactive and class dominated conception of the state has to be shifted towards a more active, interventive, independent, interest-bearing concept or even occupy a central position in the analysis. Scholars influenced by the Weberian tradition, as noted by Evans, Rueschemeyer and Skocpol, tend to consider that 'states are potentially autonomous and that the controllers of the means of coercion and administration may pursue goals at variance with dominant classes or any other social group' (1992, p.350).

This thesis is backed up by the studies which use an historical and qualitative research methodology. Usually, they focus on one or a few countries for investigation (Quadagno, 1987). This method is justified by the claim that 'comparative and historical examination of watershed periods in which state apparatuses are constructed or reconstructed may be the most promising approach' (Evans et al, 1992, p.361). The 'true potential' of the state's autonomy can only be identified by 'historical studies that are sensitive to structural variations and conjunctural changes within given politics' (Skocpol, 1992, p.14). Although the number of comparative studies of this thesis is rather limited, Skocpol and Amenta have argued that these show that it can explain cross-national differences (1986; Weir & Skocpol, 1983).

In her analysis of revolutions in France, Russia and China, Skocpol concludes that the state is not merely an arena for interests to compete in but is also a macro-structure composed of administrative and coercive organisations which serve as the basis of state power. States have their own interests and will compete with the dominant classes (1979, pp.29-30). In her analysis of the New Deal policy, she finds that the United States's political institutions and state structure contributed to shape and limit its formation. She argues that more weight should be given to the state as an independent determinant (1980, p.199). In another study by Weir and Skocpol, they contend that the power of the expert and administrator, and the higher degree of centralisation of the Swedish government explained the different responses to the Great Depression of 1930s from those of the United States (1983).

In these studies, state is perceived from an organisational perspective which comprises the appointed state officials (bureaucrats and technocrats), serving in the administrative, legislative and coercive organisations of the state (Skocpol, 1992, p.7; Nordlinger, 1981, p.11). This group of people also includes the 'welfare bureaucracy' (Wilensky, 1975, ch.3). King has argued that this group of personnel has emerged as the force defending and shaping the development of the welfare services in pursuing their own interests (1987b). The independent variable of the state is defined both in terms of the people in the state positions and the organisational structure in which they are located.

Skocpol explains that the capacity of the state to achieve its goals is based on the stability of its control of the government, a regular supply of loyal and competent officials, and adequate financial support (1992, p.16). Nordlinger has provided a detailed description of the tactics of the democratic state (or state officials) in manipulating and shifting societal preferences to pursue their own choices (1981, pp.93-94, pp.111-112, pp.130-132). Through this solid power base and a skillful application of strategies, the officials can have good chance of achieving their interests.

Yet, the thesis's explanatory power has been queried by other theoretical traditions. Certainly, the thesis will not be welcomed by those who argued for a 'society-centered' perspective, be they classes, interest and pressure groups, or forces created by industrialization, modernisation and specialisation. They argue that the state-centered thesis's account of state formation and state power has to be grounded in the context of wider socio-economic and political changes. Thus Baldwin contends that the thesis has not clarified the degree and extent of state autonomy in respect to different levels of issues. In his study, he argues that 'crucial decisions on welfare policy may have been taken by administrators, that different state structures may encourage or impede solutions, but that, in the final analysis, larger social forces have nonetheless significantly determined the nature of the legislation adopted' (1990, p.47). It is powerful social interests that the administrators work in accordance with (ibid, p.49).

Gourevitch, in his analysis of various nations' responses to economic recession, concludes that social actors and the state require each other in shaping policy (1986, p.229). The state's autonomy has to be supported by a solid social base, formed by the political support or compliance of different societal actors and intermediate associations (ibid, pp.231-238). Thus, 'the impacts of state structure, however great, cannot be shown independent of some understanding of the society it is meant to affect' (ibid, p.62). Hence, Harloe, argues 'the state-centered approach seems to promise rather more than, in practice, it delivers' (1995, p.522).

In fact, the state-centered theorists do recognise the impact of societal forces and the socio-economic-political structure on the state's action and policies. Skocpol has admitted that, 'studies of the states alone are not to be substituted for concerns with classes or groups; nor are purely state-determinist arguments to be fashioned in the place of society-centered explanations' and there is need to analyse the state in relation to the socio-economic and socio-cultural structure (1992, p.20).

In another historical analysis of the formation of the American welfare state, she argues again that 'an analysis of phases and patterns of social welfare provision in the United States needs to highlight the historical structures of the United States and politics, and needs to pay attention both to democratic pressures and to elite efforts at political reform in relation to these particular and changing macro-political frameworks' (Skocpol & Ikenberry, 1983, p.91). Yet, to make a distinctive thesis, they tend to put the state in the centre-place for study, a rather extreme reverse of the previous studies. Evans et al have suggested a more balanced understanding of the thesis suggesting that 'studying the state action should not either glorifying state power or over-estimating its efficacy' and the question of the state's role should be open to question, at the start of empirical studies (1992, p.365)..

Table 3.1
Theories of the welfare state development : a summary

Perspective of explanation	Theoretical tradition	Forces (independent variables)
Society-centered		
Socio-economic (Sociological, Economic, Demographic etc.)	Structural-functionalism	: Structural differentiation resulting from modernisation : Problems resulted from differentiation and specification : Demographic changes
	Industrialism	: Similar to structural-functionalism but the major change force is industrialisation
	Diffusion	: Geographical proximity : Channel of communication e.g. colonial rule
	Convergence	: Level of economic development : Level of economic integration into the world system
Political	Classical Marxism	: Capitalist / bourgeoisie
	Pluralism	: Interest group mediation
	Elitism	: Powerful societal elite and their interplay with the governing elite
	Corporatism	: Powerful intermediate organisations
	Instrumentalism	: Capitalists / bourgeoisie in powerful position : Logic of capitalism
	Structuralism	: Structural necessity of capitalism : Relative autonomy of state to maneuver the conflicts
	Social democracy	: Organised unions and Left parties : Participation and control of the government

'Merged'		
Socio-economic-political and state	Second-wave of Neo-Marxism	: Class conflict incl. middle class and other forms of social division : Structure of society and economy in capitalism : State structure and legacy
State-centered		
State (Political & organisational)	State-centered	: Structural arrangement of the state; : Level of centralisation; : Historical legacy; : Ideology and interest of the official; : Interaction and alignment of the : Strategies adopted to maintain state autonomy.

Divergence and convergence

The development of theories of the welfare state can be traced back to classical Marxism and functionalism. Subsequently, the focus of theories has changed from time to time and roughly in this chronological order, from structural-functionalism and the logic of industrialism, to political explanations, ranging from pluralism, elitism, corporatism, Marxism and Neo-Marxism, to the state-centered thesis. The debates are centered on the forces of determination of welfare states, whether they arise from 'society' (external) or from the 'state' (internal). The forces from 'society' include classes, groups or different kinds of social divisions and the organisations, parties and alliances that they form. The forces deriving from 'state' involve organisational structures, officials' interests and mentalities and the governing strategies they employ.

The main division concerns the relative degree of influence of these two sources. Different theories can be ranged along a continuum (Uusitalo, 1984, p.414). But in fact, the most recent theories consider both factors, for example, the second-wave of Neo-Marxism and the moderate state-centered thesis (Table 3.1).

Much research has been conducted to verify or falsify various explanations and variables. These have then been verified or falsified by other research and vice versa and all these add to the difficulty of completely denying the impact of any one variable. As argued by Palme,

> It must be recognized that a failure of an individual researcher to obtain empirical support for a variable does not always mean that the variable was rejected at a theoretical level. Proponents of specific approaches often seem to find different theoretical notions complementary rather than contradictory, although they tend to continue to lay a different emphasis on different types of causal factors (1990, p.12).

Various researchers have, in fact, proposed a multi-dimensional explanation. Cameron has found that both the convergence concept and the strength of social democracy helps to explain the growth of social expenditure (1978). Similar perspective is adopted by Flora and Alber (1981). Pampel and Williamson argue that the aging population resulted from industrialisation has been organised into a powerful group which has influence over policy decisions through voting (1989).[22] And the argument for a state centered approach does not exclude the influence of working class mobilisation, although it is put in a secondary position (Skocpol & Amenta, 1986).

An integration of all the perspectives is too ambitious to be achieved here and it may neglect the real theoretical divisions that different approaches involved. Yet, a cautious 'mix' of the variables suggested by different perspectives is still feasible. This is supported by the empirical findings of certain research and a recognition of the limitation of single-factor analysis. As Esping-Andersen has argued, 'the hope of finding a one single powerful causal force must be abandoned' (1990, p.29). This is also supported by other research which argues for a combination of different perspectives in explaining the forces behind the welfare state (Ham & Hill, 1984, p.43; King, 1986, pp.83-84; Pampel & Williamson, 1989, p.47).

Every theory has its own 'explanatory domain' and this has limited its explanatory power in relation to issues outside their domains (Alford & Friedland, 1985, p.3). To explain the complicated forces behind the welfare state, it is both fair and acceptable to start with a multi-perspective standpoint and through empirical and historical grounded research, to narrow-down and focus on more specific variables. A general model of welfare state theory, which includes the study of the socio-economic-political foundation of all perspectives, can be constructed as follows (Figure 3.1).

In such a construction, the industrialisation process is perceived as the fundamental process on which various factors are built and change. The cultural factors go side by side with the fundamental process of industrialisation and are influenced by it. This process, together with nation specific social, economic and political factors serve as the contextual factors which contribute to the shaping of the welfare state.

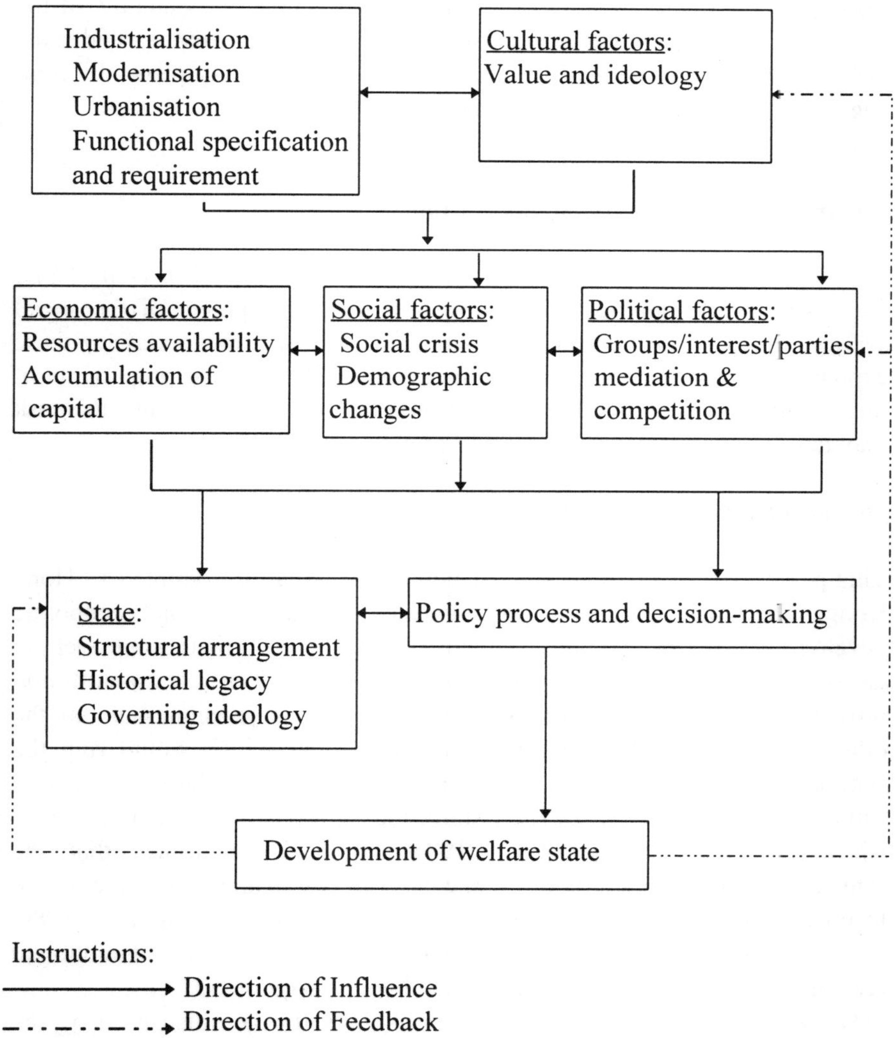

Figure 3.1 General model of theory of welfare state

The political contest over welfare is realised in the arenas of the state and the policy process. The state, is an arena where various political forces compete to have an impact on the development of the welfare state. But the state is also an active agent which has its own interests and potential to resist and re-shape the other factors. The policy process is the arena in which specific demands are raised, addressed and debated, and the outcome of this are implemented as policy. The welfare state is the result of the interplay among structural and state factors. Of course, the outcome of the policy process constitutes a feedback affecting the contextual and state factors. Within this general model, different explanations place different degrees of emphasis on different factors.

Theories of welfare state in Hong Kong

Theories of the welfare state have not been well-developed in Hong Kong but a variety of analytical explanations of the development of the social services do exist. In the following paragraphs, we will try to classify these explanations into the categories defined above. While most proponents of these explanations do not adopt any clear label for their arguments, this task may have the potential risk of misinterpreting their ideas.

Socio-economic explanation

This perspective is one of the most popular explanations adopted in Hong Kong. The basic argument, as suggested by Chiu, is that economic development serves as both the push and the pull factors of welfare development. On one hand, economic development generates wealth and provides adequate financial resources for service expansion, but, on the other hand, the 'myth' of over-supply of services which would ruin the economic success deters any further attempt to develop the services on a fuller scale (1985, 1987, p.45). A similar argument has been suggested by Chow (1979; 1985a, pp.11-13; 1985b, p.146). Ho argues that the 'unprecedented economic boom in the early 1970s enabled the Government to proceed with the Five Year Plan' of social welfare development (1980, p.14). On the contrary, welfare development is halted in times of economic recession such as in the 1970s (Cheng, 1984a, p.144).

The notions of modernisation and industrialisation are also used by the government as their explanation of decisions about and implementation of policy, referring to issues such as the deterioration of family functions, demographic changes and the aging of population, unemployment and retirement protection. Such a thesis is also echoed by scholars and policy analysts who agree that industrialisation has engendered a new style of living affecting the Chinese family system as well as the general social structure. It brings a new employment structure and unemployment. These have generated new needs for social security protection (ICSW HK Committee, 1970, p.13).

Also, the processes of industrialisation and modernisation have contributed to the fading out of traditional ideology which has been replaced by a more Western-type social-right approach to welfare (Chow, 1990, pp.16-17). The specific social situation in Hong Kong has fostered a strong self-centered, reluctant-collectivist and skeptical orientation towards social responsibility among the Hong Kong people. This attitude serves as a negative factor deterring the development of social services (1985, pp.14-15).

Industrialisation and increasing participation in the world economy are also seen as forces for education development. Sung has suggested that one of the reasons for the rapid development of technical education in the 1970s was to assist industrial development so as to maintain the competitiveness with other Newly Industrialised Countries in Asia such as Taiwan and South Korea (1984, p.6). This argument is supported by Yeung and Cheng (Yeung, 1987, p.195; Cheng, 1982, p.12).

The aging population accompanying economic development, as in other developed countries, and the overall increase of population are also seen as having influences on the expansion of social services in relevant areas (Chow, 1985b, pp.148-150). These demographic trends have also fostered the growth of medical services (Lee, 1987, p.216). Jones adopts functionalist approach in explaining the development of social services in Hong Kong. She argues that changes in the socio-economic conditions of the society and occasional crises were responded by ad hoc government policies. This intervention is considered to be a functional response to the needs of the changing environment (1990, p.290).

Hodge adopted a diffusion through lines of communication thesis in explaining the emergence of broader welfare strategies in 1960s and 1970s. He argued, based on his historical analysis of the 1960s, that the decolonisation policy of the British government served as a push factor to its colonies including Hong Kong (1973).

Yet, scholars such as Chow and Tang consider the economic and resource factors as only one of the factors affecting the development of social services (Chow, 1987, p.31; Tang 1990, p.10). Law, from an analysis of the relation between GDP and expenditure on public housing from 1967 to 1979, argues that there is no positive correlation between the growth of national income and public housing expenditure. In fact, 'government expenditures on public housing were not sufficient to keep pace with the continuous increase of national income and population' (1982, p.110).

Public housing policy has to be examined beyond the economic perspective and considered as a political issue (ibid, p.117).

Political explanation

Pluralism Cheng, though recognises the inequality of power among the pressure groups, observes that the less powerful pressure groups still have certain successes in forcing the government to give way over their policies. However, he does not give examples to support his observation (1984b, p.133). Fong also recognises that pressure groups, especially those formed by public housing residents, have affected the housing policy making process. He argues that these pressure groups are more homogenous and hence, have stronger cohesiveness than those in the private housing sector and therefore have greater chance of success and greater impact on the housing policy process (1986, pp.25-27).

Yet, Wong, Cheung and Louie find that the action organised by these pressure groups were focused more on the operational level and on resource allocation issues, and virtually had no wider impact on policy (Wong, 1989, p.91; Cheung & Louie, 1991). Cheung and Louie also argue that the government did not make real concessions to the actions and pressure initiated by the citizens and pressure groups (1991, p.53). The lack of coordinated public pressure and opinion left the government with full autonomy to decide on its own course of action and this also partially explained the reason for the slow evolution of housing policy until the 1970s (Hodge, 1976, p.11; 1981, p.18).

Elitism This perspective has gained strong support in Hong Kong. This argument stresses the domination of the elite, composed of bureaucrats and the business elite, in the decision-making process. Policy is formulated by these groups of the ruling elite. Davies (1977) asserts that Hong Kong was governed by power elite which was formed by government officials and non-officials from major corporations in Hong Kong. The group was only around 100 to 200 people but they occupied most of the appointed seats on Councils and consultative committees. England and Rear have suggested the reasons for their success,

> The groups which are most likely to succeed in pressing their philosophies and proposals are those which are organized and led by individuals with sophistication and education who have access to and can assimilate information, who can marshal and articulate arguments, who can use English language, and -- very important -- who can reinforce their

efforts through continual social contacts with decision-makers. Not surprisingly, those represent commercial and industrial interests are conspicuously successful. (1981, p.8).

Lee also observes that much decision making and power is concentrated in the hands of a few most senior officials, giant British and local corporations and experts (1984a, p.221). Lee states that the cooperation between the business elite and the bureaucrats is based on their similar holding of a paternalistic ideology; the similarity in their social and economic background and hence, the intimate social relationships and economic cooperation they have built up (1984b, p.239).

Ho has analysed the composition of the Executive and Legislative Councils (ExCo & LegCo) and finds that those with a business background have occupied many of the seats of the bodies.[23] Ho finds that in 1985 and 1986, almost ten years after Davies's study, the proportion of businessmen is still approximately 40 per cent and over 70 per cent in the LegCo and the ExCo respectively.

Corporatism Lee shows that there is no organised corporatist structure in Hong Kong in relation to the decision-making process over social policies. He finds that there are no organisations representing the interests of the users of various social services. The only exception is in the housing sector but, these organisations are not recognised by the government and cannot enter the policy-making structure (1987, pp.269-271).

However, Lau indicates that there are many intermediate organisations in Hong Kong. These include the traditional Clansmen Societies and the Kaifong Associations.[24] They have been incorporated into different district level consultative committees and District Boards. Yet, Lau's analysis points out that these traditional organisations have gradually faded out and been replaced by new political groups (1981) and the old 'corporatist structure' is fading out too. Perhaps the best example which shows a 'state corporatist' structure is the incorporation of business and manufacturing organisations into committees and Councils.[25]

Neo-Marxist Neo-Marxist arguments reinforce elitist and corporatist arguments that power rests within the business and commercial interest groups and that the state is constrained within the capitalistic logic. The notions of capital accumulation and legitimacy are the two major forces affecting the development of social services.

Along these lines, Wong adopts a Neo-Marxist approach in his analysis of the rationale for the decommodification of medical services in the 1960s and 1970s. He argues that the reason was the low income of the working class which could not form an effective demand for private medical services. However, these services are vital for the reproduction of labour power and accumulation of capital so the state had no alternative but to intervene in the provision of hospitals, out-patient services and primary health care. However, the growth of this collective consumption engenders further demands and political pressure which fosters a crisis situation (1992).

The need to maintain capital accumulation has also been recognised by England and Rear. They argued that Hong Kong is run by the bureaucracy but their actions are constrained by the need to maintain a flourishing economy (1981, pp.5-8). Scott argues that the concern for legitimacy has continuously shaped the development of social services. The dual need to attract support from the capitalists by various investments in infrastructural projects and 'social investment policies', and to maintain public support by the provision of various social services have affected the social policies (1989). The concern for maintaining 'economic prosperity and political stability' has alerted the government to deal with potential disruptive social forces and problems (Scott & Cheek-Milby, 1986, p.172). Cheung (1988) and Chow agree with the argument that the collective provision of services is an effective means to win support and recognition for the government's legitimacy (1985d, p.145; 1988, p.30). Cheng also argues that increased intervention in social policies can promote economic growth as well as retain popular support (1979).

The influence of the business sector is stressed by Henderson who mentions that its influence on policy making is both open and widely recognized in Hong Kong (1991, p.173). Leung, in arguing against a state-centered thesis, suggests that 'it is far more reasonable to argue that the predominance of business representation in the government suggests that business interests are a primary concern of the government and have a powerful influence on government policy-making' (1990, p.18).

In a specific policy case, Chow suspects that it is the opposition of the employers that made the repeated suggestions for a contributory social insurance scheme fail in the 1960s and 1970s (1982, p.26). He also argues that it is the opposition of the business and commercial sector that makes the transplant of a Western type welfare state in Hong Kong impossible (1990, p.66).

Social democracy Such arguments receive less support in Hong Kong. The reasons that scholars have suggested for this are the low level of unionisation, the political division among the unions and the lack of any political parties to represent the interest of the working class in Hong Kong. In fact, the working class is not a strong unified and conscious class. The unions in Hong Kong, the Left and pro-China, and the Right and pro-Taiwan unions, have been rather passive in social movements and have been narrowly focused on the provision of tangible welfare and recreational services for their members.

In analysing medical policy, Wong observes that the working class has internalised capitalist values and hence, there is little challenge to the fundamental capitalistic structure and the government, but only in relation to the resources redistribution issue (1989, p.96). Only those unions organised by professionals and civil servants have been more active in social action and have a greater power in bargaining with the government (ibid, p.97).[26]

State-centered explanation

Harris reviews the politics of the 1970s and concludes that the instrumentalist arguments do not have strong grounds (1978, ch.4). He suggests that ,

> In terms of interest groups analysis therefore, what this argument suggests is that the business lobby, including the banks, finance houses and myriad species of shops, stores and restaurants, can expect only a limited degree of protection from the bureaucracy. In the end the perception by the bureaucracy of the public interest predominates. There is at least some truth in this argument as we shown by the determination of the government to eradicate corruption in the private sector (1978, p.127).[27]

Harris borrows the term 'administrative state' from Fritz Morstein Marx, which describes the polity 'not as a state devoid of legislative and judicial organs but as a state in which administrative organization and operations are particularly prominent, at least in their quantitative aspects' (ibid, p.55), to describe the essence of Hong Kong's politics in the 1970s. This was complemented by the absence of major political figures, parties and politicians, and a lack of coordination and cooperation among the elite and pressure groups (ibid, pp.123-124). The strategy of the government is to 'administer without politicizing' the society and social issues. Harris observes that bureaucrats make decisions according to a rational-technical process[28] and the administrative officer forms the backbone and top-tier of the structure. Hong Kong is, in fact, governed by a structure formed by the bureaucrats, the local elite and organized interest groups but led by the state officials. To be exact, Cheng suggests that 'political power is highly concentrated in the hands of a few top government officials' (1982, p.8).

Lau explains the autonomy in terms of the notion of 'minimally integrated social political system'. The state autonomy is based on the boundary politics of the society and the polity (both are reluctant to intervene into each other's sphere), and the low expectations of the public regarding the government (1982, 1985). Lau also observes that state autonomy and its monopolisation of politics were the common practice of the British government in its colonies in the post-war era. Another reason for the state autonomy is the passive acceptance by China of the colonial rule in Hong Kong (1991, p.52).

Against such background, Scott suggests that 'generally, the bureaucracy has enjoyed a high degree of relative autonomy in this respect: it has been able to act independently of economic elite when it has felt the need to so' (1989, p.253).

> This [state autonomy] was enhanced by the absence of pressure on the policy-making process from China and Britain; by the continuing weakness of organized groups (except for business groups); by a still largely unformed public opinion; and by a complacent and generally uncritical Legislative Council. The Hong Kong government appeared to be purposive and in control. It was relatively autonomous -- and was permitted to be so by China and Britain and by business interests -- because it received credit for the success of the economy and because it was seen to be in command of the local situation (Scott, 1986, p.459).

Scott argues that the only exception occurs in the time when the state is facing a crisis of legitimacy (Scott, 1989, p.253).

To maintain their overall control, the state has retained a tight grip on the agenda, process and nature of policy debate (Cuthbert, 1991, pp.238-239). This is upheld by the centralised control of the decision making structure and power, and the appointment of people with a similar background and orientation to the Councils and committees (Jones, 1985). As a result, in Hong, Kong, 'policy-making is centralized and policy implementation, for most part, remains "top-down"' (Scott & Cheek-Milby, 1986, p.173).

Therefore, Chow argues that majority of the social services, such as the youth services provided in the 1970s, were a crisis reactive project of the state to maintain their control and rule after the Riots in 1966 to 1967 (1985b). In explaining the rationale for the 'recommodification' of medical services in the 1980s, Wong argues that the move can be considered as the state's attempt to restructure and reverse its spending pattern as 'social investments' turned into 'social expenses' (1992).[29] Cheng shows that the education policy making process, in which tactics such as public consultation, use of experts and establishment of consultative committees, are specially designed to acquire a strong legitimacy (1992).

The governing ideology is another major focus for analysis. Chan argues that the reasons for the failure of the TYHCP, were due to the conservative fiscal policy of the state. She contends that the conservative fiscal policy and reluctance to invest in the public housing programme coupled with the firm belief in the high price land policy contributed to the failure of the programme. In line with the high land price policy, the government would only allocate land in remote locations with lower market value to the public housing programme (1982). The state is the main agent in determining this policy in the light of market and social conditions. Scott agrees that the 'bureaucratic elite share the faith in the capitalist system' (1989, p.251). They strongly believe that too much welfare ('free lunch') will slow down the growth rate and destroy the economy, as seen in the case of Britain and this explains why the proposal for a contributory social insurance scheme in the 1960s and 1970s failed to be realized (Chow, 1982, p.26). Using the same perspective, the reasons for privatisation should be understood as the state's pursuit of efficiency within government (HKG, 1989; Lee, 1988, p.14). The intention is to achieve 'value for money' (Sankey, 1993).

Summary

A review of the application of welfare state theories to Hong Kong shows that the most popular arguments are the socio-economic explanation (including the impacts of industrialisation on family structures and the needs of the economy), political arguments (especially elitism and Neo-Marxist arguments about legitimation and accumulation), and the state-centered thesis (state structure, official mentality and their strategies). The convergence thesis, in terms of pressure from overseas arising from trading relationships, and diffusion thesis based on the colonial status of Hong Kong also gained some attention. Relatively speaking, classical Marxism, instrumentalism, pluralism, social democracy and corporatism (except state corporatism) received lesser attention and support. The more popular theories will receive greater attention in the following analysis.

Many scholars have attempted to study the overall development of Hong Kong's welfare system as well as specific welfare issues. However, these studies are still inadequate both in terms of quality and quantity. First of all, they are based on inadequate empirical material. Very few of the studies have actually looked into the details of welfare development either through aggregate numerical indicators or through careful examination of the historical process. Therefore, most of the arguments, although they may be valid, do not have strong empirical support. Most of the studies are based on the writer's general impressions and a general survey of government documents. Such methodologies are rather superficial and lack an adequate hermeneutic perspective, especially in justifying the state-centered thesis.

Most of studies are, in fact, political science research and welfare state issues are not their primary focus. Frequently these studies seek to apply a general understanding of power to the study of individual welfare states in their totality. However, such a generalised approach is not necessarily applicable to each area of the welfare state and may neglect the unique dynamics of power in each case.

Another major weakness of welfare state theory is the limited number of empirically grounded, well designed and systematic enquiries into welfare states on which it is based. These limitations mean that prevailing explanations often rest on shaky foundations, focusing on the certain aspects of welfare rather than the development of whole welfare states. So there is obviously a need for more systematic theory building.

Notes

1 However, Parsons did not attempt further to elaborate clearly the relationship between modernisation, differentiation and emergence of social welfare.

2 These groups included the industrial elite, middle class, communists and the reshaped traditional groups in this new environment.

3 In his study, 76 countries were analysed by regression analysis. Political variables, in terms of governmental representativeness, were only positively related to social security in the 36 most developed countries whereas economic factors consistently related to all samples.

4 Based on a study of 22 non-socialist countries.

5 Based on a study of 7 communist and seven democratic societies using time-series analysis.

6 Based on a study of 60 countries and 22 most-developed countries in the 1960s by path analysis. Nevertheless such relation was mediated by the proportion of aged in the population and the age of the system.

7 Based on a study of 18 developed countries.

8 However, when he studied the factory legislation in Victorian England, he considered that it was the fruit of successful working class struggle and, if it continued to change the mode of production, the capitalist system would be abolished (see Mishra, 1987, ch.5). Thus, welfare, according to Marx's idea, has a dual role being the bourgeoisie's tool of control and working class's object and outcome of struggle. Welfare can be generated from ruling class action or from working class struggle, though Marx seemed to be inclined to the former prediction.

9 Though it may still its own interests, these do not occupy the centre stage of the power interplay.

10 Pareto argued that human behaviour was the combination of 'derivations' and 'residues'. There were two types of residues 'instinct of combinations' which referred to 'the inclination to create new object and new social grouping' and 'instinct of persistence of aggregates' which referred to the 'inclination to preserve what has already been established'. The first type of residue engenders 'foxes' while the second leads to 'lions'.

11 In this sense, such an idea is similar to the assertion of the policy network approach that different networks are formed in respect to various policy issues and areas by different interest groups. Of course, there are still some groups who encompass most or all of the policy areas, such as the political parties.

12 The application of their arguments have constituted the 'first wave' of Neo-Marxism as proposed by Therborn.

13 Though Miliband and Poulantzas seemed have a common view regarding the relative autonomy of the state, Poulantzas put a greater emphasis on it than Miliband. Moreover, the state is constrained by the economic structure in Poulantzas's thesis while it is 'controlled' by the ruling class in Miliband's thesis.

14 In fact, in Miliband's reply to Poulantzas, he admitted that 'government and bureaucracy, irrespective of social origin, class situation and even ideological dispositions, are subject to the structural constraints of the system'. Their difference is not that unbridgeable. See Miliband, 1973, pp.310-311.

15 Based on a study of 25 industrial countries.

16 Based on a comparative historical study of Britain, Sweden and America.

17 Based on a comparative analysis of 17 capitalist democratic countries.

18 Based on a comparative analysis of 18 OECD countries.

19 Based on a historical analysis of policies in response to the Great Depression in Sweden and the United States.

20 In Offe's construction, he discovers three types of selection: negative (screen-out anti-capitalist agenda), positive (screen-in the pro-capitalist agenda) and disguising (screen-in those help to build-up a class-neutrality image). Negative selection is operated in a hierarchical filter system: structure, ideology, process and repression. See Gold, Lo and Wright, 1975b.

21 His example was the German Social Democratic Party.

22 All these three researches argue for a mix of socio-economic and political explanation. The social and economic changes are served as the contextual factors.

23 Ho finds that the proportion of members in the LegCo with a business background were higher that those without one until 1985, when indirect election to the Council was first implemented. However, the composition of the ExCo remained unchanged (as at 1986). See Ho, 1986, p.16.

24 Clansmen Societies are those formed by the residents of Hong Kong with the same places of origin in China. Kaifong Associations are those formed by residents living in the same locality in Hong Kong.

25 For example, the representatives of the Chambers (e.g. Hong Kong General Chamber of Commerce), industrial associations (e.g. Hong Kong Federation of Industries), organisations representing different occupations (e.g. Hong Kong Association of Banks), representatives from the Hong Kong Bank and the old British trading firms such as Swire and Jardine are regular members of the Executive Council. The adoption of functional constituencies in the LegCo election since 1985 has given formal status to these organisations. For details, please refer to chapter 7 and chapter 10.

26 However, they never have the upperhand in the bargaining process except in very rare cases. For details, please refer to the discussion in Parts 3 and 4.

27 Lord MacLehose set up the Independent Commission Against Corruption in 1974 to combat corruption in both the private and public sectors.

28 Which has the effect of de-politicising and legitimising their decisions.

29 Based on the typology of O'Connor (1973), Wong argues that the 'investment' in medical services, with economically-active population as the main target, in 1960s and 1970s brought positive effects on capital accumulation but the nature of the expenditure gradually changed to 'social expenses' as the people receiving care, such as hospital services, were mainly the non-productive population in the 1980s.

4 Research methodology and design

This chapter will summarise the current research methodologies applied in this field of study. The writer will describe the weaknesses of the quantitative approach and state the rationales for the qualitative approach and case study design that the current study adopted. The writer will also elaborate and discuss the data collection methods employed.[1]

Before we start the discussion, it is worth clarifying the meaning of methodology, design and method. By 'methodology', we mean the 'science of finding out' that links the theory with a method. Methodology describes the overall design of the study and provides justifications for the method as appropriate for the theory to be tested. The choice of methodology may reflect the epistemology, referred to as the 'science of knowing', of the study or the researcher (Babbie, 1992, p.18). The debate on methodology or research design is not only on its effectiveness in measuring the phenomenon but also on its validity in approaching the issue.

By 'method', we mean the techniques that researchers adopt to collect the data. This may not have any or only have a weak relation with the epistemology of the study and the researchers, it may purely be a matter of technical considerations. Thus quantitative data can also be used by a qualitative study.

Research methodology: quantitative vs qualitative

A brief review of previous research in the area of the theory of the welfare state reveals that two mainstream research methodologies have been employed, the qualitative and quantitative approaches. Of the two, the quantitative methodology is the more popular one. This methodology employs various statistical analyses, such as cross-sectional analysis (Aaron, 1967), path analysis (Wilensky, 1975), time-series design

(Namkoong, 1990) and regression analysis (Flora & Alber, 1981), to test the correlation and significance of various factors, such as political, social, organisational and economic factors, in affecting the development of welfare states.

For those researchers using the quantitative method, various independent variables informed by different theoretical strands, such as political movement, party formation, unionization and industrialism, are constructed and the dependent variables such as social security, health services and social expenditure, are defined. The statistical methods are used to prove the relationship, correlational or causal, between and among the variables by mathematical means. The method is particularly popular in comparative and cross-national research.

Such research and the methodology employed reflect the influence of the positivistic tradition. King has argued that this assumes that there is an unified scientific methodology which can cross the natural and social science fields of study, that is methodological monism (King, 1992). The task of research is to discover rules, causal relationships and regular patterns through a neutral and objective empirical analysis (Lee, 1992). This positivistic tradition emphasises the study of overt observable indicators and pays lesser or no attention to the covert human consciousness.

Such an approach has a contribution to make in studying the topic. However, such analysis, based on the statistical data, sometimes alienates the research from the 'real life' situations. The study is focused on a 'second-level construct', i.e. an 'abstracted' life-situation according to the construction of variables, instead of a 'primary-level construct', i.e. the real-life situation. The first step of the quantitative research is to re-construct the world according to its list of independent and dependent variables. Shalev has argued that, sometimes, the real factors are just too complicated to be simplified into such a list (1983, p.338). And differences in operationalising the variables and concepts have caused much confusion among various researchers (Uusitalo, 1984). Many have narrowly focused on social expenditure or on social security expenditure while ignoring other aspects of welfare state activities (for example, Wilensky, 1975, Cutright, 1965 & 1967, Castles, 1982, DeViney, 1983). Shalev has reminded researchers not to focus narrowly on expenditure because the increase in expenditure does not lead to proportional increase in welfare and in fact, the welfare state's intervention is multi-dimensional (1983, p.324).

The relationship between variables is believed to be capable of being shown statistically. In fact, these methods can seldom convincingly prove that causal relations exist between variables though different methods, such as multivariate analysis, have been developed in the attempt to do so

(Babbie, 1986, ch.16; Nachimas & Nachimas, 1981, ch.14). Shalev has highlighted some of the complications of this type of methodology,

1. A high correlation can reflect the extreme locations of a small minority of cases rather than a consistent trend;
2. The correlation looks good but the actual cases only cluster around certain segments of the regression line;
3. The correlation coefficient does not reveal the true nature of the relationship -- which may in fact be nonlinear, or else of the 'threshold' type.

In conclusion, Shalev argues that 'whatever the explanation, researchers who insist on summarising their data by means of correlation and/or regression coefficients have a clear obligation not to stop there' (1983, p.338).

Comparatively speaking, these methods are weaker in regard to the in-depth presentation of the processes and dynamics. The wider the scope the research wants to cover, the shallower it can penetrate into these details; the greater reliance on the simplified variables and the lesser it can get contact with the 'field'. Policy considerations, planning and decisions cannot be easily quantified into concrete measurements and variables. A focus on overt bahaviour, inevitably, misses out a deeper understanding based on the interpretations of those who are involved in the process. Quantitative methodology alone is not therefore adequate in this field of study.

In the qualitatively based studies, researchers draw conclusions from detailed examination of historical events. These researchers analyse the historical development of welfare states, either the general trend or particular cases, not by the statistical manipulation of variables but, instead, by in-depth analysis of the dynamics of the factors involved in the process. Examples of this type of research are Furniss and Tilton (1977), Skocpol (1980), Weir and Skocpol, (1983), Therborn (1983, 1984), and Baldwin (1990).

The sources of data can be obtained from personal information which appears in the forms of diaries, letters, notes, photos, pictures, publications, autobiographies, oral histories and, public documents such as newspapers, magazines, journals, minutes, official documents, academic research reports as well as statistics. The tasks of the researcher are to 'relive' or enter into the history by using these to 'interpret' the historical events. Such qualitative methodology is more suitable for 'delves into process and complexities' (Marshall & Rossman, 1989, p.46) and 'much documentary research in political studies, history and social policy is necessarily qualitative' (Allan & Skinner, 1991, p.178).

However, there is a potential danger that the qualitative methodology is equated to those highly abstract theoretical studies which lack adequate empirical grounding. Analysts always have the danger of imposing the theoretical construct on the objective situation and sometimes, of reconstructing the history to fit the theoretical construct. Functionalism run the danger of mixing up the outcome (function performed) as the cause of the policy if they are not aware of the differences between intended and unintended consequences. The labour reproduction and capital accumulation functions performed by the social services may or may not be the objectives of the policy in its planning. Highly abstract analysis cannot clarify situations but only distort the phenomena. If the findings and theories generated are not adequately empirically-grounded, then their reliability and validity will be questioned.

So these are the weaknesses of quantitative methodologies and statistical manipulation and the potential drawbacks of qualitative historical analysis. The major consideration for the study was the ability of the methodology chosen to penetrate into the 'real' historical world and to explain the dynamic of the various factors which this study analyses.

Research methodology and design

This study adopted a qualitative historical research methodology to examine the general trend of Hong Kong welfare development, and a case-oriented analysis in examining selected cases in detail. By 'qualitative', we mean the 'the kind of research that produces findings not arrived at by means of statistical procedures or other means of quantification' (Strauss & Corbin, 1990, p.17). Some data are presented, such as GDP, government expenditures and infant mortality rates, however, the approach is basically qualitative. These quantitative data have a supplementary role and serve as a basis for further qualitative investigation (Brannen, 1992, p.23).

Different methods were adopted to collect data from multiple sources to enrich the empirical basis of this study. Denzin describes this strategy as 'triangulation' (1989b). As argued by Denzin,

> Concepts and methods open new realms of observation, but concomitantly close others. Two important consequences follow. If each method leads to different features of empirical reality, then no single method can ever completely capture all the relevant features of that

reality; consequently, sociologists must learn to employ multiple methods in the analysis of the same empirical events. This is termed triangulation. (1989b, p.13).

Denzin further argues that 'the combination of multiple methods in a single investigation will better enable the sociologist to forge valid propositions that fully consider relevant rival causal factors' (ibid, p.26). He himself suggests four different but interrelated types of triangulation, data, investigator, theory and methodological triangulation (ibid, pp.239-244). In this research, data, theory and methodological triangulation will be emphasized.

Concerning data triangulation, different data sources will be used to ensure the 'density of empirical coverage' (Layder, 1993, p.122). Theory triangulation will be 'best seen as a method of widening one's theoretical framework as empirical materials are interpreted' (Denzin, 1989b, p.241) and it 'illuminates, discloses, and engulfs the phenomenon' (ibid, p.242). This will ensure the density of analytical viewpoints covered (Layder, 1993, p.122).

Denzin outlines two different types of methodological triangulation, the within-method and between-method. Brannen revises part of this and suggests that 'within-method triangulation'[2] is used to analyze different occasions with the same method and 'between method triangulation' is to analyze the same occasions with different methodologies (Brannen, 1992, pp.11-12). Hence, to study the same case, different methods, such as interviewing, statistical study and documentary content analysis, were all be employed whenever necessary . Also, different data sets were built up by different methods (data triangulation). Throughout the process, different theories (theory triangulation) were derived, applied and tested in the whole process of research.

By nature of the subject for investigation, experimental methods, either true and quasi, are not applicable in this research. The research subjects are entirely out of the control of the researcher. Moreover, participant or non-participant observation is also not viable as the events studied are in the past, and even when we refer to contemporary affairs, the researcher could not take a part in the policy process or be a member of the decision-making group.

We will approach the history and the interpretation given by the 'objective' data and key informants, with some propositions and potential areas for exploration as informed by the theories to observe, explain and re-construct these events. This historical approach will try to avoid an imposition of non-verified views and seeks to re-examine the current prevailing explanations of welfare state in Hong Kong. This historical analysis will also help to establish a 'baseline or background' for further research (Marshall & Rossman, 1989:95-96).

Case-study design methodology

The use of case studies in this research is to provide more in-depth analysis of events, and more accurate observation of the dynamics among factors affecting the development of social services in the period of study. This serves to enrich the data set as well as to supplement or verify the general observation of trends. In this research, I will use the multiple case embedded study design. Yin has described the different types of case study as follows,

Table 4.1
Typology of case study design

	Single-case design	Multiple-cases design
Holistic (single-unit of analysis	Type 1	Type 3
Embedded (multiple units of analysis)	Type 2	Type 4

Source: Yin, 1990, p.41, Figure 2.2

This research has adopted the Type 4 design. The reason to adopt such design is to enhance the external validity of the arguments. The choice of multiple cases is to minimize the problem of external validity by replication. Moreover, the use of embedded analysis matches the proposition of theory triangulation. Different theories have been built up on different levels and units of analysis, so to analyze the issues from various perspectives can serve to broaden the empirical base of this research. In order to have an overview of the issues and derive the most appropriate theoretical explanation, one has to study different units of analysis. As argued by Allan & Skinner, 'the notion of embedded units of analysis can be used as a design to add greater versatility and enable the basic design to be adapted to meet various theoretical and practical requirements' (1991, p.200).

The design involves choosing more than one case study and having multiple units of analysis for each case, that is to examine and interpret more than a single factor from different perspectives (Yin, 1990, pp.42-48). In this research, the study of the factors behind welfare development will not only be confined to the system level factors such as degree of industrialization and unionization but also the meso-level factors such as the operation of interest and elite groups in the decision-making process and micro-level factors such as personal preferences.

As it is impossible to examine every policy case in the period of study in this research due to length, time and resources constraints, the writer will select two cases for each historical stage, namely 1971 to 1981 and 1982 to 1992. Certainly, there is the risk that we may select inappropriate cases which will lead to the problem of 'construct validity' and generalisability of the findings of these cases to explain the whole period. So the major consideration in selecting cases is their 'representativeness'. But it is not necessary to choose at least one case in each policy area, that is housing, medical, education and social welfare services, in both periods. Furthermore, the research's objective is to study the overall development of welfare state not of individual policy areas.

To minimise the chance of inappropriate selection, we selected those cases which fitted the criteria of 'representativeness', 'relevancy' and 'significance'. To meet the criteria of 'relevancy', the case selected must be within the definition of the welfare state in this study, that is within the operational definition of housing, medical and health, education and social welfare services (including social security). To meet the criteria of 'representativeness', the case selected must be a good example showing the major characteristics of welfare development at that stage, that is 'expansion' in the 1970s and 'marketisation' in the 1980s. To meet the criteria of 'significance', the case selected must occupy a prominent position among the policies in that stage, in terms of resources mobilized and share of public expenditure, scope of people/sectors involved and attention it attracted. Moreover, it should have far reaching impacts and outcomes (Yin, 1984, pp.140-141), in other words, the cases must be significant in terms of their inputs (resources consumed) and outputs (scale of provision and impact).

Another consideration for selection of cases is the feasibility of their study which includes the possibility of getting access to the information and key informants. After preliminary fieldwork, the cases were finally selected (Table 4.2).

All the cases selected are within the operational definition of the study, that is within the services domain of the definition of welfare state. The cases selected also exhibit the major characteristics of the general policy changes within the periods specified. Ten Year Housing Construction Programme and Nine Years Free and Compulsory Education policy are the two most significant policy cases representing the government's effort to expand services provision. The Long Term Housing Strategy and the case of Hospital Authority, and subsequent changes especially in the fee charging policy, signified the trend of marketisation of social services in the 1980s. These cases are adequate to represent the overall development of the welfare state in Hong Kong.

Table 4.2
Selection of cases

	Housing	Education	Medical	Social welfare
1971-1981	Ten Year Housing Construction Programme	Nine Years Free & Compulsory Education Policy	Nil	Nil
1982-1992	Long Term Housing Strategy	Nil	Hospital Authority and fee charging policy	Nil

Finally, the cases selected are also significant in terms of their output and outcomes. The housing construction programme and the free and compulsory education policy affected a significant percentage of the population in Hong Kong and virtually all the young people aged below fifteen. The reforms in housing and hospital policy in the 1980s affected half the Hong Kong population immediately and almost all later. They demonstrate the shift from socialisation in the 1970s to marketisation of services in the 1980s.

No case in the social welfare services is selected for detailed examination. The reason is that, comparatively speaking, the scale of expansion and the coverage of these services are rather limited. The share of welfare expenditure is among the lowest compared with other social services. However, this does not mean that the writer has prejudices against or has consciously neglected this policy area nor will it lead to bias in the research findings. This policy area will be discussed in the course of general observation and analysis.

Data collection methods

Sources of data

The major sources of information can be divided into two broad types

1. Printed material:
    1.1 Academic publications
        : previous research reports;
        : analytical papers and journal articles;
        : books;
    1.2 General publications
        : magazine reports;
        : newspaper reports;
        : autobiographies or personal history reports;
    1.3 Government/public documents
        : Governor's speeches;
        : Budgets, Budget speeches and Appropriation Bills;
        : White and Green Papers;
        : consultative documents;
        : statues;
        : Legislative Council Hansard;
        : annual reports of various Departments, Authorities & public bodies;
        : statistical summaries and reports.

2. Interviews:
    The researcher contacted and interviewed those who had first-hand experience of the historical process. The major groups were current and previous senior officials including Governors and Secretaries, Legislative and Executive Councillors either appointed or elected, social activists and interest group leaders who have been involved, in different degrees in the policy planning and decision-making processes.

Data collection methods

The data collection methods involved documentary reviews and semi-structured interviews for collecting the first and second type of information respectively. Documentary review is the most popular, and perhaps the only method for some research, in Hong Kong. Comparatively speaking, interviews are a less popular method. Only a minority of the social policy studies have seriously interviewed officials, councillors and other concerned parties. One of the reasons is probably the taken-for-granted belief that these persons, especially the officials, will reject their request for interviews. While there are certain objective grounds for this belief, due to the common practice of protecting official secrets, such a belief is open to challenge.[3]

The lack of first hand information supplied by these involved persons has always handicapped in-depth understanding of the policy process and as a result, many studies relied on the 'logical reasoning' of the researchers themselves and the published documents. So the findings were largely the construction of the researchers. To compensate for this inadequacy in current research, this study interviewed those who were involved in the policy process so as to add a hermeneutic perspective by gathering information about their own interpretation of the factors which contributed to shaping the Hong Kong welfare state.

The study adopted a 'semi-structured' interview format. The researcher only prepared a broad list of questions for each individual interviewee, depending on their position in the policy process and the specific policy area. The areas for questioning were informed by the previous local studies and the theoretical perspectives. The interviewees could freely express their own interpretations within the broad topics which were defined by the researcher. However, the interviewees were also encouraged to initiate the areas and factors for discussions which they considered to be relevant. As argued by Denzin, such an arrangement can allow the interviewees to use their 'unique ways of defining the world' and to 'raise important issues not contained in the schedule' (1989b, p.125).

It must be noted that both sources of information and data collection methods have inherent weaknesses. For the secondary data available in various printed formats, one has to be alert to the position of the writers and the intention of these publications. For the information gathered by personal interview, the researcher has to be aware of the personal interpretations and limitations of the interviewees' experience and therefore, intentional and unintentional suppression or emphasis of certain aspects of understanding often occur. Denzin has suggested a list of the problems which could distort interviewees' responses:

1. Respondents possessing different interactional roles from the interviewer.
2. The problem of 'self-presentation' especially in the early stages of the interview.

3. The problems of 'volatile', 'fleeting' relationships to which respondents have little commitment and so 'can fabricate tales of self that belie the actual facts'.
4. The difficulty of penetrating private worlds of experience.
5. The relative status of interviewer and interviewee.
6. The 'context' of the interview (e.g. home, work, hospital) (adopted from Silverman, 1993, p.97).

In keeping an alert and careful attitude in examining the data from various sources, the concept of data triangulation is important. Lin has suggested three techniques for examining the validity of the data:

1. Corrobation:
   To discover more information on the questions so as to examine the validity of the current propositions;
2. Reasoning:
   To examine the 'fact' in the historical context;
3. Cross-examination:
   To cross-examine those data and arguments which are contradictory or different (Lin, 1994, pp.95-96).

These methods will never get rid of all the potential conflictual data sets and arguments. Certainly, tensions existed among them. In fact, as noted by Silverman, 'this suggests that we need not hear interview responses [as well as secondary data] simply as true or false reports on reality. Instead, we can treat such responses as displays of perspectives' (1993, p.107). It is hoped that through such careful examination of various data sets and arguments, a more accurate explanation of Hong Kong welfare development can be provided.

Notes

1 The details of data collection by interviews, list of interviewees and interview schedules are provided in Appendix 1. A sample of the in-depth interview is provided in Appendix 2.
2 Denzin suggests within-method triangulation means to select one method and use different strategies within it. See Denzin, 1989, p.243.
3 This was shown by Alvin Rabushka around 20 years ago when he came to Hong Kong from United States to research the budget policy of the

Hong Kong government. In his research, he interviewed more than 50 officials and councillors. See, Rabushka, 1976.

Part Two
THE CONTEXT OF WELFARE STATE IN HONG KONG

5 The context: Hong Kong in pre-1970s

The context

This chapter will focus on elaborating the contextual factors. As argued in the previous chapter, different explanations have suggested that different factors shape the welfare state. These factors can be grouped, as shown in the general model, under the categories of political, economic, social and cultural, although they are, in fact, inseparable relationships between them. Changes in one context will inevitably affect another context. The relationships between them are neither linear nor static but dynamic. In this chapter, we shall discuss these factors and then describe the context up to the start of the 1970s and how this context shaped the development of the welfare state in Hong Kong before 1971.

Political factors

The description of political factors focuses on the two aspects of external forces and the state and the interaction between them. The external forces, suggested by various theoretical perspectives, include classes, parties, interest groups, elite groups and the interactions and coalitions among them.[1] Within class analysis, the interests and actions of the capitalist and the middle classes are worth further attention. The social democracy thesis has suggested the factor of working class mobilisation. The state factor will include the structure of the administration, the rules and regulations which govern it, the historical background and legacy, and the orientation of the officials. This will also include state's (officials') reaction and response to these forces and the strategies that it adopts to counteract those pressures, or the contradictions embedded in the capitalist system.[2]

Moreover, considering the unique status of Hong Kong, as the colony of United Kingdom (UK) while at the same time, maintaining a close relationship with China and being the Special Administrative Region (SAR)[3] of China after 1997, it is certainly necessary to take account of the influence of these states into account in the construction of political context.[4]

Economic factors

The economic factor can provide us with several reference points for our analysis. Firstly, as argued by Marxist theorists, the most powerful economic interests occupy an advantaged position, by appointment into the formal political structure by informal influence (as in Hong Kong). Therefore, understanding the economic context will help us to analyse the powerful economic groups within the political process. Secondly, as public expenditure is heavily reliant on tax income, economic prosperity or recession can constrain or generate the resources for state spending. Therefore, the general economic situation and the overall level of GDP,[5] may play a part in constructing the economic context. Similarly, the level of overall economic prosperity can have a determining effect on individual incomes.

Thirdly, the development of Hong Kong's economy is very much reliant on exports, especially to the OECD countries and the United States of America. Such a dependent trade relationship could be used as a tool by the trade counterparts to support various objectives, within or apart from economic policies. Factors suggested to be relevant include the nation's participation in world trade and international organisations, and its strategies to promote competition and its status on the world stage (Skocpol & Amenta, 1986, pp.144-147; Thomas and Lauderdale, 1988).

Social factors

Industrialism is the fundamental process of modern society. The industrialism thesis suggested that the welfare system is an offspring of the social problems brought about by the economic development. Therefore, the consequences, including the social problems (especially the ageing population and family disintegration), of the industrialisation process must be considered. When an ageing population has voting power, it can become a powerful factor shaping the political agenda. Social tension and unrest, such as the Riots in the 1960s, intensified social conflict in the 1970s, the issues concerning '1997', the 'June 4th' issue, and the migration problem in the 1980s, are all potential factors which might impact on the development of welfare state.

Cultural factors

Culture consists of the values that people hold, the norms that they follow and the material goods that they create (Giddens, 1992, pp.31-32). It guides people's behaviour within a social context. It forms the reference frame for people's action and choices. It is very rare to find that there is a consensual orientation and uniform values on anyone issue within a society. Also, it is not unusual to find that the orientations held by the public and the officials are different though not necessarily contradicting. Thus, we have to explore both the orientation and belief of the public and the officials. As the state's ideology will be discussed under political factors, this part will only analyse the public culture. We will present relevant research and arguments which are aimed at portraying the Hong Kong people's perceptions, values, orientations and beliefs on such matters as politics, economic policy, social policy ideology and the roles of state and other sectors in providing care.

The setting of the stage: pre-1971

Political context

Hong Kong has been a colony of UK from 1841.[6] After almost a century of development, the colony has experienced significant changes in its economic, social and political aspects. However, concerning the politics, there were, unfortunately, only small and insignificant changes until the end of 1960s. Until 1966, Hong Kong came under the Office of the Secretary of State for the Colonies.[7] In principle, the final veto power over all Hong Kong affairs was vested in the Whitehall.

Similar to its sovereign state, Hong Kong has no written constitution. The structure of government was based on two documents, the Letters Patent and Royal Instructions, issued by the British government. The Letters Patent outlines the power of the Governor, the creation of the ExCo and LegCo. The Royal Instructions supplements the gap left by the Letters Patent and deals with the details of the Councils, such as the appointment and dismissal of members and decision-making procedures.

The ExCo is the highest advisory body to the Governor[8] and its members are all appointed by the Governor. Its agenda, discussion and minutes are all confidential and there is only limited access to these by a few top officials. It is operates on the principle of 'collective responsibility' that disregards the members' individual views, they have to support the final decision when facing the public. The LegCo serves two major functions: to debate and pass the budget, and legislation. The members, until 1985, were all appointed by the government. LegCo has a Finance Committee which is responsible for discussing and approving the expenditure listed in the annual budget.[9]

Apart from this, councillors can set up task forces to study specific issues or laws that they are concerned about. Occasionally, Legislative Councillors can use their power to initiate an 'adjournment debate' on policies and issues that they are concerned about in the Council. However, such debates have no legal binding force on the government. The most significant control over the government from LegCo concerns the financial aspects of the policy.

This constitutional structure gives the Governor supreme power and authority within the government. The structure has also given the government a leading position with respect to LegCo. Of course, in practice, the Governor also has to take advice from and respond to pressure from the Councils' members. In any unresolved dispute, the Governor has to explain to the Secretary for State in London the reasons for his final decision. Nevertheless, such disputes are rare in Hong Kong. The government is operated by an 'administrative-led' structure, governed in the name of 'consensus', which enjoys much power over policy decisions.

The dominant position of the officials was further strengthened by two factors: the inability of the advisory committees and the LegCo to monitor the government and the apathetic attitude of the public toward participation in the policy making process and in monitoring the government. The limitations of the LegCo have been mentioned above. Apart from appointments to the LegCo, and limited direct election to the Urban Council (UC) there were very few accessible and significant channels for the public to participate in policy making.

However, voting for UC elections was highly restricted.[10] The only relatively significant channel of influence them was through appointment to advisory committees. The ExCo, as well as LegCo were restricted to those who seemed to support government policy. At least, those who held different and 'radical' positions compared with the government were never selected. Even the Legislative Councillors seldom employed their power to hold adjournment debates on government policies. Most important of all, after the 1890s, all official members[11] of the LegCo were instructed to vote for the governor (Scott, 1989, p.58). As the official members remained as the majority until the 1960s, the government could never lose a vote during this time.[12] The advisory committees played an entirely advisory role and therefore, depended on the attitude and response of the officials to their suggestions. In fact, the officials could always find reasons to accept or reject these proposals.

In the administrative structure, the Governor and the Financial Secretary (FS) were the two most powerful officials. The Governor, appointed by the British government, represents the Royal family and Britain's rule over Hong Kong. Under the Governor, there was a Colonial Secretariat headed by the Colonial Secretary. However, in the 1960s, the leadership position of the Colonial Secretary was challenged by the FS.[13] Structurally speaking, the Colonial Secretary has no power to overrule the decision made by the FS on the fiscal, revenue and expenditure policy of the government. Rabushka had interviewed an Acting Colonial Secretary who held the office in early 1970s and he has recalled his experience thus,

> The Colonial Secretary virtually never became involved with the Financial Secretary. Although in theory there should be a good deal more intertwining between the two men and their aides, in fact the Financial Secretary was virtually autonomous dictator in matters of expenditure, and hence, policy. At times, heads of department sought aid and comfort from the Colonial Secretary in their continuing friction with the Financial Secretary, but it was more the exception than the rule. In all matters of irreconcilable disagreement, the Governor was called into the picture and as often as not, the Governor would side with the Financial Secretary (Rabushka, 1975, pp.54-55).

According to another officer served in the Secretariat until early 1970s interviewed by Rabushka, 'the Financial Branch of the Secretariat ran the government by default throughout the 1960s'. After the departure of Claude Burgess as the Colonial Secretary in 1963, no one could keep John Cowperthwaite[14] 'in line' and 'his brilliance and argumentation prevailed, and he thus made policy by ruling on all items of expenditure' (Rabushka, 1975, p.55). There is no doubt that Cowperthwaite had the dominant influence over government revenue and expenditure policies until his departure in 1973. As every social service policy involved spending, then, every policy was under his or the Finance Branch's scrutiny. The growing dominance of the Finance Branch may have had the effect of imposing economic considerations over other considerations.

Social context

Until the 1960s, Hong Kong society was still facing great uncertainty and instability. This resulted from the instability, failure of reforms and the attacks on landlords in China, its ambiguous attitude to the position of Hong Kong, and the influx of illegal immigrants. Hong Kong was a typical refugee society and, it was claimed, deeply influenced by the refugee mentality. It was argued that as the majority of the Hong Kong people were refugees from Mainland China, Hong Kong was in fact their 'life boat' or temporary shelter (Hoadley, 1970; 1973). It was a relatively safe haven for those who had escaped from the Communist China and also a stepping stone for migration. There was no strong sense of commitment and belongingness to the place. Such factors contributed to the potential instability of the society but, paradoxically, provided a favourable foundation for political stability.

The population growth in Hong Kong was relatively steady, except when refugees flooded in again in the mid-1950s due to the failure of 'Great Leap Forward' reform in China, but it kept increasing throughout the 1950s and 1960s (Table 5.1).

Table 5.1
Population growth in Hong Kong, 1950-1970*

Year	Population	Year	Population
1950	2,360,000	1963	3,503,700
1956	2,440,000	1964	3,594,200
1957	2,583,000	1965	3,692,300
1958	2,748,000	1966	3,732,400
1959	2,857,000	1967	3,834,000
1960	2,981,000	1968	3,926,500
1961	3,133,131	1969	3,987,500
1962	3,346,000	1970	4,089,000

* All are mid-year estimates except year 1961 which is from the 1961 Census.

Sources: HKAR, various years

There was a significant increase in the number of children and youth in the 1960s as a result of the first baby boom after the War.

Hong Kong's economy had gradually recovered from the adverse impacts of the Second World War, the China civil war and the Korean War gave the local economy a chance to develop its industries. However, the early development of the economy was insufficient to provide adequate job opportunities for the rapid increasing population. In these circumstances, working conditions and wages could be kept at a minimal level as there was no problem of recruiting adequate workers. Hence, there were potential grievances among the workers.

To maintain their households, families had to push their children into full-time employment as early as possible. Of course, at that time, the inadequacy of school places and the high cost of schooling made studying for this young population seemed a remote possibility.[15] Thus, the phenomenon of child labour was prevalent in Hong Kong. The problem increased as the younger population increased. The frustration of this sector of population gradually built up and was considered to be one of the reasons for the riots in the late 1960s.

Another social division that existed in Hong Kong society was the political conflict between those loyal to the Communist Party or the Kuomintang.[16] Those loyal to Communist China opposed the pro-Kuomintang groups and the colonial government and there were overt conflicts between them.[17] The government had to be very cautious in handling this conflict and the potentially destabilising forces created by the pro-Communist groups.

Although Hong Kong society remained stable during this period, there were still three riots. The first was in 1956, started by the supporters of Kuomintang in Hong Kong.[18] After the riot, the Governor, Sir Alexander Grantham suggested that it had a certain relationship with resentment of social conditions,

> The people themselves for the most part live at a bare subsistence level; they own little or no personal property; the great majority have no real stake in the Colony. Employment is difficult and in some cases indifferently paid. They are people who have fled from their homeland and it is not surprising if their fate has engendered a sense of frustration and bitterness (quoted from Scott, 1989, p.77).

Although the Governor noted the social hardship of the public, this analysis was not followed by corresponding social measures. There were few significant developments of social services at that time except the continuation of the housing programme and the unfulfilled promises made in the Fisher Report and the subsequent Five Year and Seven Year Plans, in 1952 and 1955, on primary education.[19] So the perceived threat had little effect on the government. Comparatively speaking, the second and third riots in 1966 and 1967 were far more effective in pushing the government into changes.

The 1966 riot was sparked off by an increase of Star Ferry cross-harbour fare by 25 per cent.[20] The riot started with a sit-in protest by several youths outside the Star Ferry terminal on 4 April 1966. After they were arrested by the police, scattered riots broke out in various streets in Kowloon for four days and finally, peace was restored in 8 April. The Report on the riots drafted by the government came to the conclusion that they were, again, sparked off by economic causes[21] and feelings of non-belongingness. The majority of the rioters were young men, poorly educated and poorly paid, inadequately housed and overworked. The Report called for reforms in social policy such as quickening the pace of provision of housing, education and services directed towards youth (HKG, 1967a, pp.136-146). The Report also noticed the failure of communication between the government and the public[22] and recommended widening public access by developing representation on its advisory, consultative and executive bodies at the local level, and improvement in public relations (ibid, p.128). On the economic aspect, the Report called for improvements in working conditions (ibid, p.136).

When the government was still debating the follow-up measures for the 1966 riot, another riot broke out in May 1967 and lasted until December. This was, as argued, a spill-over effect of the Cultural Revolution in China as pro-Communist Party people in Hong Kong staged a series of protests against the colonial government. This was the first time since the strike in 1921 that there was a disturbance which directly challenged the legitimacy of the government and lasted for such long period of time. It was generally agreed that such riot had a great effect in pushing the government towards more reforms.

Cultural context

Until the 1960s, there was a general consensus that Hong Kong people had rather little social awareness and were apathetic towards public affairs. These were some of the reasons to explain the dominance of the officials in politics. Scholars have suggested several reasons for this social attitude. The first explanation was based on the notion of the ‘refugee mentality’ in which people did not have a strong commitment to the place and at the same time, no or low expectations of government (Miners, 1991, ch.3; Lau, 1982). They did not have much resentment over the denial of their political rights.

The other explanations of this rather apathetic attitude were based on an analysis of Chinese culture and values. The Chinese were portrayed as politically apathetic (Miners, 1991, p.32). Though there were no research data to support such an image of the Chinese people in Hong Kong, it was not that difficult to prove such an argument by the fact of low social and political participation by them before the 1970s. For example, the candidates and the elected Councillors for the UC, the only election open to the public before 1982, were mainly Westerners. The voting percentages were always around 5 per cent of the qualified voters.[23] The Chinese were more active in forming philanthropic associations, clansman organisations and kaifong committees.

The Chinese were used to authoritarian rule and Lin argued that such a long history of submission and patience under oppression has formed a part of the typical Chinese personality (1938, p.44). In conclusion, Hoadley has suggested that the Hong Kong people maintained a typical 'parochial' or 'subject' civic culture (1970, p.207; 1973). Democracy was never the concern of the wider public at this period of time.[24]

Another feature of the Hong Kong Chinese was their belief and dependence in informal care, from family and kin, instead of formal care from the public sector. They were rather reluctant to accept the state's assistance which was always related to a sense of stigma. Another significant source of help was the clansman[25] and kaifong associations.[26] The third source of help was the traditional philanthropic organisations, such as the Tung Wah Group of Hospitals and the Po Leung Kuk. This informal care reflected the deep-rooted belief in self-care, family care and charity and helped to sustain the limited state intervention in social affairs (Chow, 1984b, p.20-22; 1990, pp.2-4).

Economic context

Hong Kong was only a small fishing village when the British took it over and maintained it as the place for British merchants, and businessmen from other countries to do business with China. It maintained a steady but not distinguished economic growth until the end of the Second World War. After the War, Hong Kong suffered from tremendous destruction, an influx of refugees and the international economic recession. Without secure and adequate revenue from taxation, the post-War Hong Kong government had inadequate resources to rebuild the ruined economy.

However, the Communist victory in China and the outbreak of the Korean War in 1950 gave Hong Kong an unpredictable opportunity to rebuild its economy. The Communist victory over the Kuomintang forced many wealthy Shanghai merchants running the textile industry to move to Hong Kong with their skills, experience, capital and machines, to restart their businesses. Hence, job opportunities were created for the population (Youngson, 1982, pp.3-4). The fast expanding industries, textiles as well as the plastic industry, were accompanied by a regular supply of cheap labour, the refugees from China. The embargo imposed on China due to the Communist victory and the Korean War forced the Hong Kong businessmen to search for overseas market instead of remaining as an entrepot of China. In 1953, only 30 per cent of Hong Kong's exports were local products and the rest were all re-exports. The situation reversed dramatically, by 1959, 70 per cent of exports were of local origin.

The threat from the Communist party to march across the Lo Wu border[27] became less possible when the Chinese government became deeply troubled by internal conflicts.[28] Hong Kong, thus, enjoyed a relatively stable and safe environment for investment and doing business though, the confidence in the future was still fragile.[29] The growth of GDP in the 1960s was remarkable.[30]

Such economic growth, especially in such a difficult situation, also served to gain the support of the public for the colonial authoritarian government even in the urban riots in 1957, 1966 and 1967. This success also legitimised the belief that the administration of the city should be left to the efficient bureaucracy no matter how authoritarian or how inadequate public participation was. The success of the economy was perceived, at least by the officials, to be based on capitalism, free trade, low taxes and non-interventionism. Thus, a prosperous economy was one of the primary tasks of a successful administration and in turn, this strengthened the legitimacy of the government.

The growth of economy engendered a new class of Chinese merchants. They formed associations of their own to promote their own interests.[31] This sector of the population gained the respect and recognition of the government and therefore, they occupied the seats in the advisory committees and the Councils alongside the economic groups organised by traditional corporations such as Swire and Jardine.

Policy making: process and structure

Given the interaction between the government and the people was kept at a minimal level and participation in and expectation of the government kept low, the bureaucrats could maintain a high degree of autonomy in ruling the colony. Moreover, pressure from both the British and Chinese merchants was effectively solved by co-optation and inclusion of them the government structure. The government at this period and in fact, until the 1970s, was 'ruled by small communities with interlocking memberships of bureaucrats and businessmen became a characteristic of government. Government decisions were legitimised by the consensus reached by different elite within what had become a closed system' (Scott, 1989, p.60). However, this did not mean that power was really shared with them, or that the state was captured by them. The businessmen's support was essential but lack of it from time to time was not disastrous. For example, the government had successfully ruled against the business sector's interest by passing labour legislation in the late 1960s (Scott, 1989, ch.3). So, the government was in the leading position.

It was quite clear that one of the major concerns for the government was its survival. In times of peace and stability, the government tended to adopt a piecemeal and incremental approach.[32] However, in crisis situations, the government was willing to make more changes if these were meet its interests. Such policies were largely crisis management projects[33] but were not necessarily short-term.

The governing principles of the government, until the 1960s, were fiscal conservatism and the 'limited' role of state. These principles could be found from the very early days of the colony. They were the product of the early political struggle between the British merchants (and in late nineteenth and early twentieth century they were joined by the rising class of Chinese merchants) and the government. The merchants were the major tax payers and thus, any increase in government taxation would be inevitably shouldered by them.[34] Therefore, they had every reason to reject expansive government budgets (Chan, 1991). Moreover, the colony's government was expected to be self-reliant as quickly as possible by the British government. So, from its very early onset, the Hong Kong government was 'under pressure from two sources to provide 'value for money' in government expenditure', the Secretary of State which tried not to burden the British tax payers and the local merchants (Scott, 1989, pp.55-56). Such forces made the government very cautious in spending money, trying to keep the budget in balance or more desirably, to achieve a modest surplus and to control the growth of spending.[35] This contributed to the fiscal conservatism of the Hong Kong government.

Another principle, the limited role of government, was partly due to the limited budget which put an upper limit on the size of the public sector. Also, it was partly due to the reluctance of the bureaucrats to intervene in social affairs, which would inevitably involve the government in potential crisis situations and partly, the Chinese reluctance to let the government intervene into their 'internal affairs'. The Chinese community's problem were best, it was thought by both sides, to be solved by Chinese ways, usually by family and local charity organisations (Lau, 1982). These two principles were built-in as the governing philosophy, shared by the officials and the co-opted elite, the businessmen and community leaders and basically left unchallenged until the late 1960s.

The riots, as a result of the social problems in the 1960s, served to modify part of the political context. The 1966 Riot had engendered some changes within the public sector. The Dickenson Report (Report of the Working Party on Local Administration) and the Report by the Inter-Department Working Party to consider certain aspects of Social Security were published in 1967 in response to the riot. The Dickenson Report called for the setting Municipal Councils consisting of both elected and appointed members in the ratios of 3:1 or 3:2 respectively, in several districts (HKG, 1967b). The Report on social security acknowledged the fact that Hong Kong lagged behind in the provision of social security and called for the establishment of such system (HKG, 1967c).

The 1967 Riot had intensified the changes. In 24 January 1968, the Colonial Secretary announced the setting up of the City District Office (CDO) scheme in urban areas.[36] In 28 February, the Governor, Sir David Trench, announced in the LegCo that Chinese was to be made the official language in government communications.[37] Although the idea of an ombudsman[38] was rejected by the Governor and the LegCo, the unofficial members of the LegCo were given greater powers to receive complaints from the public and to investigate.[39] But further reform in the civil service structure was rejected by the senior civil servants such as Cowperthwaite,

> If people want consultative government, the price is increased complexity and delay in arriving at decisions. If they want speed of government, then they must accept a degree of authoritarianism. I suspect that the real answer is that most people prefer the latter so long, that is as the government's decisions conform to their own views (Hong Kong Hansard, 1968, p.85).

His logic, widely shared by other government officials, was that 'government by consensus' was the right approach to governing (the reform of the civil service did not occur until the McKinsey Report was published in 1973). Apart from these limited but significant changes, there were also labour legislation which served to increase the workers' welfare, despite resistance from the employers associations (Scott, 1989, pp.122-123).

Further reforms were not accepted by the officials as most of them considered the disturbances as a minor event or as merely a failure in the government's public relations efforts. The government preferred gradual improvements in access to and the public relations of the government. The real changes only occurred in the next decade.

Summary

Hence, we can observe that with the weak control of local affairs from United Kingdom, the Hong Kong government could enjoy a high autonomy from its control. As there were only weak local pressure groups, except the business groups, the government also enjoyed high autonomy from societal forces. The most powerful business groups had been incorporated into the governing principles, policy and decision making process of the administrative structure.

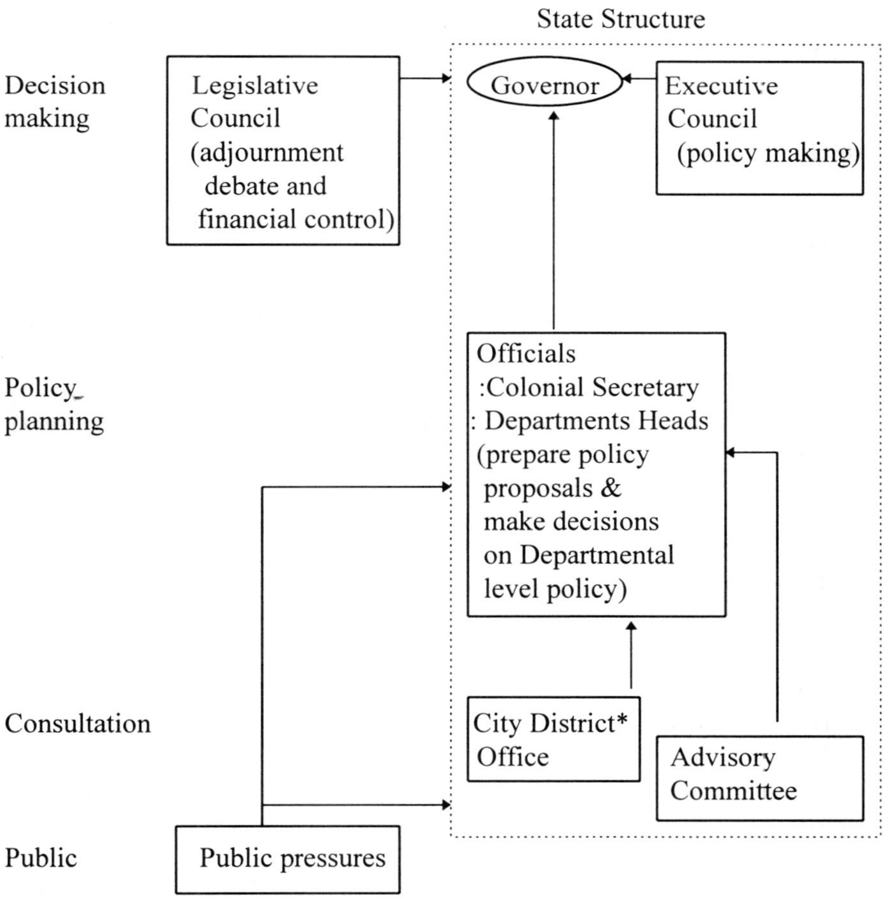

* Established in January 1968.

Figure 5.1 Policy process and structure, pre-1970s

Other social pressures and demands that arose from economic and social factors served to form the context for the officials to deal with. Yet, as they were constrained by the policy process and structure, such social pressures or problems could not be guaranteed acknowledgement and corresponding actions by the officials. This was not to say that the social pressures had no impact but the impact was rather limited. Only in exceptional circumstances, such as the riots, did the officials take more active measures.

Although the LegCo played the role of monitoring the government and reflecting the public opinion, the narrow base of appointment to it, the orientation of the Councillors and structural constraints on its power, in effect, had made it unable to direct the government's policies to meet social demands (Figure 5.1).

Notes

1 These are the propositions of the political perspectives and classical Marxism.
2 These are mainly the propositions of the state-centered thesis.
3 As agreed in the Joint Declaration between China and United Kingdom signed in 1983, Hong Kong will be returned to China in 1 July 1997 and after that date, Hong Kong will be the SAR of China, enjoying high autonomy in its internal affairs. It is the principle of the 'One Country, Two Systems'.
4 These are the propositions of the diffusion thesis.
5 The Hong Kong government does not have data for GNP and only started to prepare it from 1995.
6 The Kowloon peninsula was ceded to Britain in 1860 and the New Territories, was leased to Britain in 1898 for 99 year until 1997.
7 Later, renamed as the Secretary of the State for Foreign and Commonwealth Affairs.
8 Hence, the decisions are all named as by 'Governor in Council'.
9 Within that Committee, there are two sub-committees, the Establishment Sub-Committee and the Public Works Sub-Committee. The former focuses on the issues of the civil service while the latter attends to public works.
10 The election of the UC started in 1953 with two seats out of 11 directly elected. However, until 1981, the election was restricted to a minority of sectors of the society. Miners has reported that 'a potential voter had to satisfy the registration officer that he was qualified in at least one of the 23 categories. Broadly speaking those eligible included those who had

passed the School Certificate Examination or a similar or higher certificate or diploma, who were jurors, salaried tax-payers, ratepayers, or business men, or who were members of some listed professional organisation, ranging from air pilots and barristers to midwives, nuns, and newspaper reporters' (Miners, 1989, p.168).

11 At that time, the members of the Legislative Council were divided into three types, the ex-officio members, that was the Colonial Secretary, Financial Secretary and the Commander-in-chief of the army, the official members, that was the bureaucrats of the government, and the unofficial member that were all appointed by the Governor.

12 However, it must be noted that the ex-officio and official members could not be members of the most influential Finance Committee.

13 Perhaps until the mid-1980s when Sir David Ford took over as the Chief Secretary (formerly known as Colonial Secretary) that the Chief Secretary regains its leadership position in the government structure.

14 Sir John Cowperthwaite was the Finance Secretary from 1965 to 1973 and was succeeded by his follower, in terms of fiscal policy, Sir Philip Haddon-Cave.

15 For example, only 35 per cent of the school age population was studying in government, grant-aided and subsidised primary and secondary schools in 1949. The rest were studying in private schools with high school fees. Nevertheless, it was estimated that 50,000 children and youth could not receive any education. The situation changed gradually after the effort was narrowed to primary education. Yet, until the mid-1960s, there was still inadequate primary places for all children, not to mention the issues of fees and the severe shortages in the secondary and tertiary sectors. See, Jones, 1990, pp.190-193.

16 The Communist Party took over the mainland in 1949 and the People's Republic of China set up. The Kuomintang had withdrawn to Taiwan and set up the Republic of China.

17 The most popular example was, perhaps, the conflict in Western District. The pro-Kuomintang residents have to moved to Rennie's Mine to escape from the pro-Communist's attacks in 1950.

18 In 1956, the resettlement policy committee of the Urban Council decided that flags of the Republic of China (Taiwan government) should not be posted on wall and following such policy, a junior government officials attempted to remove two large 'double ten' symbols from a wall in resettlement estate. Angry crowds gathered and riot started. The riots lasted for three days.

19 The Fisher Report in 1951 and the two Plans called for expanded education, and places for all primary school age children by 1961.

Although the government managed to reach the places target, the increase of population was faster. For the development of education services, please refer to chapter 6.

20 It increased from HK¢20 to HK¢25 for a single trip.

21 Hong Kong suffered from economic recession in 1965 and later, several banks have ran into trouble. Moreover, there was accumulated frustration resulted from poor employment and working conditions.

22 One of the reasons for this was the use of English as the official language which created a distance between the government and the public. See HKG, 1967a, pp.127-128.

23 Compared with the voter turn-out in Singapore and Japan in 1963, of 94.2 per cent and 71.1 per cent respectively. Of course, it would be depend on the type of election. See United Nations, 1991, Table 2.8.

24 This has been used as an argument against the development of democracy even in the debate on further development of representative government in mid-1980s.

25 As most of the Hong Kong people migrated or fled from China as refugees, they set up these associations to take care of those who came from the same places in China as most of their family networks were weak or non existent.

26 Examples were Shamshuipo Kaifong Association, Aberdeen Kaifong Association and Mongkok Kaifong Association.

27 Lo Wu is the major customs check-point on the border between China and Hong Kong.

28 These conflicts resulted from an internal power struggle, the failure of reforms, and chaotic social and economic situations especially during the Cultural Revolution.

29 Thus the migration of Hong Kong people to overseas countries never stopped in the 1950s and 1960s and this 'movement' was stimulated by any crisis situation in Hong Kong, mostly because of political factors (the riots).

30 For the details, please refers to Castells, 1986, p.72.

31 Hence, The Chinese General Chamber of Commerce, Hong Kong and Federation of Hong Kong Industries were formed in 1900 and 1960 respectively. The oldest business organisation in Hong Kong was the Hong Kong General Chamber of Commerce formed in 1861.

32 There were plans but the problems were in their monitoring and implementation of these.

33 This was seen in the labour legislation after the 1967 Riot.

34 The first complaint from the merchants over the colony's expenditure was received by the Secretary of State as early as in 1845.

35 Such a principle was also valid even in the immediate post-war years. See Tang, 1992, Table 5.2.

36 Hong Kong Hansard 24 January 1968, p.20

37 Noted that Trench also stated that it was a 'process of taking numerous small and specific steps, not of making one sweeping gesture'. See Hong Kong Hansard, 28 February 1968/69, p.50.

38 The idea was suggested by a committee commissioned by the government in 1969.

39 The power to redress grievances was formally given by the Colonial Secretariat directives of 21 August 1970. Hence the Office of Unofficial Members of Executive and Legislative Councils (UMELCO) was set up.

6 Development and legacy: Hong Kong's welfare state in pre-1970s

This chapter provides a brief account of the development of the welfare state from the early post-war years to 1971, when Sir Murray MacLehose[1] became the Governor of Hong Kong. All welfare states evolve over time. Hence, later development is often based on the previously established system and its legacies. This chapter also attempts, using the theories of welfare state and the general model of welfare state development, to relate the contextual factors to the development of the Hong Kong welfare state in this period.

Development of the welfare state in Hong Kong: 1945-1971

For the first hundred years of the colony, there was hardly any systematic provision of social services nor any attempt to build up a welfare state in Hong Kong. There was no provision of housing or of social security. Social welfare was mainly restricted to relief work and the education service was mainly for the elite and the wealthy class due to the high school fees and very limited supply of places. Health services provided by the government were primarily concerned with communicable diseases. Services for vulnerable groups were largely provided by the missionaries and local Chinese philanthropic organizations[2] with very limited government subsidies. The Second World War had brought all the administrative and social services efforts to a standstill. After the War, Hong Kong gradually recovered and had more resources for social services development. At the same time, the input and assistance from overseas churches and missionaries had contributed to the establishment of a strong NGO network.

Medical services

The first 'long-term' plan for medical development was in 1957 and there followed an increasing role of government in providing medical services. As communicable diseases became eradicated in Hong Kong by the 1960s, the government diverted resources to building clinics and hospitals. In its planning, hospitals and clinics were primarily provided for those who 'could not afford to pay economic charges' and clinics were the higher priority, not because they were better but they were more economical (HKAR, 1966). From 1945 to 1957, there was only one new government hospital[3] but three new government-assisted hospitals operated by voluntary organisations were opened.[4] According to the 1963 revised plan and the subsequent White Paper 'Development of Medical Services in Hong Kong'[5], a network of clinics supported by specialist and large hospital facilities would be constructed and the number of beds would be increased from 2.91 per thousand of population in 1963 to 4.25 in 1972 (ibid). In the 1960s, the hospital construction programme accelerated. Several government hospitals opened and continuously expanded thereafter[6] and the growth rate of government hospital beds surpassed the growth rate of assisted hospital and private hospital beds (Table 6.1). By 1970, the percentage had grown from 2.25 in 1956 to 4.2 beds per thousand of population (HKAR, 1956; CSD, 1978). Infant mortality, though it was still high, was reduced to 19.6 per thousand's births by 1970 (CSD, 1978, Table 15.1).

Table 6.1
Increase of hospital beds in Hong Kong, 1965-1970

Year	Government (including dispensary)	Assisted	Private
1965	5,176	5,975	1,511
1966	5,253	6,109	1,489
1967	5,551	6,716	1,490
1968	5,832	7,010	1,609
1969	6,142	7,556	1,731
1970	6,788	7,533	1,806
Increase	31.1%	26.1%	19.5%
% of total bed	42.1%	46.7%	11.2%

Source: HKAR, various years

Education services

In 1951, the Fisher Report proposed an expansion plan from 1954 to 1961, eventually providing primary school places for every child. Such a grand idea and enthusiasm were not shared by both the government and the public[7]. The idea of free primary education was raised in 1965 by the White Paper on 'Education Policy'. The proposal was accepted, in principle, by the government but progress was rather uncertain.[8] Until 1968, the government only planned to provide places for 80 per cent of the children aged 6 to 12 in 1971. However, after the riots in the late 1960s, the government speeded up the plan and finally reached its target, set 20 years before by the Fisher Report to provide free primary education for all in government and government-aided schools, in 1971 (HKAR, 1971).[9] Primary education was perhaps the first recognized social right to social services in Hong Kong enjoyed both by the rich and the poor.[10]

Secondary education and especially tertiary education were still restricted to a small percentage of the student population. Due to the limited supply of places, only those who could pay or achieve very good results in open examinations could proceed to secondary and tertiary education. In August 1971, the government implemented a plan for three years free secondary education for 50 per cent of the primary school graduates. Those who wanted to attend secondary school had to take a highly competitive 'Secondary School Entrance Examination' (HKAR, 1970; 1971).

The cost of attending school had been reduced, especially after the riots. The annual school fee for primary education had been reduced from HK$50 and HK$40 to HK$20 and HK$10 in 1967 and 1969 respectively,[11] and finally free education in 1971. However, school fees for secondary schools were kept at a higher level and were basically unaffordable for majority of families, not to mention fees for tertiary education. The student loan and grant scheme which aimed to enable students from poor families to enter higher education only started in the 1969/70 academic year.

According to an estimate made by the government, by 1966, 99.8 per cent of those aged from six to eleven had been enrolled in primary schools. The government admitted that this provision was made possible by the payment of school fees which contributed to the expansion programme (HKAR, 1966, p.81). The growth was dominated by the subsidised and private sector. For example, in 1965, the ratio for student enrollment in government and grant schools, subsidized schools and private schools was 6 per cent, 32.3 per cent and 61.7 per cent respectively. The growth rates of each sector, measured by the number of places provided, over 1965-71 were 3.5 per cent, 83.6 per cent and 22.4 per cent (HKAR, 1965-1971). This growth was made possible by the relatively cheap option of subsidy to voluntary organizations.[12]

Table 6.2
School enrollment in Hong Kong, 1964-1971

Year	Primary	Secondary	Post-secondary	Total (% of total pop)
1964	596,971	177,680	6,693	781,344 (21.7%)
1965	627,621	197,237	5,926	830,784 (22.5%)
1966	657,585	222,890	9,549	890,024 (23.8%)
1967	689,561	235,387	9,629	934,577 (24.4%)
1968	724,450	253,458	10,484	988,392 (25.2%)
1969	752,171	264,056	11,522	1,027,749 (25.8%)
1970	765,397	279,318	11,739	1,055,454 (25.8%)
1971	764,313	295,820	11,799	1,071,932 (26.5%)
Increase	28.3%	66.5%	76.3%	--

Notes:
a. All figures calculated by the enrollment in September.
b. Increase of places in the post-secondary sector was largely due to the opening of the second university, The Chinese University of Hong Kong, in 1963 and its expansion thereafter.
c. The increase of secondary school enrollment was largely due to the rapid expansion of the private sector due to the increased number of primary school graduates.

Sources: HKAR, various years

Housing services

The housing service was probably the best showcase of the government's intervention in the period from 1946 to 1971. The watershed occurred in 1953-54 when fires swept over several major squatter settlements, especially in Shek Kei Mei which produced nearly 100,000 fire victims.[13] Such a crisis could hardly be neglected by the government. The government opted for a cheap relief scheme, that was to build very low cost accommodation (resettlement estates) with minimal facilities to accommodate as large a population as it could. The origin of the public housing programme was never a well-planned one but just an ad hoc measure, which was continued later, for resettling the squatters and receiving land for redevelopment purposes.[14] Such a motive was made clear by the Commissioner for Resettlement who stated that these squatters must be resettled because 'the community needs the land of which they are in illegal occupation' (Chan, 1985; HKAR, 1966, p.6). The land was cleared for commercial and industrial use and the squatters were resettled to other outlying areas 'which it was then thought would not need to be redeveloped for some time' (HKAR, 1965, p.125).[15]

The continuous expansion of the public housing programmes covered more and more categories of household. The Hong Kong Housing Authority (HA) was set up in 1954 to cater for the housing needs of the lower middle income class, for example, with HK$500 to HK$1,000 (HKAR, 1971) or above as their monthly family income (at 1971 prices). The Hong Kong Housing Society (HS) was set up in 1948 to serve the needs for the category with monthly incomes between HK$400 to HK$900 (at mid-1960s prices) (HKAR, 1966). Apart from income level, families' living conditions such as sanitary and overcrowding were also considered as eligibility criteria. In 1959, the government announced a plan to build a new type of housing, 'low cost housing', for those lower income groups not covered by the resettlement plan nor eligible for the flats provided by the HA and HS (HKAR, 1966, Chan, 1989, pp.45-52). Low cost housing was entrusted to the HA for management. The major advisory body, the Housing Board, was set up in 1965 to advise the government on various housing matters.

The population rehoused by these programmes was enormous. In 1970, the resettlement estates had provided accommodation for approximately 1,100,000 people. The HA provided housing for another 187,000 and managed the Low Cost Housing for a further 173,000. The HS served for another 100,000. Thus public sector housing had provided accommodation for approximately 38 per cent of the total population in 1970 (HKAR, 1970). The housing sector was the only one to which the government had committed significant portion of its resources. Although there was still much to do in the following years, the housing services had achieved a remarkable record by 1970.

Social welfare services

Social welfare development, comparatively speaking, fell behind in this period. In 1948, social welfare was only the responsibility of a 'sub-office', the Social Welfare Office,[16] within the Secretariat for Chinese Affairs. As late as in 1956, the office was only responsible for women and girl protection, probation, boys and girls clubs[17] and relief work. The service role of the government only became more significant from mid-1960s (Lau, 1991, p.46). Such a limited range of duties reflected the government's limited role in social welfare provision.

The first White Paper on social welfare, 'Aims and Policy for Social Welfare in Hong Kong' was published in 1965. The government admitted that the situation at that time was far from satisfactory. 'It was drawn up in a context which lacked many of the provisions that are common in the West: a society without a national assistance programme, without family allowances, without much of the legislative provision of the welfare state, and without the relatively stable economic conditions on which to base such provisions (HKAR, 1966, pp.19-20)'. However, the government did not have any ambitious plan but instead, a reinstatement of its role and that of the family. The major strategy was to strengthen the family to cope with individual and family problems, and help individuals to become independent and productive (HKAR, 1966, p.20). The only major breakthrough was the setting up of the public assistance scheme in 1971 for poor individuals and families to assist them to live at a minimal standards.

The majority of the services were provided by the voluntary organizations, either operated by the overseas churches or by local charitable organisations. Although in the 1960s, more and more organizations received subsidies from the government, still 'substantial sums are raised locally to support welfare programmes, while large sums continue to be made available through international agencies' (HKAR, 1967, pp.141-142).

Characteristics of welfare development

Table 6.3
Social service expenditure by items, 1966/67 - 1970/71
(percentage of government total expenditure)

Fiscal Year	Education	Medical	Housing	Social Welfare
1966/67	14.9	9.1	10.8	1.2
1967/68	16.3	9.3	12.3	1.2
1968/69	18.3	10.0	10.0	1.6
1969/70	19.3	10.3	8.9	1.8
1970/71	20.3	10.0	8.4	1.6

Sources: HKAR, various years

Comparatively speaking, the growth of social services and the size of the welfare state, in terms of its share of the government's total expenditure and GDP, rather steadily increased in the post-War era (Table 6.4). Social services expenditure did expand faster than before and took 40 per cent of the annual budget by the 1970/71 fiscal year. The expansion of the welfare output was easy to recognise especially in housing services. Yet the greatest share of the resources went into the education service (Table 6.3).

Table 6.4
Government expenditure and social services expenditure, 1949/50 - 1970/71 (index: 1949/50 = 100)

Year	Indices of GDP & government expenditure		Total expenditure on social services	
	Government expenditure	Total GDP	% of government expenditure	% of GDP
1949/50	100	100	16.7	1.4
1951/52	115	113	19.6	1.6
1953/54	142	108	27.6	2.9
1955/56	189	134	30.4	3.5
1957/58	256	156	31.3	4.2
1958/59	276	164	36.9	5.1
1959/60	319	168	36.1	5.7
1960/61	388	186	36.4	6.2
1961/62	470	226	37.8	6.2
1962/63	536	250	38.1	6.3
1963/64	604	277	39.8	6.7
1964/65	634	308	38.7	6.4
1965/66	738	354	34.7	6.0
1966/67	767	378	36.2	5.9
1967/68	767	378	39.5	5.8
1968/69	778	436	40.3	5.8
1969/70	800	487	40.7	5.2
1970/71	850	511	40.7	5.3

Source: adapted from Schiffer, 1991, p.192

However, facing with the increasing demand, the programmes were still weak and inadequate. Scott's comment on this, though harsh is relevant,

This meant, in practice, that the provision of social services throughout the period of the unreformed colonial state [period from 1842-1966] was often subjected to cost-cutting and penny-pinching measures, for the missionaries became increasingly unable to meet public demand without government support. Social services were minimal in quality and quantity or non-existent. By the 1960s, there was an enormous, accumulated, century-old, social debt (Scott, 1989, pp.50-51).

Redistribution by the government intervention in social services was not on its agenda, as made clear by Sir John Cowperthwaite, the Financial Secretary in the 1960s,

I myself have no doubt in the past tended to appear to many to be more concerned with the creation of wealth than with its distribution. I must confess there is an elements of truth in this, but to the extent that it is true, it has been because of my conviction that the rapid growth of the economy, and the pressure that comes with it on demand for labour, both produces a rapid and substantial redistribution of income directly of itself and also makes it possible to assist more generously whose are not, from misfortune, temporarily or permanent, sharing in the general advance (quoted from England & Rear, 1981, p.22).

The notions of justice and equality were also hardly mentioned in government documents. Citizenship was never a concern of the reforms and there was no such thing as social entitlement[18]. Therefore, Lau argues that 'on the whole, up till the early 1970s, the government was extremely reluctant to expand its role as a deliverer of basic social services' (Lau, 1982, p.45).

Although there was ample evidence to show the shortfall and inadequacies in many service areas, there is no doubt that this period of growth laid the foundation for further development. MacLehose's progressive reforms in the 1970s were not started in a complete vacuum, instead, they were based on the platform built largely in 1960s, for example, the public housing programme, the free education programme and the public assistance scheme. Moreover, this period also laid down the basic structure of services for the later development to be modelled on. The respective responsibilities, roles and relationships between the state, the market, the NGOs and the individual (the informal welfare sector), were consolidated in this period. The government still maintained a very cautious attitude in intruding into domain of the other sectors in provision of social services. These were the results of its governing principles of the limited role of the state and fiscal conservatism.

Implications for the theories of the welfare state

The development of the welfare state services until the start of 1970s was both a continuation of the limited intervention ideology and, contradictorily, the emergence of selective expansion of involvement in several areas. Several explanations were put forward to explain this phenomenon. The most frequently cited explanations were the social factor of the urban riots and the functional needs of economic development. It was correct to point out that much of the improvement came after the riots. Although the services, such as the expansion of primary education, were initiated before the riots, it seemed that they contributed to the speeding up of several services, such as the adoption of free and compulsory primary education, the Public Assistance Scheme and social welfare services for the youth.[19] The usual explanation was that the government recognised the inadequacies of current services provision and its relation to the riots and therefore, it had to start to reluctantly implement changes and make concessions to these manifest threats.

However, such a notion has to be further elaborated and refined. The riots did have impacts on society and the government. Nevertheless, such effects might not be all that significant. The major social programmes, except the above-mentioned, were introduced in the 1970s. Considering such delay in timing, it is plausible to suppose that there were some intervening factors in the process which made this happen in the 1970s but not in the 1960s. Moreover, even after the riots, some officials were still reluctant to make concessions in certain matters.[20] Yet, it is still fair to argue that the riots had made the government more alert and so it had responded with limited immediate reforms. However, there was, definitely, no significant change in the government's power in decision making and the administrative-led style of governing was maintained. The 'riots notion' was, at best, one of the significant factors in shaping the reforms in the late 1960s.

Another factor that contributed to the development of social services was the functional needs engendered by economic development. The first factor was the need for land resumption for further development and the better-trained labour force arising from the expansion of the economy. The resettlement programme was the best example to illustrate such an argument. Hong Kong had been a capitalist economy since its cession to the British. In such a context, when the government had to rely on economic success to prove its legitimacy and gain popular support (or at least, not open opposition), to maintain this success was certainly the primary task of the government. Another factor was that the economic boom, which contributed income to the government through taxation and the sale of land, could now allow more resources to finance the welfare development and make easier and more feasible. This argument was valid as a deficit budget or raising loans to finance the social programme were definitely ruled out by the government.[21] Yet, this increase of resources did not guarantee an increase of expenditure on social services. This was still subject to the decisions of the people who controlled the allocation of resources. Therefore, the policy and decision-making processes were important. So these social and economic factors served as the policy context which generated needs and problems which required solutions by the policy makers. The policy process in Hong Kong, at this time, was a product of the capitalist structure, the relative passivity of the public and the administrative-led style of governing.

The primacy of economic success to the colony, had given the business sector a significant position in Hong Kong . Its cooperation with and support for the government was decisive and given this, there should have been some influence from that sector on its policies (Henderson, 1991). However, it is hard to conclude that, in this period, the businessmen had firmly 'captured' the state as their instrument for their own interests. If this had been so, the government would not have been blamed for its lack of support to the manufacturing sector and objections from the capitalists to the labour legislation programme in the late 1960s. Neither classical Marxist nor instrumentalist explanations could be applied in this context. Instead, the structuralist arguments threw a clearer light on the power relationships involved and their outcomes.

The social democratic thesis was not applicable to Hong Kong, working class mobilisation could not be a strong force to counteract the officials' power. The trade unions were deeply divided by their political standpoints, the pro-Communist China Federation of Trade Unions (FTU) or pro-Taiwan Trade Union Council (TUC) (Jao et al, 1988; Turner et al, 1980; England & Rear, 1981, ch.7). They were not strong enough to alter or influence government policies (ibid, pp.13-14, p.155). Moreover, the general fear of the Communist Party and the Communist's involvement in the 1967 riots had caused its loss of popularity among the public. After the 1967 riot, the pro-Communist FTU suffered from public criticism for threatening the stability and prosperity of Hong Kong. Apart from the unions, there were no political parties nor strong intermediary organizations to act as powerful bodies of opinion.[22]

The government could maintain a high level of autonomy and freedom by claiming to follow a 'consultation and consensus' strategy (Cheng, 1992; Scott, 1989; Lau, 1982), though occasionally, they had to made concessions in exceptional circumstances such as the riots. But the favourable conditions generated by economic development had put the government in a more vulnerable position in responding to demands for more services. Cowperthwaite's address in LegCo in 1964 showed this,

> I have said that money has not been the limiting factor in recent years; this is in the short term. For longer terms it is not quite as true. We have to look ahead as far as we can, and assess as well as we can ... I pointed out that we were at present able to meet the high cost of certain services based on imported standards only because we were providing them for a small part of the population, a situation which had arisen by historical accident [refer to housing] (HK Hansard, 1964/65, p. 52).

Cowperthwaite did not totally reject the improvement of social services but he was very worried by the potential financial burden in the long run and the inappropriateness of provision to a high standard (Rabushka, 1975, p. 90). Hence, he strove to control the expenditure. In the 1968/69 budget debate, the government was under pressure, partly from the LegCo, to provide more social services, but the FS resisted such pressure, and argued that 'the implication that the people of Hong Kong have to be given a reward, like children, for being good last year, and bribed, like children, into being good next year' and proceeded with a conservative budget (Miners, 1975, p. 33).

The provision of six year free and compulsory education from 1971 was another example which showed the government's reluctance. Cowperthwaite's argument was that those who could afford to pay primary school fees should not receive a subsidy. Though he finally agreed with the policy, he still hoped that 'we shall be able to do something to limit free primary education, and possibly, for that matter, heavily subsidised primary education, to the schools which do not cater for the affluent' (HK Hansard, 1971/72, p. 419).

These examples have shown us that although the government did enjoy high degree of autonomy and control over the policy process and decision-making, it was not immune to all external pressures. The government's autonomy was based on its success in managing the economy and hence, in getting support from the business sector and the public. Thus, legitimacy was gained from its ability to contribute to capitalist accumulation and public acceptance. The autonomy of the state was also aided by the general apathy of the public over public policies and their fear of the Communist Party in view of the poor conditions in mainland China at that period of time. All these factors gave a free-hand to the officials to decide on their response to the social problems and needs. There was some external influence, but not in an explicit manner and its effect was not openly manifest.

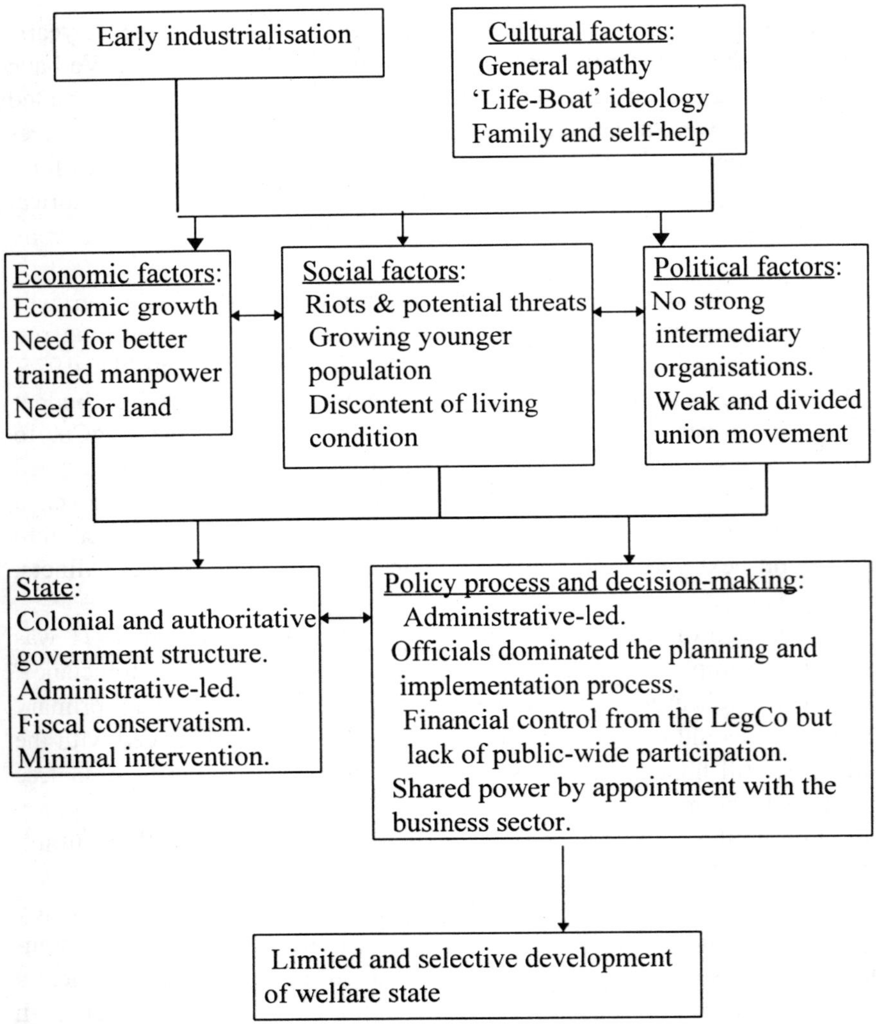

Figure 6.1 General model of theory of welfare state, pre-1970s

The contextual factors had generated needs and demands. However, the relationship between these needs and the corresponding policies was not unidirectional. The relationship was mediated by the state, screened by the governing ideologies, officials' interpretations and the business interests represented in the policy process. The dominance of these elements was safeguarded by public apathy and lack of intermediary organisations to represent and articulate alternative demands to the state and the policy process. Within this process, there was still room for largely autonomous government.

Summary

The state was situated in a capitalist society. The origin and survival of the society and the state very much relied on the sustaining of the capitalist structure. Because of the structure of the state and its success in maintaining support from the business sector and avoiding rejection by the public, its autonomy was sustained. The policies it did adopt were scrutinized by the logic of capitalism and measured according to their impacts on the economy. The more positive the effects, the greater the chance they would be accepted and supported by the business sector.

However, social services projects were not merely a tool of the capitalists or state to pursue their own interests. The social services also served the interest of the public[23]. The study of the welfare state evolution up to 1971 can be seen as state-centered. Particular attention should be paid to the administrative and decision making structure, and the governing ideology of the state versus the degree of influence from external factors, both in an explicit and implicit ways.

Notes

1 Upon his retirement in 1982, he was awarded a peerage.
2 Examples were the Tung Wah Group of Hospitals and Po Leung Kuk. Tung Wah was founded under an ordinance passed in 1870 and provided the first medical services, hospitals and out-patient clinics for the Chinese. Po Leung Kuk was founded to prevent the kidnapping of women and young girls and formally recognized by the government in mid-1890s. Both of them served social services as well as political representation functions at that period of time. See Scott, 1989, ch.2.
3 This was the Tsan Yuk Maternity Hospital with 200 beds.

4 They were the Ruttonjee Tuberculosis Sanatorium (1949), the Haven of Hope Tuberculosis Hospital (1955) and the Grantham Hospital (1957).

5 The White Paper was published in 1964.

6 For example, the Castle Peak Hospital (the first mental health hospital in Hong Kong) opened in 1961 and the Queen Elizabeth Hospital in 1963.

7 Although Chinese traditionally put a high value on education, parents at that time were more concerned to feed their families.

8 Because the secondary school sector rejected the method of financing the expansion by increasing their school fees to re-divert part of the resources to primary education. See HKAR, 1966.

9 The plan was announced before MacLehose came in 1971.

10 Health is another universally provided service but, in fact, the poor had a greater chance to use the services and the rich were more inclined to consume the far better services in the private sector.

11 HK$20 per month for the schools in urban areas and HK$10 per month for those in rural areas. Moreover, the poor families could get assistance through the fee remission scheme as well as book and stationery grants.

12 It was a cheaper option as the teacher-student ratio was more favourable in the government schools and those concerned voluntary organizations had to contribute part of the capital costs and recurrent expenses.

13 The fire in Shek Kei Mei produced 58,000 victims and other fires followed until December 1954 and produced another 42,000 victims. The total number of victims was nearly 5 per cent of the Hong Kong population in that year. See HKAR, 1954 and Chan, 1989.

14 In an interview with South China Morning Post (SCMP), Sir Ronald Holmes, the proponent of the resettlement estate scheme recalled that in 1952, 'there wasn't really a resettlement policy at all'. The report also contained the following description, by Sir Ronald, of the Executive Council meeting on the resettlement plan: 'I can clearly remember appearing before the Executive Council when our multi-storey resettlement plan was first put to them. After the members had asked a variety of questions, the Governor, Sir Alexander Grantham, said to me: 'Well, Holmes, what do you think? Is this the best we can do?' I said that we couldn't think of anything better. Then, he asked the Director of Medical & Health Services, who said, 'Sir, I feel bound to oppose it. These are standards of overcrowding which are simply intolerable and we shall be criticised all over the world.' So, the Governor asked him 'Well, what would you do?' He replied 'I don't know, Sir.' And that was the key. There was nothing else we could do in the circumstances'. This shows that the government was forced to intervene and had no

intention to use the service as a mean to vacate land for redevelopment at first. See SCMP, 30 April 1977.

15 The demand for land from the entrepreneurs was made clear when they had settled in Hong Kong. Sir Ronald Holmes had recalled that 'at first we didn't realize what was happening, but by 1952 it was very clear that these chaps meant business... However, what they chiefly wanted was land and the great influx of people made it very much more difficult to make land available.' See SCMP, 30 April 1977. Although such awareness did not relate to the initial resettlement policy, such need for land from the business sector and the intention to assist them in the acquisition of land was certainly the reasons which maintained and modified the initial early resettlement effort.

16 The Office was upgraded to a Department in 1958.

17 These clubs were provided for street-children, who could not find a school place or could not afford to pay the fees to have an alternative chance of education. In these clubs, there were small libraries and some literacy classes. These served to compensate for the inadequacy of formal education.

18 Though services were provided to the citizen, the government did not intend to interpret this provision and consumption as based on the principle of citizenship.

19 Youth were the major participants of the 1966 Riots and therefore, it is logical to think that the government would invest more resources to counter this potentially disruptive force. Labour legislation was another example but as the operational definition of the welfare state in this thesis does not include labour services, this will not be discussed in here.

20 Such as the constitutional reforms.

21 However, the Hong Kong government did welcome donations from overseas and grants from the United Kingdom after the Second World War.

22 Except the organisations representing the interests of the business, commercial and industrial sectors.

23 As the finance of public expenditure did not result in increase of tax, the business sector would not strongly oppose these as they were not required to contribute additional tax. Considered the overall economic situation at that period of time, such services provision, 'free' or priced at a low cost to the public was already beyond the public expectation.

Part Three
DEVELOPMENT OF THE WELFARE STATE, 1971-1981

7 The context: 1971 to 1981

Welfare state development is here seen as a dependent variable of the interaction between the contextual factors, the state and the policy process. Therefore, the changes in these factors and the relationships among them will result in changes in the welfare state. In the 1970s, the socio-economic-political context changed and there were also changes in the policy process and the degree of state autonomy.

Economic context

The local economy continued to develop in the 1970s, though it faced crises in the middle of the decade. These crises included the oil crisis in 1973, a stock and property market crash which started in 1973 and lasted two years and the following banking crisis. There was less growth in 1974 and 1975 but Hong Kong then managed successfully to recover from the hardship caused by the local and international economic recession from 1973.

The growth of the economy also contributed a stable and adequate source of income to the government. Although there were some problems, the government was generally successful in maintaining a balanced budget and accumulating a huge reserve throughout the 1970s. So, stable growth and the remarkable recovery from recession provided the government with a firm and safe sources of income to make new expenditure possible. Moreover, the accumulation of huge sums reserve also engendered criticism of the government for being over-conservative in spending money on needs, such as the social services.

Table 7.1
Growth of GDP, 1971-1981 (1980 price)

Year	GDP (HK$m)	Change (-/+%)
1971	60,536	7.4
1972	67,197	11.0
1973	75,725	12.7
1974	77,309	2.1
1975	77,616	0.4
1976	90.967	17.2
1977	101,893	12.0
1978	110,824	8.8
1979	123,923	11.8
1980	136,775	10.4
1981	149,585	9.4

* In 1973, the CSD changed the calculation method for GDP and hence, figures for 1973 onwards are not exactly comparable with earlier figures.

Source: Mok, 1993, Table 2.3

There were two major changes in the local economy, the growth of new industries and the gradual development of commercial activities (Mok, 1993, pp.111-124). Apart from clothing, plastic and electrical products employed more and more of the working population. Now, the percentage of the total working population engaged in manufacturing industries declined while the percentage in finance and commerce business gradually increased.[1] There was a growing new class of employees, skilled workers and the professionals.

However, the local industries were facing growing competition from Taiwan and South Korea. To deal with the challenges from these 'Little Dragons', the Hong Kong government responded by its 'diversification' policy (ibid, pp.158-165).[2] The changing nature of industries and employment patterns generated needs for a more well-educated and appropriately trained working force. The need was more urgent when it was estimated that in 1979, 55 per cent of the working population did not have a qualification beyond primary education (Youngson, 1982, p.18).

Table 7.2
Surplus/deficit for the budget and accumulated fiscal reserve
1971/72 - 1980/81 (HK$m)

Financial year	Estimated deficit/surplus	Actual deficit/surplus of General Revenue Account	Accumulated fiscal reserve
1971/72	256	640	2,204
1972/73	47	636	2,916
1973/74	513	72	3,089
1974/75	98	(380)	2,809
1975/76	(431)	488	2,522
1976/77	(355)	903	2,810
1977/78	30	1,236	3,713
1978/79	(20)	1,467	4,890
1979/80	1,455	2,500	6,549
1980/81	2,594	7,826	8,916

* The calculation of fiscal reserve varied across the decade. The data are generated from the General Revenue Account. For 1971/72, the data included the Revenue Equalisation Fund and the Foreign Exchange Fund which is used to stabilise the Hong Kong currency. In the devaluation of the British Pound in 1972, the Fund virtually lost all of its reserves. From 1975, the amount in the fund was kept secret until 1992. Apart from these funds, the government also has other funds for construction, development, capital investment, lottery, student loan etc..

Sources: Youngson, 1981, Table 2.1
HKAR, 1981 and 1982
Tang, 1992, ch.5; Table 5.3 & 5.4

Social context

The changing of the employment pattern and the growth of the income[3] of the population gradually engendered a middle-income group[4] in society. This group of people were better educated and occupied higher posts in different sectors. A significant group of them were engaged in careers which stemmed from the growth of the social services, such as doctors and nurses, teachers and social workers. These more active groups formed strong pressure groups to pursue their own interests.

The growth of pressure group politics was the main feature of informal politics in the 1970s. According to Lau's analysis, the traditional intermediary organisations were further weakened and finally collapsed in the 1970s. Industrialisation and accompanying value changes had rendered them both ideologically unattractive and functionally redundant. The government's increasing involvement in public welfare provision had taken over their private charity function. The changes in formal politics, the centralisation in decision-making and co-option of the elite directly into the government structure, had weakened their intermediary function.[5] The decline of community feeling and lack of identification with the traditional elite and organisations, especially among the younger generation, also weakened their popular support (Lau, 1981, pp.873-874). Pressure group politics was also stimulated by the limited success of the CDO scheme and UMELCO as the grievances channels (ibid, p.875).

The new pressure groups filled the gap left by the old organisations. These groups were actively involved in opposing socially injustice, as they saw these. They initiated various action-type organisations[6] and helped grassroots groups to form their own residents organisations to fight for their interests. Several residents organisations were formed on the public housing estates[7] and they fought either individually or in a coalition.

Another new initiative was the formation of new types of trade union that resulted from the changing employment structure and the expansion of social services. Apart from the low profile FTU and TUC, in the 1970s, three new groups of trade unions emerged and gained wide recognition. The first group were the 'neutral' and 'independent' trade unions,[8] with the Christian Industrial Committee (CIC) as an typical example. The second group was the civil servant unions, such as Hong Kong Chinese Civil Servants Association and Civil Servants' General Union.[9] The third group were the white collar unions, such as the Professional Teachers Union (PTU)[10] and the Social Workers General Union. All these types of trade union were more active in social movements than the traditional unions. They collaborated together to form ad hoc alliance on various issues, such as housing policy and the Golden Jubilee Incidents.[11] Their participation might be seen in terms of protecting their own interests in respective services or in terms of a claim for social justice.

Though these pressure groups and alliances were mostly short-lived and loosely organised, such a new form of challenge to government was unprecedented and, difficult for it to respond to. The government established a confidential committee, the Standing Committee on Pressure

Groups (SCOPG) to monitor the group's activities in 1978 (Leung, 1990, p.45). Its attitude, in the 1970s, was the one of hostility and suspicion.[12]

Cultural context

The new social movements and pressure group politics show us that there was a sector of the population who had by now deviated from the passive and submissive Chinese personality, the 'life-boat' ideology and 'refugee mentality'. Though there were very few studies on this changing culture, in research carried out by the Reform Club[13] in 1977, 50 per cent of the respondents were in favour of having elected members in the LegCo, a progressive suggestion at that period. A detailed analysis of the results showed that among those with post-secondary education, 71 per cent were in favour of elected members and 64 per cent of those with secondary education were in favour. By contrast, only 27 per cent of those with primary education or below were in favour of the idea. This shows that those with a higher education level were more radical and progressive than those with a lower education level. These higher educated people were the backbone of social movements in the 1970s. Miners has suggested that,

> ... it seems likely that 'Confucian' ideals of government were more influential among older people who had been born in China and had little education. The younger generation, born in Hong Kong and with no memories of the chaos of the Chinese civil war, have been brought up in a cosmopolitan city ... Almost all have been educated to secondary school level. For most of them Confucian influence would seem to be confined to the traditional Chinese pattern of teaching children how they should behave: to respect their elders, avoid conflict, and keep silent rather than express open disagreement (Miners, 1991, p.36).

However, there was still a considerable proportion of the people who maintained the traditional type of views. King's research[14] discovered that only 14 per cent of respondents thought that they could do something about an unjust government regulation (1972). The figure was particularly low when compared with figures for other countries. In those countries where similar research was conducted, the proportion who believed that they could influence government policy was 79 per cent in Britain, 77 per cent in United States, 62 per cent in West Germany and 52 per cent in Mexico (Almond & Verba, 1963, p.185). Lau's study[15] also found that less than 20 per cent of the respondents had joined any voluntary association and among these, only 3 per cent (i.e. 0.5 per cent of total respondents) were members of a political organisation. Those data show us that most Hong Kong people were still unattached and not associated with any organisation. Among these respondents, more than 87 per cent put a higher value on social stability than other factors, even including economic prosperity. It was clear that the majority of them favoured stability rather than any radical action, including active participation in social movements, which might 'rock the boat' (Lau, 1982, pp.71-72).

These findings were also supported by other studies by Lau.[16] In these studies, he concluded that Hong Kong was a 'minimally integrated' social-political system (ibid) in which there were limited linkages and exchanges between the bureaucratic polity and Chinese society and each of them were 'boundary-conscious' wary of 'intrusion' by the other. The bureaucratic polity strove to maintain its political autonomy by limiting its functions, by preventing the emergence of rival political actors and by depoliticising Chinese society, and the Chinese society, a politically conservative and stabilising force in society, was primary concerned to meet the needs of the Hong Kong Chinese (ibid, pp.18-19). Lau argues that the 'small groups of disgruntled and socially unattached individuals' could not significantly change the relationship and distribution of roles between the state and the society (ibid, p.20). The low participation and interest in politics and public affairs were evidenced in the only elections at this time, the UC elections.[17]

These contrasting findings, however limited, indicate that Hong Kong society had gradually divided into two group of people, differing in their social and political awareness and participation in the 1970s.[18] The first group, probably the majority, still retained the residues of the traditional Chinese personality while the second group, the minority, had a more active interest in politics and higher awareness than the first group. For them, the 'refugee mentality' was replaced by a strong sense of belongingness and attachment to Hong Kong. Low or no expectations of the government were replaced by requests for more government intervention especially in social problems.[19] It seems that a 'Hong Kong society' was gradually emerging and the image of Hong Kong as a temporary 'life-boat', stepping stone to migration and as transient society was fading away.

Political context

The emergence of new politically active groups, and more covert conflicts with the government, coupled with the residual effect of the riots had engendered changes in the government structure and policy process.

Concerning the riot's impacts on the legitimacy of the colonial government, Scott writes that,

> The disturbances was a watershed in Hong Kong's political history. They illuminated the weaknesses of the system and pointed to the need for change. They showed that prevailing justifications for state action were inadequate; that the structure and functions of government were inappropriate for an industrial society; that there was widespread resentment of the arrogance of office which was often associated with the colonial civil services; and that a new political order and a new basis for legitimacy were urgent requirements (1989, p.81).

The first half of this period was dominated by the government's major concern over the reconstruction of the government-citizen relationship after the riots. The government recognised the inadequacies of the old structure which was ruled by 'consensus' and an elite-to-elite communication, and the 'failure of communication' between itself and the public (HKG, 1967a, p.110).

But basically, there was no revolutionary change in the formal structure. What seemed to be the most significant change was the widening scope of consultation, from the grassroots up to the LegCo. The objective was to maintain the existing structure and 'government by consensus' and deal with rising social pressure and covert conflicts when it was possible. King refers to the further penetration of 'administrative absorption' to the grassroots level (1975).

The first new measure was the setting up and strengthening of the CDO scheme. The scheme was a 'political communication agent' to rebuild the 'bridge' between the government and the people by this decentralised and debureaucratised offices which were located in the neigbourhoods. The CDO scheme involved setting up offices which the residents could recognise as 'the government' in their districts (King, 1975, p.432).[20] The CDO Scheme certainly expanded the government's 'consultation' target from the elite to the grassroots.

Another method to expand the government's consultative politics was the setting up of a three-tier local consultative system, the City District Committees (CDC), Area Committees (AC) and the Mutual Aid Committees (MAC). There was no formal tie between these three committees but they could be arranged in a hierarchy according to the size of the locality that were supposed to 'represent'.

The CDC discussed district affairs, the AC commented on the sub-areas' affairs in the district and the MAC, formed on a housing block basis, was only be consulted on the minor matters relevant to the block. They were all government sponsored advisory bodies and, except the MAC, all members were appointed on an individual basis. Leung criticised the system as dominated by pro-government voices, well-represented by the traditional organisations who hence, successfully excluded different voices. Consensus was the norm of these committees and members seldom challenged the government's policy (Leung, 1990, pp.45-46).

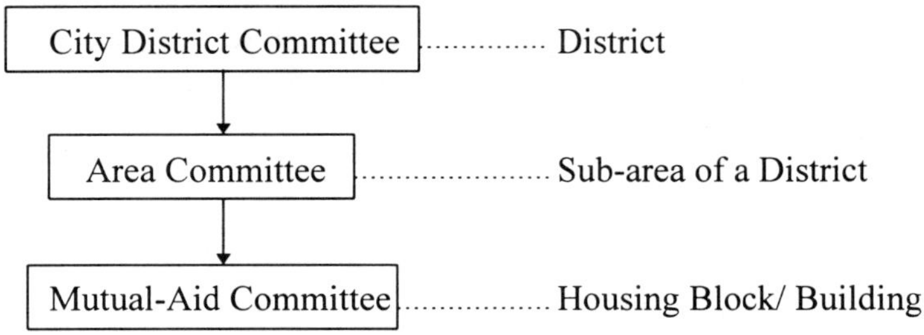

Figure 7.1 Three tiers of district advisory and consultative structure

The third change in the 1970s was in the composition of the LegCo. It was always claimed that the LegCo only represented the interests of the businessmen and the commercial sector which were the traditional elite and, in that sense, the voice of the rest of the society had no proper 'channel' in the Council. Until 1976, the unofficials were equal in number to the officials, but it was still possible for the government to win any debate as, the Governor, being the chairman of the Council, had the casting vote. Such arrangements had guaranteed that the government could pass any decision. Of course, in line with the 'consensus' politics, disagreements were always resolved before the formal meetings and there was no case when the Governor had to use the casting vote.

However, from 1976, MacLehose and the successive Governors have followed the practice of not appointing the full numbers of official members and therefore, the unofficials maintained a majority in the Council (Miners, 1989, ch.9). More interestingly, from 1976, the Governor expanded the targets for appointment from traditional elite, the British and Chinese businessmen, to the professional groups such as doctors, lawyers, teachers and even 'ordinary' citizens.[21] The aim was to build up a wider representation without opening up the membership to the public more generally. As a result, the professionals did get a larger share of seats on the Council but not the grassroots bodies.

Also, the government had modified its administrative structure in 1973. MacLehose appointed the United Kingdom-based management consultant company, McKinsey & Company, in 1972 to review the administrative structure. A preliminary report was circulated within the government in November 1972. The Report, 'The Machinery of Government: a new framework for expanding services', was published in May 1973 and recommended changes in the government structure in order to achieve better coordination, reduce the large span of control of the Colonial and Financial Secretaries and create a balance between the policy and resources branches.

Table 7.3
Composition of the Legislative Council, 1971-81

Year	Officials (incl. chairman)	Appointed unofficial	Total
1971	13	13	26
1972	15	15	30
1973	15	15	30
1974	15	15	30
1975	15	15	30
1976	20 (23)	22 (23)	42 (46)
1977	21 (25)	24 (25)	45 (50)
1978	21 (25)	24 (25)	45 (50)
1979	21 (25)	24 (25)	45 (50)
1980	23 (27)	26 (27)	49 (54)
1981	23 (27)	27 (27)	50 (54)

* Figures in brackets show the maximum possible membership when this differs the actual membership

Sources: Miners, 1989, Table 7, p.124
HKAR, various years

The major suggestion was the creation of new branches. Apart from maintaining the Finance and Establishment branches,[22] six new branches[23] were created and each was headed by a Secretary. The Secretaries had the power to plan, coordinate and control policies and programmes. This power, which previously belonged to individual departmental heads, was largely relocated to the newly created Secretaries. The department heads were left to deal with operational and executive decisions and administration of the department.

‘Programme Plans’ were executed for the different areas of policy, planned by the senior government officers with the help of consultative committees and co-ordinated by the Secretaries.[24] For example, in the preparation of the Programme Plan for social services, there was participation from the social service sector and professionals and the planning mechanism was installed for the later Five-Year Plan for social services.

Therefore, under the new structure, power was centralised within the hands of a few Secretaries and within them, the FS still retained most influence. ‘The centralised system of finance still in effect accords to final approval on almost every submission to Finance Branch’ (Rabushka, 1975, p.153). Moreover, as only the Finance and Colonial Secretaries could have a seat on the ExCo, the FS had have more opportunities to argue for his policies and put forward his view than the six new Secretaries. Although the objective of the McKinsey Report was to delegate authority and increase efficiency, this new arrangement only led to further centralisation of policy-making decisions. This was ‘to delegate without diluting central authority’ (ibid, p.150).

So the public participation in planning was still far from satisfactory. Of course, the primary concern of the McKinsey Report was to increase efficiency in view of an ever-expanding bureaucracy. However, the result was centralisation instead of delegation. Although the new pressure groups had managed to gain some concessions in the operation of policies and their presence had been recognised by the government, and the modification of the consultative structures and the composition of LegCo reflected such recognition, no real redistribution of power had been gained within the policy process.

Impacts from external forces: United Kingdom and China

Impact from United Kingdom

Generally speaking, the Hong Kong government had gradually gained autonomy in most of its administrative and financial affairs from UK, ever since its economy expanded in the 1960s, which enabled this tiny colony to be self-sufficient. From 1958, Hong Kong had its budgetary and financial autonomy and administrative freedom from Whitehall. The power to appoint councillors, though they still had to be endorsed by the Secretary of State, was virtually in the hands of the local government (or Governor). Other than the Governor himself, all of the officials were recruited by the Hong Kong government locally.[25]

As expressed by Sir Charles Jeffries,[26] 'to overrule the considered and maintained advice of a Governor is a thing which no Secretary of State would do lightly or unless he was convinced that his action was right and could be publicly defended' (Miners, 1989, p.221). The 1967 riots had attracted the attention of British MPs to local conditions and the Labour government found itself under pressure from its back-benches to take actions. MPs and labour advisors visited Hong Kong to 'advise' on the improvement of labour legislation and welfare.[27]

Yet, the power relationship was never uni-directional. For example, in 1970, Sir S.Y. Chung, at that time only a junior appointed member of LegCo (he became a long serving member of ExCo and LegCo),[28] had strongly criticised such interference from the British government. Without adequate support, by 1971 the labour advisors sent by the British government had all returned home (Miners, 1989, p.228). As expressed by Lord Goronwy-Roberts,[29] 'on internal matters, there was never an occasion during 1974-1979 when it became a question of issuing a directive to the Governor over his objections' (Miner, 1989, p.221). Tom McNally,[30] who had served in the Labour government from 1975 to 1979, also suggested that Hong Kong's issues were never on the top of the agenda.[31]

The UK government did not grant full autonomy to this local government but the intervention focused on certain aspects, such as severe social unrest, labour issues and welfare and, the external liaison with China.[32] Of course, UK experts were frequently invited to Hong Kong to advise on local services development and planning (Jones, 1990, Part II) and there were many similarities between the two welfare systems.[33] But the UK government, above all, respected the autonomy and freedom of the Hong Kong government. Certainly, influence from Britain was one factor but it was certainly not a very significant or determinant one.

Impact from China

There was certainly no example of explicit intervention from China on domestic social policies. Henderson explains that such a passive policy was due to China's pre-occupation with the domestic chaos caused by the Cultural Revolution and in order to maintain its economic benefit from the flourishing Hong Kong economy (1991). The de facto embassy in Hong Kong, the New China News Agency (NCNA) gave the public a secretive and closed image. The pro-China FTU, was also at a standstill with very little involvement in labour affairs, not to mention wider social issues. Moreover, there was a consensus among the Left in Hong Kong about not joining any committees or serving in the Councils of the Hong Kong government which were considered to be colonial institutions and opposed to the Chinese government (Turner, 1980, p.32, ch.12).[34] So, there was no significant influence from China and local Left groups during the 1970s. Of course, the historical visit of MacLehose to Beijing to meet with Deng Xiaoping in 1979 reflected the potential influence of China through the uncertainty of the 1997 issue.[35]

Impacts on the policy making process

The changes in the social structure, the growth of middle class and professional groups, the formation of new types of unions, the increasing demands for participation from the grassroots, coupled with the rising expectations of government in dealing with social problems and intervening in social affairs did have impacts on the policy-making structure. The initiation of the CDO, the widening basis for appointment to LegCo and other committees, together with the introduction of participation and public consultation in the planning process, modified the policy-making structure.

There was a widening consultative structure down to the grassroots level and more channels for the public to voice their grievances and opinions through. There was also greater influence from the public, through the social action movements and the small-scale organisations, on government decisions. The professionals and the middle-class had gained greater recognition. However, such influence was rather implicit and never in a position to counter-balance the power of the traditional elite and the officials.

At the decision-making level, there were different perceptions of the power of the Council to influence the government's policy. Those ex-government senior officials that the author interviewed, held a similar view, namely that the Councillors did have a certain influence in policy-making through, for example, the Finance Committee of LegCo. Moreover, they argued that the influence of the Councillors was only shown in their lobbying activities behind the scene. This viewpoint was shared by Sir S.Y. Chung. Critical comments from the unofficials on government policies could also be found in the Hong Kong Hansard. As argued in the previous chapter, LegCo did have some power to influence government's policy. It is difficult, therefore, to conclude that the Councillors were merely a 'rubber stamp', manipulated by the officials though, in reality, they virtually always endorsed or did not oppose government proposals. The absence of unity among the unofficial members, who could not form a strong coalition to press the government, the lack of concrete, firm attempts to do so[36] and the similarity (or absence of unbridgeable gap) between the standpoint of the officials and the unofficials rendered the differences between them largely insignificant. England and Rear found that the unofficials' attitudes generally coincided with the bureaucracy and 'any disagreements are not over ends, but over methods and the detailed application of agreed principles' (1981, p.10). This may have also been due to the careful selection in appointing members of the Councils.

The government's expectation towards the unofficials was one of support not opposition. This attitude is best be represented by a speech of the then Chief Secretary (CS), Sir Denys Roberts, in a debate in 1975/76 Legislative Council,

> The task of unofficial members is not to oppose, but to participate in the formulation of government policy, to improve proposals presented to them and to monitor their effective implementation. They ensure that the government does not become divorced from reality or more influenced by the enchantment of its own programmes than by the needs of our citizens (quoted from Miners, 1989, p.151).

Such an expectation regarding the unofficials was shared by Sir S.Y. Chung,

> Legislative and Executive Council do not serve as opposition to the government but as a bridge between the government and the public. The members interpret public opinion. They will support those views they think are right and put these forward to the government. Those they think are not right, they pass on to the government but not support them. We have a very intimate dialogue with the government. The government uses us as its eyes and ears.[37]

So widened consultation and appointment seemed only to have brought limited changes in the power relationship. Of course, there was some limited impact, the bureaucrats could not totally neglect all these pressures and conflicts. Within the bureaucracy, the planning process was centralised and sometimes decisions were made at the top level -- Governor, the ExCo, Secretariats and the LegCo. The FS was still the most powerful Secretary. Haddon-Cave, the FS after Cowperthwaithe, was a follower of Cowperwaithe's line in managing the budget, on expenditure and on the role of government.[38] In the time of financial crisis and economic recession in the mid-1970s, the FS was in an even stronger position to argue for a tight rein in controlling the purse and defining the size of the 'pie'. The only official who could override him was, perhaps, the Governor.

The governing principles, maintenance of a budget surplus, fiscal conservatism, limited intervention, remained largely unchanged. Expenditure was determined by the amount of expected income received every year and the fiscal reserve could only be used in very exceptional circumstances. However, the willingness to spend and the boundary of state intervention was expanded in this decade.

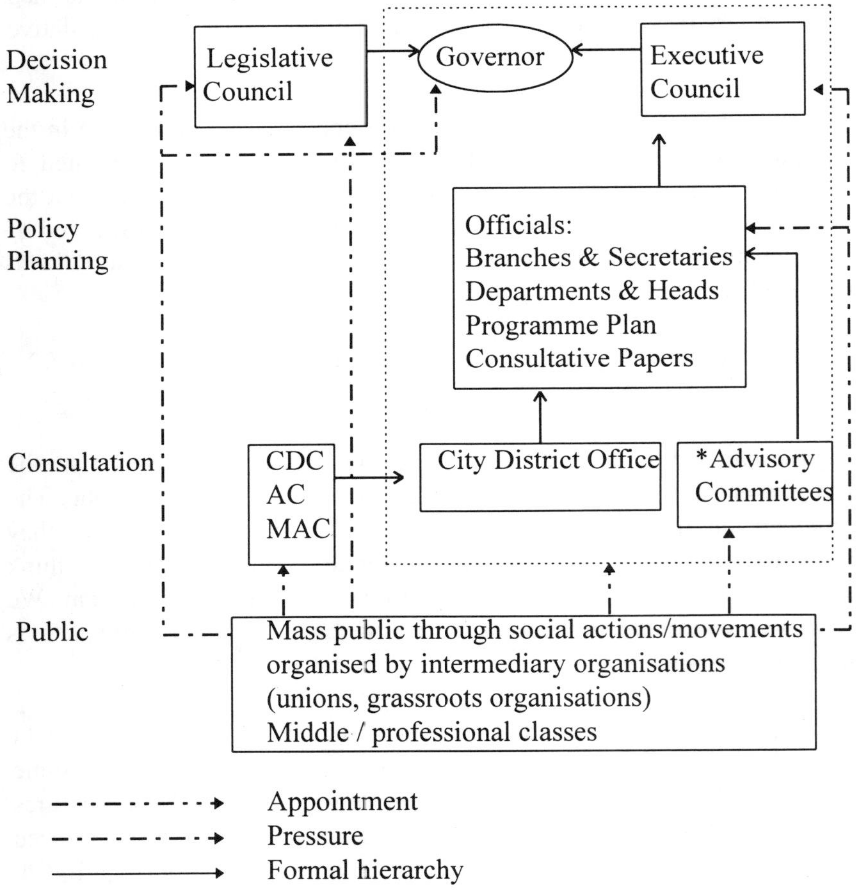

* Examples are the Medical Development Advisory Committee and Social Welfare Advisory Committee. They have greater power than others and were with the same levels of Department or Branch.

Figure 7.2 Policy-making process, 1970s

Notes

1 For example, the population employed in manufacturing industries increased by 17.1 per cent, while for the retail, wholesale and trading, and the financial services industries, the increases were 30.4 per cent and 114 per cent respectively from 1976 to 1981. See CSD, 1987, Table 2.4.
2 The policy was to diversify the industry to different products other than textile, plastic and electrical appliances manufacturing. Income from different sources, such as tourism, was also encouraged to bring a more diversified and hence safer base for public finance and Hong Kong's economy.
3 For example, the nominal GDP per capita from 1974 to 1981 increased from HK$10,320 to HK$32,080 respectively. The real growth was approximately 90 per cent.
4 The so-called middle income group is rather a general term here. For a conceptualisation of the middle class and its impact on the society and politics, see Cheung et al, 1988.
5 For details, please refer to Chapter 7 below.
6 Such as Tai Wo Hau/Kwai Chung Community Development Project (later renamed as Tsuen Wan Ecumenical Social Service Centre), Society of Community Organisation and Neighourhood Advice-Action Council.
7 With the assistance from the above-mentioned organisations, residents organisations were formed in public housing estates, hot-beds of grievances and complaints, in Kwun Tong, Kwai Chung and various squatter areas.
8 They were named 'neutral' because they had no political affiliation and were 'independent' from the two traditional types of unions.
9 However, due to a restriction imposed by Ordinance, the civil servants could not actively participate in the social movements.
10 The PTU was formed in 1974 and since 1982, has been the largest single occupation union. See Jao et al, 1988, p.163.
11 The Chinese Language Campaign aimed at legalising Chinese as the official language and it succeeded in the mid-1970s though it took a very long time for the government to change all its daily practices. Tiaoyutao was a small island 'occupied' by Japan during the World War II and did not return to China after Japan surrendered. So, there were always disputes about these tiny islands. The Golden Jubilee Secondary School had a financial scandal and the Department of Education was

severely criticised over its way of handling the issue, thus aroused wide discontent.

12 The government occasionally adopted a high-handed policy to them. For example, a group of protesters and social workers (the protest organisers) were arrested on their way to a protest outside the Governor's House in 1979.

13 One of the few political organisations in Hong Kong in the 1970s which had a different standpoint from the government but at the same time, participated in elections (Urban Council). Other groups or individuals included the Civic Society and Ms Elsie Elliot (also called as Mrs Elsie Tu, a missionary who came from Britain to Hong Kong in 1950s and then was actively involved in actions against injustice, unfairness and corruption).

14 The research was done in 1971 in Kwun Tong, a new town at that time which was the, if not the most, popular place for doing surveys because of its mix of population and mix of housing types.

15 The study was conducted in 1977.

16 The studies were conducted in 1977 and 1978.

17 For example, in the UC election in 1981, among 440,000 eligible voters, only 34,381 registered and eventually only 6,195 bothered to vote. Of course, the low turn-out rate could also be explained by the limited authority of the Council and its lack of promotion. Elections alien to people's daily life. See Miners, 1989, p.168.

18 Therefore, contrasting studies and constructions of the society and its value orientation might only reflect a partial view of the subject matter. Lau's construction might be valid when applied to certain sector of the society.

19 Certainly, education was one of the characteristics of this group of people. Their high involvement in social affairs might be attributed to other explanations or individual preferences. There were, of course, well-educated people who still held to conservative and traditional types of culture and orientation.

20 The CDO Scheme was under the auspices of the Secretary for Home Affairs. Each City District Office has a City District Officer and two Assistant City District Officers assisted in internal administration and external liaison respectively. There were usually five to eight liaison officers in each office who dealt with external liaison duties and grassroots contacts. King's study in Kwun Tong's CDO in the mid-1970s listed the functions of the CDO as:

1) to facilitate communication between the governors and the governed;

2) to articulate the demands made known to them through Monthly Meetings, the Study Groups and Town Talks;
3) to redress the grievances, either of individuals or groups, and refer these to responsible departments;
4) to set up of a Public Enquiry Service Counter to familiarise people with the government bureaucracy;
5) political socialisation and recruitment of the local leaders and youth into CDO sponsored community services (ibid, pp.433-435).

21 In this new initiation, a bus conductor has been appointed as a member of LegCo. According to an interview with Sir S.Y. Chung, the former Senior Member of LegCo and ExCo, this idea was in fact, initiated by the unofficials who took the view that the government had to widen the basis of appointment to incorporate a wider spectrum of ideas in the Councils.

22 When the preliminary report was circulated among the officials, there was serious objection from the Finance Branch as the report recommended that it would be converted to a resources operation department and its influence on policy making would be reduced. After objections from the Branch, the consultant modified this section and suggested that 'the responsibilities of the two resources branches, Finance and Establishment Branch, should remain largely as present'. See Rabushka, 1975, p.146.

23 These covered Economics, Environment, Home Affairs, Housing, Security and Social Services.

24 The Programme Plan was gradually abandoned by the bureaucrats in the late 1970s although the chief proponent of the idea, Sir Murray MacLehose was still the Governor. But, Programme Plans were adopted in education, medical and social welfare services (e.g. rehabilitation) planning.

25 Of course, there were still a lot of expatriates in the government and the three most senior official positions, Chief Secretary, Finance Secretary and Commissioner of Police were all filled by British people.

26 He was a Deputy Under-Secretary of State in the UK government in 1956.

27 For example, the Minister of State of the Foreign and Commonwealth Office, Lord Shepherd, visited Hong Kong in 1967 and insisted that the Hong Kong government should take measures to improve labour legislation. Groups of Labour MPs also attacked the local 'sweated labour' conditions. See Harris, 1978, pp.20-22 & pp.127-128.

28 He served in the LegCo from 1968 to 1978 and in Executive Council from 1972 to 1988.

29 He was the Minister of State responsible for Hong Kong's affairs in the 1975-79 Labour government.

30 He was the advisor to the Prime Minister, Lord Callaghan.

31 From a personal interview.

32 The relationship with China was always considered a very sensitive issue. The government had a political advisor appointed by the Whitehall to advise on the matter.

33 For example, the education system.

34 Anyway, the Hong Kong government was also highly suspicious about these Left organisations and certainly not willing to appoint them to such positions.

35 Sir Murray visited Beijing in 1979 and met with Deng. One item of the agenda, which remained secret, was the future of Hong Kong beyond 1997. At that meeting, Sir Murray was told that China had the intention to reclaim Hong Kong in 1997. The year of '1997' was crucial because the New Territories's lease ran out then. Without the largest part of Hong Kong, it could not survive. However, the result was kept secret from the public. But China has made public that it did not recognise the unequal treaties signed by the Qing Dynasty and would reclaim all the land, i.e. Hong Kong and Macau, at a suitable time.

36 For example, LegCo members seldom used their power to initiate adjournment debates to discuss government policies. See Miners, 1989, pp.154-155.

37 From an personal interview with Sir S.Y. Chung. Translated from Chinese.

38 However, his style of dealing with requests for resources from Branches was different from Sir John. According to an interview with a senior official done by Rabushka in mid-1970s, the interviewee described that 'Sir John's style was to attack the estimates in a thousand ways; find flaws; chip away. By the end, expenditure will not exceed revenue. Philip is different. He's going to tell them he hasn't got the money and let the 'super secretaries' fight among themselves to divide a limited pie, rather than have them agree that the Financial Secretary is competent and the most important man for the good of Hong Kong, they let their own personal drive for advancement take them into a power struggle to get what they can from the Financial Secretary for their empires'. (Rabushka, 1975, p.160).

8 Development of the welfare state, 1971-1981

This chapter will describe the general development of the social services from 1971 to 1981. There was significant development and growth of these services in this period. To gain a deeper understanding of this development, two policy cases have been chosen to illustrate the dynamic process involved. This will be used to support the analysis in later chapters.

General development of social services

Development in the 1970s was more remarkable than in any previous period. MacLehose, in his first speech to the LegCo in October 1972 argued that 'people will not care for a society which does not care for them' (Jones, 1990, p.210). To achieve the vision of making Hong Kong 'a better place in which to live' (HKAR, 1973, p.2), he announced a major development plan, covering housing, education and social welfare. In his second speech to the LegCo, he added medical services to these three as 'pillars on which the future well-being of the community would be built' (Scott, 1989, p.162). Expenditure on the social services continuously increased in this period (Table 8.1).[1] The growth of social services expenditure was in line with the growth of GDP and for several years it was much higher than the GDP growth (Table 8.3). The share of social services in total government expenditure was kept at around 40 per cent. Though this share was not affected by the economic recession, it was clear that recession did have effects on individual services, especially housing (Table 8.2 & 8.3).

Table 8.1
Social services expenditure, 1970/71 - 1980/81 (current price)

Fiscal year	Expenditure on social services (HK$m)			
	Education	Medical	Housing	Social welfare
1970/71	497.8	252.2	171.7	39.9
1971/72	586.9	304.7	178.6	60.4
1972/73	710.6	378.9	253.7	93.0
1973/74	990.0	456.7	215.3	153.2
1974/75	1144.8	560.4	446.9	275.5
1975/76	1268.1	561.9	438.9	359.2
1976/77	1402.7	648.2	217.5	365.1
1977/78	1624.9	755.7	932.2	392.7
1978/79	1929.8	954.9	1304.1	533.3
1979/80	2444.1	1233.4	1339.0	681.6
1980/81	3344.1	1635.3	2443.5	867.4

Sources: HKAR, various years

Table 8.2
Social services expenditure as percentage of total government expenditure (1970/71 - 1980/81)

Fiscal year	Percentage of government total expenditure
1970/71	38.8
1971/72	38.5
1972/73	32.5
1973/74	34.7
1974/75	38.1
1975/76	43.2
1976/77	39.7
1977/78	41.2
1978/79	42.6
1979/80	41.1
1980/81	35.1

Sources: HKAR, various years

Table 8.3
Comparison of growth rate (percentage) of GDP, public expenditure and social service expenditure, 1971/72 - 1980/81 (current price)

Fiscal year	GDP	Public exp.	Social services expenditure				
			Ed	Med	Hou	Soc Wel	Total
1971/72	13.8	18.5	17.9	20.8	4.1	51.4	17.6
1972/73	18.2	50.5	21.1	24.4	42.1	54.0	27.0
1973/74	30.7	18.4	39.3	20.5	(-15.1)	64.7	26.4
1974/75	14.2	21.8	15.6	22.7	107.6	79.8	33.7
1975/76	4.6	(-4.5)	10.8	1.5	(-1.8)	30.4	8.3
1976/77	27.7	9.0	10.6	15.4	(-50.4)	1.6	0.2
1977/78	16.1	35.6	15.8	16.6	328.6	7.6	40.9
1978/79	17.8	23.2	18.8	26.4	39.9	35.8	27.4
1979/80	31.9	25.1	26.7	29.2	2.7	27.8	20.7
1980/81	28.2	70.4	36.8	32.6	82.5	27.3	45.5

Notes:
a. The growth rate of GDP is calculated in calendar years.
b. In 1973, the CSD changed the calculation method for GDP and so, figures for 1973 onwards are therefore not exactly comparable with previous figures.
c. Ed: education; Med: medical; Hou: housing; Soc Wel: social welfare; exp: expenditure.

Sources: CSD, 1981, Table 7.1; 1986, Table 7.1

Medical Services

In 1974, the White Paper, 'Further Development of Medical and Health Services in Hong Kong' was endorsed by the government as the blueprint for the next ten years. To monitor this long term development, the Medical Development Advisory Committee (MDAC) was set up in 1973. The major long term objective of the White Paper was to provide 5.5 beds per thousand of population by the end of the plan, as compared to 4.1 beds per thousand of population in 1973, and the establishment of a network of regional hospitals and clinics (HKG, 1974a).[2] In 1976, the plan was modified and became even more ambitious.[3] The increase of hospital beds, especially in the public sector, was very impressive (Table 8.4).[4] Of course, many NGOs also played their part in the expansion programme in the assisted and private sectors.

Table 8.4
Increase of hospital beds in Hong Kong, 1971-1981

Year	Government	Assisted	Private	Total
1971	6849	7664	2176	16689
1972	7037	7621	2075	16733
1973	6927	7868	2053	16848
1974	6743	8165	2126	17034
1975	8533	7849	2179	18561
1976	9041	7913	2316	19270
1977	9181	8199	2399	19779
1978	9380	8347	2408	20135
1979	9445	8630	2531	20606
1980	9684	8585	2537	20806
1981	10281	8755	2550	21586
Increase	50.1%	14.2%	17.2%	29.3%

Sources: HKAR, various year

The fee charged for medical services was kept at a low level. The charge for out-patient treatment was increased from HK$1 to HK$2 in 1979 and to HK$3 in 1980. The daily charge for a hospital bed in a general ward was increased from HK$2 to HK$3 in 1975, and to HK$5 in 1978.[5] For those who could not afford this cost and also claimants of the Public Assistance Scheme, the charge could be waived.

The results of this improvement of health services were reflected, partially, in the decrease of the infant mortality rate[6] and the improvement of life expectancy. The figures show that Hong Kong now reached a state comparable to that of the developed countries (Table 8.5 & 8.6) (Youngson, 1982, p.44)[7].

Table 8.5
Infant mortality rate, 1971-1981

Year	Infant mortality rate (per thousand)	Year	Infant mortality rate (per thousand)
1971	18.4	1977	13.9
1972	17.5	1978	11.8
1973	16.8	1979	13.3
1974	17.4	1980	11.8
1975	15.0	1981	9.7
1976	14.3		

Sources: CSD, 1978, Table 15.11
CSD, 1983, Table 16.11
CSD, 1992, Table 1.1

Table 8.6
Life expectancy: comparison (1980)

Countries		Life expectancy	
		Male	Female
Asia	Japan	74.2	79.7
	Hong Kong	72.6	78.3
	Singapore	69.2	74.6
America	Canada	72.4	79.6
	USA	70.6	78.3
Europe	Sweden	73.4	79.3
	Netherlands	72.8	79.5
	France	70.7	78.9
	UK	71.0	77.2
	Austria	69.6	76.8
Oceanic	Australia	71.9	78.7
	New Zealand	70.7	76.9

Source: United Nations, 1991, Table 15

Education services

Free primary education had been introduced in September 1971, before the arrival of MacLehose. During his term of office, development was focused on secondary education, to provide three years of free education to children aged 12 to 14 was the first priority. In September 1972, 81.4 per cent of primary school graduates went to secondary school, but only 41.3 per cent were awarded governmental, government-aided or government-assisted places (HKAR, 1974).[8] However, even those who enjoyed government places had to pay HK$400 per year as school fees. In MacLehose's speech to LegCo in 1972, he planned to provide subsidised education up to Form 3 for all primary school graduates (i.e. for those aged 12 to 15) and forty per cent of higher form places for the junior form graduates by 1979. It was a difficult task to achieve within seven years but the government achieved it a year ahead of schedule in 1978.

Table 8.7
Increase in secondary students enrollment, 1973-1981
(no. of places)

Year	Government & aided	Assisted private	Private	Total
1973	99,314	48,526	197,123	344,963
1974	109,046	50,151	230,101	389,298
1975	114,908	49,400	251,383	415,691
1976	125,308	50,107	278,376	453,791
1977	138,996	50,694	298,354	488,044
1978	196,925	7,430	325,357	529,712
1979	204,945	7,238	312,209	524,392
1980	210,143	7,038	309,078	526,259
1981	218,893	6,056	296,632	521,581

Notes:

a. All figures are at September each year.

b. From 1978 onward, nine years free education started and the government transformed the majority of assisted private schools into aided schools which had better facilities and student-staff ratios.

Sources: HKAR, various years

Another priority was the expansion of technical education. In MacLehose's term of office, four additional technical institutes were opened[9] and there was also the formation of Hong Kong Polytechnic in 1972 which provided more advanced technological training. An Apprenticeship Ordinance came into effect in 1976 which make 'contracts of apprenticeship obligatory for the employment of young persons in some designated trades, and requiring employers to release their apprentices in these trades in order to attend part-time day-release courses at technical institute' (Youngson, 1982, p.47). Hence, Hong Kong gradually established another system of education, apart from the grammar school system, for the training of craftsman and professionals. This provided adequate technically-trained manpower for the economy.

To provide adequately trained teachers for the expanded education sector, the College of Education expanded its intake throughout the 1970s. The number of students in the government supported post-secondary sector, including the university and polytechnic, was also planned to be tripled by the early 1980s.[10] The increase of places at every level of education improved the overall education level of the population (Table 8.8).

In the 1970s, another characteristic in education was the systematisation of planning. The Board of Education was restructured in 1973 to become the chief advisory committee to the government. The ED was regionalised in 1977 to enhance its contact with district affairs, and its flexibility and sensitivity. From 1971 to 1981, two Green Papers and two White Papers outlining developments in secondary, senior and tertiary education were published and accepted by the government.[11] Finally, in 1981, the government invited an overseas panel to conduct a comprehensive review of the entire education system.

Housing services

MacLehose announced the TYHCP which, if it succeeded, would provide permanent housing for 1.8 million population by 1983, eliminate overcrowded living conditions and clear all squatter areas.[12] Moreover, there was a gradual improvement in the quality of newly built housing and a redevelopment plan for the Mark I and Mark II resettlement blocks. To implement this grand plan, the government reconstituted the policy planning and implementation structure, creating the new HKHA and the Housing Department (HD). The HA took over all the duties of the old Housing Authority, UC, Resettlement Department (RD) and Public Works Department (PWD) with the Housing Department as its executive arm.

Table 8.8
Population by education attainment, 1971, 1976 and 1981 (percentage)

Level of Ed.	1971			1976			1981		
	M	F	T	M	F	T	M	F	T
No sch./kindergarten	9.9	35.9	22.7	9.2	31.6	20.2	7.6	25.5	16.1
Primary	49.5	38.4	44.1	43.2	36.2	39.7	36.8	31.5	34.2
Lower secondary	16.2	10.5	13.4	18.7	12.4	15.6	21.3	14.6	18.1
Upper secondary				19.8	15.3	17.6	22.2	20.2	21.3
Matriculation	20.5	13.9	17.2	3.7	1.7	2.7	5.3	3.7	4.6
Tertiary: non-degree				0.8	1.0	0.9	2.3	2.4	2.3
Tertiary: degree	3.9	1.3	2.6	4.5	1.9	3.2	4.5	2.0	3.4
Total	100	100	100	100	100	100	100	100	100

Notes:
a. M: Male; F: Female; T: Total; Sch: school.
b. Figures confined to population of age 15 and above.
c. Figures of upper secondary level included craft courses offered in technical institute.
d. Figures of matriculation included diploma/certificate course offered in technical institute and polytechnic.
e. Figures for tertiary non-degree level included higher diploma/ endorsement, associateship and other non-degree courses in polytechnic, college of education and other post-secondary colleges.

Source: CSD, 1987, Table 13.1

Other than providing rental flats, the Authority also began a new programme of 'sale flats' for the middle income families. The HOS started in 1976 with the first estate sold in 1979. Another similar programme, the PSPS[13] started in 1979. The progress of the plan was delayed in the early and late 1970s when Hong Kong's economy encountered crises. Though the government speeded up its building for 1979 onwards, it could not catch up with the accumulated deficit. The construction programme failed to achieve its goals[14] but the progress of housing construction was still remarkable (Table 8.9) and approximately 40 per cent of the total population were living in various forms of public housing in 1981 (Table 8.10). The low rents of public rental housing and low prices for HOS have contributed to improving the living standards of households. By reducing households' housing expense,[15] public rental housing tenants could deploy a larger share of their household budget into other areas.

Social welfare services

Shortly after MacLehose's first speech, in April 1973, the White Paper 'Social Welfare in Hong Kong:the Way Ahead'[16] was endorsed in LegCo. The first White Paper in 1965 was basically a restatement of the roles and responsibilities of the state and other sectors. But now the government recognised its own responsibility to finance the services and the division of responsibilities between itself and the NGOs (Chow, 1980, p.37). Such a commitment from the state in supporting social welfare, which was largely operated by the NGOs and financed by overseas donations at that time, was crucial. 'With a dwindling flow of aid from overseas, the voluntary sector has become increasingly dependent on this assistance' (HKAR, 1979, p.112). The Paper also suggested new directions for various social welfare services, and covered the training of welfare personnel as well as the consultative structure of social welfare planning (HKG, 1973a).

The Paper was drafted by a joint effort between Social Welfare Department (SWD) and the Hong Kong Council of Social Services.[17] The White Paper agreed that this joint planning mechanism should be continued. The first Five-Year Plan in 1973, a blueprint for social welfare development for the next five years, was the first product of such mechanism. To cope with the ever-increasing need for financial support for the NGOs, the government restructured the subsidy system and divided the services into Category 1 and 2 services.[18]

Table 8.9
Annual production of public housing, 1973/74 - 1980/81

Year	Resettlement estate	Government low-cost housing	New HA flats	HOS/ PSPS	Total
1973/74	1,970	6,200			8,170
1974/75			9,200		9,200
1975/76			14,900		14,900
1976/77			9,620		9,620
1977/78			13,020		13,020
1978/79			14,130		14,130
1979/80			29,759	2,439	32,198
1980/81			26,763	8,857	35,620

* The lower standard resettlement estate and low-cost housing ceased to be provided when the new Housing Authority was established in 1973.

Source: Castells, 1986, p.9

Table 8.10
Population accommodated in different types of housing, 1972-1981

Year	Govt quarter	Public		Private	Others	Total
		HKHA	HS			
1972	68,800	1,483,200	115,000	2,025,200	375,300	4,067,500
1973	70,700	1,553,300	116,600	2,084,800	338,700	4,164,100
1974	61,900	1,586,100	119,900	2,156,000	305,700	4,229,600
1975	63,400	1,622,500	120,700	2,218,400	312,000	4,337,000
1976	49,000	1,682,300	117,400	2,143,700	444,600	4,437,000
1977	53,100	1,735,000	124,400	2,163,500	418,000	4,494,000
1978	58,900	1,754,700	126,700	2,187,800	450,900	4,579,000
1979	67,000	1,780,100	129,100	2,382,200	420,600	4,779,000
1980	76,000	1,883,000	126,700	2,422,900	477,000	4,985,600
1981	62,900	1,862,900	131,100	2,579,200	469,400	5,105,500

Sources: HKAR, various year

In the 1970s, several consultative documents and Green Papers were published on elderly services, personal social services for youth, and social security,[19] outlining government plans in response to the changing needs,[20] These papers' recommendations were integrated into the White Paper 'Social Welfare into the 80s' published in 1979. Following the format of a 'Programme Plan', the Report, 'Integrating the Disabled into the Community: A United Effort' was published in 1977[21] and a Commissioner of Rehabilitation was appointed to monitor and coordinate the development of the rehabilitation services provided by various departments. Similar to the ED, the SWD was regionalised to enhance its contact with and sensitivity to the local needs.

The eligible clientele for Public Assistance was widened to the able bodied aged from 15 to 55. After the basic scheme introduced in 1971, a Disability Allowances Scheme and Criminal and Law Enforcement Injuries Compensation Scheme were added in 1973, and Old Age Allowance, Old Age Supplement and Long Term Supplement were added in 1978. A Traffic Accidents Victims Assistance Scheme was adopted in 1979.

Although intervention from the state in social welfare services was widening, the state still upheld a residue of the previous system. The notion of 'community care', the emphasis on support from the informal systems such as family members, relatives, kin, friends and neighbours, was adopted in the planning of elderly and rehabilitation services (HKG, 1973b; 1977a; 1977b).

Characteristics of the services development in 1970s

Certainly, the most notable characteristic of this stage was 'expansion', in terms of quantity and 'improvement' in quality. Only in times of economic recession was the growth rate kept at a lower level. More and more target groups were included as the welfare state's client groups. For example, the housing programme included more lower income housing families and the middle class, the Public Assistance Scheme included the elderly, the disabled and crime and traffic accident victims. The expansion of education services and the medical services signified the provision of universal services to every citizen of Hong Kong without any means test. The services could be enjoyed by lower, middle or even the upper class at equal cost.

The provision of these universal services to the citizens signified a shift in the philosophy of social services provision. It signified the concept of welfare rights versus the traditional belief in self-care and individual responsibility. The provision of free and compulsory education was the best example showing this shift. The government in this period, was increasingly concerned about human welfare. MacLehose had mentioned that 'the inadequacy and scarcity of housing and all that implies ... offends alike our humanity, our civic pride and our political good sense' in his first speech to LegCo (Scott, 1989, p.154). Social services were now provided and consumed, to a certain extent, as a social right of citizens. Of course, the residue of traditional principles still applied to those services with means-tested mechanism. The concept of self-care, individual responsibility and family care were still important among the public and the government. Moreover, the new approaches were not fully agreed to by the mere pragmatic and conservative senior officials (ibid, p.155). Yet, there was the emergence of an alternative ideology in the provision of social services.

The emphasis on planning and monitoring of implementation was another characteristic. More reports, consultative documents, White or Green Papers were published for every social service. The restructuring of the government structure and introduction of the 'Programme Plan' reflected a new form of planning and monitoring. There was also some wider participation, especially by the welfare professions, through appointment to various advisory committees and public consultation about the planning process. However, participation from the mass public or clients in the services planning, except the public housing tenants, was rather limited.

However, the relationship between social services and capital accumulation remained unchanged. Although the scale of service provision had been enlarged, it did not compete with the market but instead, supplement or complemented it. The targets of the social welfare services and public housing (even the HOS/PSPS) were mainly those who could not purchase services from the market. Welfare state intervention was to fill the service gap and prevent social tensions from building up. These two services, coupled with medical and education services could also help with the reproduction of labour force, socialising production costs and maintaining social stability. In fact, the wider provision did not hamper the private market but helped to maintain capital accumulation.

Generally speaking, the reforms in the 1970s greatly enlarged state intervention in the provision and production of social services. The scale of the welfare state seemed to have transformed from a 'minimal residual' type to an 'optimal' type.[22] Ho has calculated that the lower income group gained additional resources through the redistributive effect of welfare state output. He estimated that the social services increased the income of the lowest decile five-fold (1979, p.130).[23] Lin argued that social services helped to modify the overall income distribution by 9 per cent in 1981 (Tang, 1992, p.249).[24]

The Ten Year Housing Construction Programme

Historical development

When MacLehose announced the TYHCP in October 1972, a group of officials from various departments met together to formulate the plan which formally 'commenced' in April 1973 and, at the same time, the HA was reconstituted. The plan did not start in a vacuum. According to Mr (later Sir) Ian Lightbody[25] and Mr Bernard Williams,[26] the TYHCP was a continuation of the previous building programme.[27] According to them, MacLehose had shown great interest in housing issues at a very early stage of his governorship. Lightbody said in an interview,

> He [MacLehose] must, in very early on, came to the opinion that we should not live and no one should be lived in this environment permanently ... state action must be taken to get rid of this and to improve housing. But certainly, he took on this idea in very early when he took over the governorship. He was on the housing very early.[28]

Such an attitude was clearly shown in his first speech to LegCo. Though he was impressed by the development of housing programmes at that time, he expressed his concern for the inadequacies,

> ... the problem still remains. 300,000 people still live in squatter huts or temporary housing. Many units in resettlement estates are badly overcrowded, or have no separate wash places or lavatories. It is estimated that a further 310,000 people would need rehousing if all of those in shared private flats and tenements were to have a self-contained home, and few of these can afford the rents asked by private landlords. It is my conclusion that the inadequacy and scarcity of housing and all that this implies, and the harsh situations that result from it, is one of the major and most constant sources of friction and unhappiness between the Government and the population. It offends alike our humanity, our civic pride and our political good sense (HK Hansard, 1972/73, p.4).

He announced that the objective was to provide sufficient permanent accommodation in a reasonable environment for every inhabitant of Hong Kong within ten years. The further details were revealed in his 1973 Governor's Speech to LegCo. MacLehose also announced the organisational reforms of planning and management of housing services. The two major changes were, first, to create a new HD which took over all the fragmented management duties.[29] The new Department 'will be responsible for the planning, administration and construction - in cooperation of course with the PWD - of all public housing in the Colony, and also for all the duties hitherto carried out by the RD and the staff of the HA' (HK Hansard, 1972/73, p.6). The second change was the reconstitution of the HA to handle the policy planning duties.[30] Although the HA had been an offspring of the UC, the new Authority's composition was largely of new appointees with few of its old members from the UC left.

The merging of all the administrative duties under one roof was due to the increasing division of quality of housing between the old HA flats and the RD's estates. At the time of restructuring, the most senior officials in charge of housing policy were Lightbody and Mr Donald Liao.[31] Liao was a professional architect and the majority of the staff in the HA were also professionals, such as architects and housing managers. The situation was totally different in the RD where the staff received no formal training in housing management. It was not difficult to imagine the chaotic situation in the resettlement estates[32] and the comparatively better conditions on the HA estates. Liao criticised the design of these resettlement block as 'ridiculous' and the people who were responsible for building this type of block 'had no appreciation for the people who would be living in them' (SCMP, 21/8/77).

The intention to professionalise the RD received very little support from the bureaucrats. Even the Governor at that time, Sir David Trench had his support for the move handicapped by the bureaucrats.[33] However, the situation changed when MacLehose became the next Governor from 1971. Impressed by the achievement of old HA, Lightbody was a keen supporter of the professionalisation of housing management and unification of the structure under the HA model. He had argued that involvement of so many agencies in the housing programme was 'confusing and irrational and resulted in unsound divisions of responsibility and uneconomic use of the limited supply of staff experienced in Hong Kong's public housing problems' (SCMP, 12/7/73). Liao also argued that the new system would not work if the managers and the architects were not under the same roof and the change must integrate the two in one structure.[34] This idea, to unite the two systems into one, though received with skepticism from some, gained support from other officials and very importantly, MacLehose himself.[35] Given this background, the proposal was accepted and the HA was given the power to run the TYHCP.

MacLehose instructed a group of officials to form a working group to draft the details of the plan. Mr (later Sir) David Akers-Jones[36] describes the situation at that time as,

> So, MacLehose said to us, I want you to let me know how much housing needed to be built in ten years if we have to provide everyone in Hong Kong with decent self-contained accommodation. And so, a few officials got together, to look at the squatter population, the coolies housed in shared accommodation, roof-top squatters and then the growth of population. Put all these factors together, to add them up and see what they came to. We had the data more or less available from various resources. So, we were able to come up with the figure fairly quickly, and in fact, in the course of one meeting on one morning, we worked out the figure of 1.5 million. A further 300,000 who were poorly housed in New Territories. So, we had 1.8 million and we said to MacLehose that provided nothing else happened, we could house 1.8 million and we could solve our problem.[37]

The plan was to reach a plateau of production in 1976/77 of new homes for 200,000 people a year and to maintain the production rate thereafter. The plan's allocation ratio was calculated at 35 sq.ft. (previously 24 sq.ft. per person) for each adult and the total cost and floor space that had to be built were calculated according to this ratio.[38]

The TYHCP was began in 1973 and spanned 10 years to the 1982/83 fiscal year. Lightbody was appointed as the first Secretary for Housing (SecH) and the first chairman of the new HA in April 1973. Liao was made the first Director of Housing and the vice-chairman of the HA.

While introducing the detail of the TYHCP in the LegCo, MacLehose repeatedly argued for the top priority of housing issues. He said,

> Everything that I have seen in the city and read at my desk during this second year in Hong Kong confirms my conclusion that the inadequacy and scarcity of housing, and all that this implies, and the harsh situations that result from it, is one of the major and most constant sources of friction and unhappiness between Government and the population. It also has implications for our twin problems of crime and corruption. It is therefore vital that we press on with our target of self-contained homes for all in a reasonable environment, by the fiscal year 1982/83 (Hong Kong Hansard, 1973/74, p.3).

Responding to this ambitious plan. Lightbody was very enthusiastic and confident that the plan could be achieved,

> Some of the timing assumptions on which the 10-year housing programme rests will no doubt change in some degree as new town

> development plans are further refined ... but taking the 10 year period as a whole, we have grounds today for expressing confidence that we have not set an impossible task (SCMP, 29/11/73).

However, in 1973, the economy of Hong Kong was hit by the Oil Crisis and the worldwide economic recession. In addition, the acquisition and preparation of land for construction required a longer time than expected. The programme made no significant progress in its first years. A source in the Finance Branch commented that, the ten years housing plan was no more than a 'catch-phrase' and that the Governor's promise of houses for 1.8 million people was 'only a target figure' (SCMP, 28/3/75). This showed the half-heartedness (or the 'realistic' attitude) of some of the officials.

A month later, the Census and Statistics Department (CSD) released a projection that, showed that due to increasing demand for smaller flats, the building programme could only house 1.2 million people.[39] In August 1975, Williams[40] made it clear that the redevelopment programme would have to be put back and would take 15 to 20 years, as compared with the initial target date of 1983. The main reasons, as expressed by him, were the economic recession, budget cuts and the difficulty of finding sites for rehousing (Star, 8/8/75). In the annual report of the HA tabled in LegCo in 1 October 1975, Lightbody outlined these constraints and reviewed the disappointing progress. In the recession, Lightbody stated, the HA had to compete with other important social programmes for the limited sum of money available from the government (SCMP, 2/10/75). So the progress of the programme was very disappointing in its first two years due to the technical constraints and the softening in support.

In the initial stage of the plan, rent policy was also raised on the agenda of HA. In the past, the rent for the resettlement and low cost housing was very low and just adequate to cover the construction costs while the HA's rents were comparatively higher and various factors like the location and facilities were considered in determining these. After the unification, the HA had to construct a new unified rent policy for these old and the new estates. Lightbody hinted that higher rents in the future would be expected,

> Given the many competing demands on public funds, I am confident that the people of Hong Kong would prefer that we should accept the need to charge higher rents than has been the case in the past for these new estates, rather than contemplate any reduction in our housing programme (SCMP, 21/2/75).

Therefore, the rent policy of the HA, in the initial stage was based on the dual considerations of the establishment of a unified policy and the financial income of the Authority, especially when government subsidies were unreliable in economic recession. When the economy recovered from 1975 and HA's restructuring was completed, the housing programme switched back into 'top gear', as described by Liao (SCMP, 27/10/76).

Apart from the public housing programme, a new type of housing began in this year. Different from all the previous public housing, this new type of subsidised housing was for sale. In 1973, the Authority had considered whether to sell some of flats to the tenants. However, the idea was rather short-lived and was shelved in November that year. In 1975, the idea was retabled at the HA's meeting but was once again postponed. Liao explained that 'we [HA] have discussed this a number of times in the past, and we have postponed selling of flats because the number of applicants for public housing was greater than our production of new flats' but he said that the HA would consider this again in the future (Star, 8/8/75). The idea was to improve the financial situation of the HA which was heavily indebted to the government from borrowing money for the TYHCP and to promote home ownership.

According to Williams, MacLehose had thought about the idea of selling rental flats in 1974 and 1975. However, at least two senior officials, Liao and Williams were not in favour of this idea. Williams said that Liao was convinced about the extreme technical difficulties involved and persuaded MacLehose that it was not a good idea but that instead, the government could build higher standard housing in order to attract buyers.[41] In fact, at that time, the HA had thought about policies to induce sitting tenants with better incomes to move out in order to vacate flats for the more needy.[42]

The idea of building another type of housing for this type of tenant had also been suggested by the LegCo Unofficials (HK Hansard, 1975/76, p.114). Apart from inducing sitting tenants to move out, Dr Harry Fang argued that such a new scheme could help those who could not afford private flats and were not eligible for public housing. The scheme would also 'create a sense of belongingness and of responsibility' (ibid).

MacLehose was convinced by these ideas. He was also concerned about how to increase the supply of housing within budget limits and without any adverse effects on the economy.[43] The effect on the private sector was also mentioned by Haddon-Cave who noted, 'terms of sale would have to be carefully devised - very carefully devised - so as not to inhibit private development' (HK Hansard, 1975/76, p.537). Lightbody, in preparing the policy, met the Real Estate Developers Association and assured them that the scheme was not in competition with them as it was for a different target group (ibid, p.763). Hence, the impact of the private market was seen in the preparation of the scheme.

In MacLehose's Speech to LegCo in 6 October 1976, he said that the promotion of home ownership was 'such a desirable social objective in its own right' (SCMP, 7/10/76). Before the Speech, in July, he had already set up a working group chaired by Haddon-Cave and its task was to work out a practical scheme and to recommend how and by whom the scheme should be managed.

This policy was a significant departure (or enrichment) of the initial TYHCP which was primarily focused on building public rental housing. It was supported by the officials and parts of the LegCo and the HA, to meet the needs of those who aspired to own a flat. The scheme was primarily for sitting tenants on rental estates so as to encourage them to move out and vacate the rooms for others in need (SCMP, 26/11/76). Clearly, the scheme could help to meet the housing needs of different classes and by this mean, achieve the goal of social integration and stability. The HOS was well-received by the public and the Councils.

Apart from the HOS policy, a new rent policy and financial arrangement between the government and the HA were adopted in 1977. The government argued that the new financial arrangement would relieve the HA of the enormous debt to the Government incurred since its reorganisation in 1973. Haddon-Cave announced this new arrangement in the 1977/78 Budget. The government cancelled all the debts but the HA was to receive no further loans from the government (SCMP, 19/4/77). People used the term, 'self-balance finance' to describe this new arrangement.[44]

At almost the same time, in 1976, the HA formed a Rent Policy Steering Committee to examine long-term rent policy. During this process, Mr Alan Scott, the SecH who had replaced Lightbody in 1977, was faced by a serious protest from the residents over rents. The residents feared that the outcome of the review would be an increase in rents. Scott responded with a tough attitude and said that, 'if there was no protest, I would not feel at all happy. I would expect it to erupt at some time' (SCMP, 1/6/77). This was the probably the first cross-district residents' protest against housing policy.

MacLehose stepped in and tried to assure the public that rents would still be reasonable.[45] However, a wider coalition, the Public Housing Rent Action Group Committee was established in 9 October 1977. It challenged the new self-balance finance arrangement and the calculation of the HA's costs.[46]

The pressure was responded to by some concessions in rent policy in 1977 but not over the new financial arrangement. For those estates built after 1973, rents would be kept at the same levels for the time being but it would be reviewed periodically in the future, taking into consideration increases in management and maintenance costs and the general income levels of tenants, an well as assessments of the 'relative value' of estates.[47] Rents for those estates built before 1973, which housed the largest group of tenants, would not be changed for the moment. However, when tenants were rehoused to new estates due to the redevelopment programme, they had to pay higher rents for the new flats and these levels would be reviewed every two years.

So the public protest could not stop the new rent policy but contributed to shape certain components of it. For example, the rent for the estates built before 1973 was 'exempted' from a substantial increase in rent at this moment. After the disputes, the residents movement shifted its attention to estate management and the improvement of the living environment. This joint effort among many estate residents, with the organisers (most of them were social workers) as catalyst, was transformed into a permanent cross-district organisation, the Hong Kong People's Council on Public Housing Policy (HKPCPHP) in 1980.

The addition of the PSPS to the HOS signified the growing importance of home ownership. MacLehose announced this new scheme in his Speech to LegCo in October 1977 and his argument was to tap the resources from the private sector to provide subsidised owner-occupied flats to those in need.[48] The HOS working group 'intends to invite real estate enterprises to take part in an experimental project, the purpose of which is to determine whether the private sector could make a contribution towards promoting home ownership' (SCMP, 11/10/77). MacLehose said in October 1978 in his Speech to the LegCo that, 'in view of the popularity of the scheme, we must be alive to the possibility of varying the balance between the programmes for renting and sale in the light of public demand, and the design of new estates provides for this degree of flexibility' (SCMP, 12/10/78). These ideas were gradually implemented thereafter.[49]

Home ownership had a boost in the late 1970s in response to the housing needs of the growing middle class. From the building boom in 1977 and 1978, the price for private flats rocketed and the middle income group increasingly found it difficult to purchase a private flat. However, they could not enjoy either subsidised rental or HOS housing as their incomes were beyond the income limits. This aroused the attention of the Unofficials. In the Governor's Speech debate in November 1978, Mr Lam Wong called for a thorough review of housing policy for the middle-income group (SCMP, 3/11/78). Scott argued that the middle class housing need was not a priority for the HA[50] and 'we cannot, for the present, consider extending these priorities' (SCMP, 16/11/78). However, the government subsequently changed this attitude. A government official mentioned the dilemma of the 'sandwich class' and disclosed that 'the government has recently accepted a commitment to produce at cost homes for sale to these households' (SCMP, 27/2/79).[51]

MacLehose gave more details of this middle-income housing policy in his Speech to LegCo in October 1979. He admitted that this group of families were having real difficulties in purchasing flats and 'although priority must continue to be given to those who need help most, the Government should not ignore the position of this relatively small group' (SCMP, 11/10/79). The progress of this review was, similar to the HOS/PSPS review, extremely rapid. In November, Scott informed the LegCo that sites for middle-income group housing had been identified and the review group had been formed to study the policy, to identify the target group of households and how to increase the production of flats to meet the need. The first estate was completed in 1981 but the response from the middle class was extremely poor. This might have been due to the location of the estates which was considered to be unfavourable by the middle class and, more importantly, because the prices of private market flats reduced in the early 1980s to a more affordable level. As the crisis was over, the government decided to terminate the policy, without any objections being raised.

The increase of private flats price had also affected the prices of HOS/PSPS as their prices were set at a discounted market price. As the prices of private flats rocketed, HOS flats gradually became unaffordable by their potential applicants. Miss Lydia Dunn[52] had argued this issue in the 1981/82 Budget debate and had criticised the provision of free land for rental housing but full market price for land for HOS.[53] Haddon-Cave's initial response was not favourable, and argued that, 'under the HOS, flats are sold, not rented, and there is no compelling arguments for public funds to be used to subsidise individuals in the acquisition of permanent assets' (FEER, 23/12/81). However, six months after Haddon-Cave's statement, MacLehose announced in his last Speech to the LegCo in October 1981, that the new HOS estates would have free land from the government as the Governor was clear that rising costs were in danger of putting the scheme beyond the reach of its original target population (SCMP, 15/10/81).[54]

The construction of public rental housing, the core of the TYHCP, did now make greater progress than in the first five years. Liao was still optimistic and argued that, 'by 1980, we will be turning our flats for 250,000 people a year and that will put us ahead of the previous target'. However, he refused to push the programme further as 'if we try to produce more, we may overheat the industry and this is not good for the economy' (SCMP, 21/8/77). However, MacLehose, in his 1978 Speech to LegCo, admitted that the plan might fail to meet its target even though the current progress to build 40,000 to 50,000 flats (to house 250,000 each year) and private sector building continued to make a substantial contribution. He stated that such a shortfall would only be eliminated by 1985 or might even be 'rolling forward' after it (SCMP, 21/10/78). He explained that the trend to smaller families had increased the demand. To add to the problem, the HA had increased the standard rate of space allocation to 50 sq.ft. per adult from 35 sq.ft.[55] in 1977.

Finally, on 4 April 1979, Scott formally admitted that the government could only achieve the housing target two years later than the TYHCP had projected, i.e. 1984/85. The announcement was followed by public criticism which pushed the government to speed up the programme to fulfill the outstanding housing need. However, the HA did not yield to this demand. Scott, speaking in at a luncheon meeting on 30 April, disagreed with such a demand and criticised it for ignoring the fact that this would increase pressure on the building industry, increase imports and cause serious inflation. He argued that the request 'will hurt everyone including particularly the low income group for whom public housing is being built' (SCMP, 1/5/79). MacLehose also admitted the failure and in his 1979 Speech to the LegCo, he stated that the target of 45,000 flats per year had been made in the 'mistaken belief that domestic demand, and in particular domestic demand affecting the construction industry, would shortly ease'. That target, if pushed ahead, would place an intolerable strain on the whole construction industry (SCMP, 11/10/79).

Their major concern was about the possible adverse effect on the economy. At this time, the construction industry was under pressure as Hong Kong was in a building boom and the private sector continued to provide a vast amount of flats. The government's decision to lower the building programme was certainly an initiative to sacrifice the programme for the benefit of the private sector and the overall economy. Such a decision to delay progress received a 'regret' from the unofficials on LegCo (SCMP, 2/11/79).[56]

Apart from the demographic explanations, the recession in the early 1970s and the overheated economy in the late 1970s,[57] Scott argued that the influx of illegal immigrants in the 1970s was another cause of the failure (SCMP, 20/11/79). Mr John Walden,[58] disagreed and argued that the shortfall in the housing programme 'as a great deal to do with a lack of corporate determination within the system to do what was necessary to honour the Governor's promise'. However, Liao described this as 'utter nonsense' (SCMP, 6/4/80) and MacLehose also rejected this explanation. He recalled that 'the programme was strongly supported by Officials and Unofficials though there were some differences between the Finance Branch and the HD, but the programme did not fail and these differences were ephemeral'.[59] Lightbody and Williams also rejected Walden's comment and argued that, though there were disagreements within the bureaucracy, the decision to scale down the programme was jointly agreed between the Finance Branch and the HA, the disagreement was only on the pace of the remaining programme.[60]

Overall, it is clear that the considerations of the effects on the economy had constrained their decision. However disappointed MacLehose was, he could only accept this unavoidable delay of the programme (HKS, 2/10/80). The public reaction was not in favour of this decision and the HKPCPHP strongly criticised the HA and the government (SCMP, 26/5/80; 28/9/80). Nevertheless, the programme was scaled down and only returned to full-speed in later years.

Table 8.11
Development of the Ten Year Housing Construction Programme

Year	Historical development
1972	Announcement of the TYHCP
1973	Formation of the TYHCP planning group. Initial consideration to sell the PRH to tenants but dropped later. Restructuring of HA & HD.
1974	First delay of TYHCP due to economic recession.
1975	Second consideration of sale of PRH but dropped again. HOS plan mentioned.
1976	'Top Gear' of TYHCP. HOS plan formally announced. Rent Policy Steering Committee established. LegCo member asked for providing mortgage benefit for middle income group to buy private flats but rejected by Haddon-Cave
1977	PSPS plan announced. Self-balance finance policy installed. New rent policy announced. Mortgage benefit for middle income group called for again in LegCo but rejected by Liao.
1978	Second delay to TYHCP due to overheated economy. Housing need of middle income group discussed in LegCo. Scott resisted initially but government changed its attitude subsequently.

1979	Scott formally admitted that TYHCP would be delayed. MacLehose admitted the TYHCP was incorrectly planned. MacLehose announced the middle income housing (MIH) plan.
1980	'Full-speed' of TYHCP again. New design PRH which can be changed for sale. HOS Land policy debated in LegCo but rejected by Haddon-Cave.
1981	Free-land for HOS accepted and announced by MacLehose. MIH completed but poor response and plan halted.

Observations

The programme had been revised and modified but it ended with a failure to reach its target of housing 1.8 million people in self-contained housing. This was an expanded and extended version of the previous fragmented construction programme. The programme received wide support from the public, the business sector, the LegCo Unofficials and the government. The major arguments between them were not on the major policy direction, except over the rent issues, but rather on the implementation of individual programmes of redevelopment, estate management and environmental improvement.

Yet, during the process, we could observe the influence of officials in the initiation of ideas, planning, implementation and monitoring of progress. There were several modifications to the plan, such as the 'delays', over rent policy, the self-balance finance policy, the HOS and PSPS[61] policies and the middle income housing, during the process. Almost all of these decisions were made by the state itself. Of course, there was the impact of the macro-economic situations, especially on the delays of the programme and the design of the HOS/PSPS and middle income housing schemes. This economic crisis only hit the housing programme, not the other services. This may have been due to the special nature of housing and the close relationship between the private and public housing sectors which did not exist in the other services.

Social factors also played a part in the process, such as the middle class housing crisis. The presence of such problems, if they had imposed a real threat to the government and gained support and attention, would have required some reaction from the state. However, the process was never that smooth. The officials did not generally yield to demands, in their early stages but 'suddenly' changed their attitudes. Provided that there was no drastic change in the context, such changes might be resorted to by the state system itself. Several interviewees argued that the personal interest of

MacLehose had an impact on the programme.[62] Lightbody suggested that his personal enthusiasm had given the proposal a 'big push'. Williams argued that his attitude had made the programme a higher priority on the government agenda. He also observed that if MacLehose decided on a policy, no one would dare to oppose it. In the case of land policy for HOS, the negative attitude of the FS was soon replaced by MacLehose's support and a green light was shown to this idea. Yet, in the case of the economic problem, even MacLehose had to temporarily yield to the key principle, that was to keep the market prosperous.

Comparatively speaking, the pressures exerted through the social actions had limited impacts on the process. The programme and the significant changes in it were not significantly related to social pressure. The officials, Lightbody and Williams, commented that this pressure was not difficult to handle. Lightbody said that the officials' attitude was 'if it was reasonable, we will consider it'. If the pressure groups' ideas were not that good, as judged by the officials, the HA would try to explain this to them and if that still did not work, the HA had to ignore them and adopt the appropriate policy. Fung, from the perspective of a social activist in this period, also concludes that the impacts of the pressure groups were rather limited.[63] The main contribution of the groups was to exert pressure on the authority continuously and hence, maintain the demand for the programme. This pressure, though not very powerful, could not be easily neglected and sometimes concessions had to be made, as in the case of rent policy.

Another exception was the middle income housing crisis which forced the government to take action. The Unofficials' attitude might also have contributed to the swift reaction to this problem. Of course, the government's policy would not have an adverse effect on the market[64] and the previous successful experience of the HOS/PSPS schemes had given the government confidence in assisting people in home ownership. However, when the crisis was over and support for such scheme faded away, the programme was terminated.

The success of the officials' firm stand on their own interpretation of the situations and corresponding policies in rejecting the pressures from the Councils reflected the relative power of the LegCo and the officials. Compared with the LegCo, the HA was more involved in the planning of policy. The HA were all appointed members, a majority of them had a business background, including property-related business. It was rather difficult to imagine that they would put forward any drastic proposals which would be against their own interests and beliefs. This was not to say that they were self-interested but, it might be valid to argue that their mentality would be more inclined to the traditional free market-oriented philosophy than be massively interventionist and would certainly be cautious about keeping the expansion going in the economic recession. This attitude was also shared by the officials, either willingly or reluctantly. This is not to conclude that the HA, the Unofficials and the pressure groups did not have effects on the policy process but rather to suggest that the officials were in the leading position.

The Nine Years Free and Compulsory Education Policy

Historical development

The Nine Year Free and Compulsory Education Policy (NYFCEP) was a continuation of the Six Years Free and Compulsory Education Policy. In fact, the government's policy in developing the education services in the post-war period was a 'step by step approach' moving from primary, to secondary and technical education and, finally to tertiary education.

The intention to expand secondary, as well as technical education, was made in the mid-1960s.[65] In July 1970, the government announced its intention to provide three years of aided post-primary education for all children in the appropriate age-group who sought it.[66] The extra school places would be provided directly in government or aided schools, in private non-profit-making schools which would be assisted by Government, or by buying places in suitable private schools (ED Annual Report, 1970-71).

MacLehose, in his 1972 Speech to LegCo, restated this intention.

> But I think honorable Members will agree with the proposition that during the rest of the 70s the main thrust of our educational effort must be in secondary and technical education ... Our absolute objective of course is the provision of 3 years secondary education for all in the 12-14 year age group, and your Government proposes that we should address ourselves to this objective forthwith (HK Hansard, 1972/73, p.7).

MacLehose also announced a proposal to reconstitute the Board of Education and appointed, for the first time in its history, an unofficial from LegCo, Mr Pak-chuen WU, to be the chairman of the Board. This reconstituted Board was to advise the government and draw up detailed plans to speed up achieving the target by 'as soon as possible' (HK Hansard, 1972/73, p.8).

Such intention to provide places for all primary school leavers, had never been mentioned in any previous government document and certainly, the idea had not gone through public consultation or discussion before the announcement. However, it was well received by the Unofficials and the education sector on the grounds of the need for better quality manpower and concerns for child welfare.

The new Board of Education began work in January 1973. The Board presented its report to the government in August 1973 and in the form of a Green Paper, to the LegCo in October 1973. Although in support of the government's proposal, it was rather cautious about the timetable. The Board considered that it was impossible to achieve the ultimate objective by 1980 and, instead, set an interim target of providing places for 80 per cent of 12-14 year olds by 1981. The Board also argued against free secondary education for all in Forms 1-3 as it would result in a misuse of public funds to provide free education for those who could afford to pay fees, thus preventing the money from being spent on other areas. It concluded that there was inadequate justification for free education for all (HKG, 1973b).

Apart from seeking public consultation, MacLehose expressed his dissatisfaction over the proposed schedule which he considered to be too slow. More than thirty organisations joined together to give a concerted opinion to the government. They supported the idea of providing subsidised junior secondary education and agreed that the Green Paper's proposal was too slow (Wong, 1982, p.281). At the same time, the Councils' unofficials had organised an ad hoc group and this was assigned to draft the White Paper instead of letting the Board continue the job.

In October 1974, the Group published its White Paper on 'Secondary Education in Hong Kong over the Next Decade' and the government endorsed it. It recommended a faster pace to provide subsidised secondary education to all primary leavers in 1979 and to provide subsidised places to 40 per cent of 15-16 year olds, with no mention of the issue of compulsion.[67] It was clear that at that stage, the government, the Councils and the publics' (including the education sector) concerns were to provide adequate 'subsidised' places, instead of 'free' and 'compulsory' education. The events showed that the attitude of the Governor had a certain impact on pushing the proposal forward and this attitude was shared by the education sector and the Unofficials.

When the White Paper was announced, Hong Kong's economy was in trouble. Most government policies were affected by this, though in different degrees. On 5 March 1975, Mr Kenneth Topley, the Director of Education (DoE), said that the lack of funds would delay the government's main objective of providing nine years of subsidised education for all children by

1979. In view of the financial situation, Topley would not request funds for other White Paper proposals until the economy improved (SCMP, 5/3/1975). This shows how the economy affected policy implementation that 'lower priority' policies were sacrificed but there was less effect on the top priority of nine years subsidised education. This suggests that the government had decided, because of the strong support from the public, that the policy would not be terminated though its pace might be adjusted.

In the 1975/76 Budget debate, a LegCo councillor, Mrs Catherine Symons,[68] questioned 'free to all' education and suggested that fees should be re-imposed on those who could pay. She argued that, 'when many of these children from homes where there is no financial difficulty' and if it was not for the blanket subsidisation policy, the government could 'stretch the education money further' (SCMP, 29/3/75). However, this challenge did not get favourable response. Topley replied that he disagreed with the suggestion as it would be harmful to the system. He argued that 'if primary education is to be compulsory it should be free' (SCMP, 3/4/75).[69]

The government had repeatedly rejected the option of increasing fees to support the policy.[70] However, Topley disclosed that the ED would accept alternative measures such as permitting a temporary increase in class sizes[71] and redeploying some government primary school teachers to teach extra classes in government secondary schools to meet the schedule. He explained his concern,

> if we can expect a lot rather quickly we could hardly modify our educational plans at all but wait for the revenue upturn. If at the other extreme, there were really sound reason for pessimism - a little and late - then we should thoroughly restructure our expansion plans to suit our assumed resources. Otherwise we would be waiting for a day that was never coming (SCMP, 6/11/75).

These new measures meant that the government had not sacrificed the nine year education policy but had reduced the quality of education instead.

The Education Action Group (EAG),[72] a pressure group formed in 1972, rejected the increasing of class sizes and called for the government to implement the proposals immediately even at the cost of a higher tax on the rich and the use of the fiscal reserve (Star, 21/11/75). This request, of course, received no positive response from the ED. A month later, Mr Q.W. Lee,[73] in view of the fact that there were still 68,000 children aged 12-14 who did not have a place in a secondary school, called for compulsory schooling for them. Topley admitted that the lack of places caused this problem to persist and he hoped 'we shall be able very soon, to make progress with our plans for secondary education expansion under the White Paper arrangements' (SCMP, 18/12/75).

In 1976, the economy gradually recovered and the government had returned its budget from deficit to surplus. Topley stated that 'the ED and the Finance & Social Services Branches of the Secretariat have been locked - not in battle - but in-depth discussion of how we can meet the deep-felt wish of members, indeed of the whole community, for decisive action in the realm of secondary education' (SCMP, 8/1/76). Very soon, in the 1976/77 budget, increased funding was allocated for the expansion of secondary schools. The increased resources were used to,

1. build new schools;
2. implement 'floating class' and 'extended day' policies in public schools;[74]
3. convert under-utilised primary schools;
4. buy places from the private sector.

All these measures aimed to increase the supply of secondary school places as quickly as possible. The FS announced the intention of providing every primary 6 leaver with an aided Form 1 place by September 1978 instead of September 1979 as proposed by the White Paper (SCMP, 27/2/76). Such a decision was certainly not expected by the public, the Councils and the pressure groups. Later, MacLehose spoke optimistically in his Speech to the LegCo in October 1976, expressing with confidence that, 'by 1978, extra places will be funded for all primary school leavers by building or conversion to create 48 new schools, by floatation and extended day classes, and by the purchase of places in private schools' (HK Hansard, 1976/77, p.13).[75]

To fulfill this target was not an easy task but the government had shown its determination to achieve it. In 1976, it announced a plan to convert 18 under-utilised government primary schools into 16 new secondary schools (8 fully-aided and 8 government secondary schools). The officials had to deal with the concerns of the teachers within the public sector on the issue of re-deployment.[76] Moreover, the school building programme and the purchase of places from the private sector also had to be organised to meet the target.

As the success of the plan required co-operation from the private schools, their interests and concerns had to be fully considered.[77] The Hong Kong Private Anglo-Chinese Schools Association (HKPA-CSA) had repeatedly bargained with the government about the future of these independent schools (formerly known as profit-making schools) when the bought places scheme ended. In 16 November 1976, Topley made it clear to the independent schools that the government would stop buying places in the early 1980s. He said at a luncheon meeting of the Rotary Club of Peninsula that, 'the buying of places in private independent schools has never been regarded by the Government as a long term aim but rather as necessary until more long term plans can be brought to fruition'. A 'source' from within the Department frankly admitted that, 'the government has no obligation towards the profit-making schools. So, if they say we are using them, they are right' (SCMP, 17/11/76).

Though the Department was tough in dealing with the independent schools, ED agreed to fully consult the HKPA-CSA on all matters relating to the operation of and any modifications to the bought places scheme (SCMP, 19/11/76). The ED also agreed to increase the benefit level for pupils under the bought places scheme in non-profit and independent schools by more than 40 per cent from 1 September 1976 retrospectively (SCMP, 11/12/76).[78]

Topley realised that the private sector was essential in meeting the target. While reluctant to have any long term commitment to the private schools, Topley promised that there would be 'full and fair' consideration of any application by them to join the aided school scheme (HKS, 20/1/77).[79] This shows that where the government had to rely on others, such parties were in a better position to bargain for their interests.

However, such a relationship would fade away when the government could provide adequate places in the public and aided sectors. When the private schools exerted further pressure to ask for their inclusion in the bought places scheme and subsequently in the aided scheme, Mr Basil Board, the Acting Deputy DoE, replied to the HKPA-CSA that the government would not consider any automatic inclusion of them in the subsidised scheme, as the government perceived they had a duty to protect the public from sub-standard private schools. According to the Department's information, only 66 out of a total of 150 private independent schools would be included in the scheme by September 1977 (SCMP, 5/4/77). Although the Association condemned the government's position, they also recognised their own weaknesses.

> If [the private school] fails because of their incompetence, there can be no cause for complaint. But if a school is well supported by the parents and yet is artificially cut off from its source of students, the Government is to blame ... there should be a fair and carefully worked out plan to effect the changes in the best possible and the least disruptive way (HKS, 5/4/77).

A month later, Topley restated that the role of the private sector was rather transitory and the ultimate aim of the government was to provide places in government, aided and non-profit making schools, though the private sector contribution was important at present (SCMP, 2/5/77). The government would not, certainly, entertain all requests from private schools to change to grant status (HKS, 2/5/77). The private schools were clear about their 'gloomy' future and it was noted that 'the golden era for running a school as a commercial business is over' (HKS, 3/7/77).[80]

To make sure the government did not rely on the private sector for any longer than necessary, it pressed ahead with the school construction plan. Mr S.K. Ho, senior education officer of the ED, stated that the government would have built 52 schools by December 1978 instead of the 48 that were planned. He explained that this advance was due to the sound financial situation which was far better it had been a few years previously when the massive building programme was initially planned (HKS, 29/8/77).

Another relevant issue, the child labour problem, had continuously attracted the attention of local people and overseas groups. The phenomenon was prevalent in the early stage of industrial development in Hong Kong and it continued into the 1970s. The CIC carried out a research in Sau Mau Ping[81] district in 1975 and found that the failure of the government to provide more Form 1 places was the greatest cause of the widespread evidence of child labour (SCMP, 29/1/76). The president of HKPA-CSA, Mr Y.C. Au Yeung, also commented that the problem would continue if the government did not provide five years of assisted secondary schooling for all pupils (SCMP, 19/1/77). In 1976, a group of MPs also criticised the situation and Frank Hooley, Robert Parry and 72 other MPs had signed a letter condemning the 'sweated labour' conditions in Hong Kong.

On 5 October 1977, MacLehose unveiled the government's decision to provide nine year education for all and also that fees would be abolished and that education would be made compulsory up to a child's 15th birthday or until the completion of Form 3 study (HK Hansard, 1977/78, pp.26-28). He said 'the coming year will witness a milestone in the development of education in Hong Kong' and 'I feel convinced that it is not the wish of this council or the public that any of the benefit of the places now provided should be lost to any children through the indifference of parents, or pressure to take up full-time employment instead' (ibid, pp.26-27). MacLehose also explained the argument for 'free' education,

> ... legislation will be introduced to abolish fees for junior secondary education in the public sector. This is a corollary of making this type of

education compulsory ... Since abolition of fees is linked with education being made compulsory, strict logic would dictate that fees should be abolished as compulsion is applied to each age group, from 1979 onwards (ibid, p.27).

The government's decision to make junior secondary education free and compulsory was beyond the expectations of the most of the individual parties though most of them supported this move. However, this unexpected move[82] to provide free and compulsory education (the previous aim was only to provide subsidised places) attracted some criticism, for example, Rev Erik Kvan[83] later argued that Western-style compulsory education had caused juvenile delinquency and criticised the government for not discussing the policy with the concerned groups before the decision was made. The proposal received general support from the Councils but a few members expressed their reservations. Dr Rayson Huang[84] supported free education for all but worried that making it compulsory remove families' choice about allowing children either to work or to study (SCMP, 28/10/77).

The education sector was divided over the policy. Another opponent of the policy, Father Barrett, principal of Wah Yan College, said that the government should upgrade vocational and technical education instead of introducing free secondary education for all up to Form 3. 'It should have complete priority over free education if funds are not available' and the money should be used to 'restore a proper primary school organisation' (SCMP, 25/11/77).

However, according to Mr James Wu,[85] the policy would enable Hong Kong to keep pace with the better-off neighbouring regions. He did not believe industrialists with a social conscience would complain if 14 year olds were not allowed to work, 'rather, their concern is for the adequacy and relevance of higher education in our industrial and commercial society' (SCMP, 27/10/77). In fact, industrialists always supported the policy but argued for a greater practical and technical training component. Later, the Chinese Manufacturers' Association[86] issued their support for this policy and argued that 'people should realise that is definitely good for the community to have well-educated workers' (SCMP, 26/12/77). The major pressure group, the EAG, also supported this policy and called for the government to take steps to provide more places in senior forms.

The debate on this policy centered on its two fundamental principles (free and compulsory) and the potential problems engendered by them. MacLehose did not yield to these criticisms and argued that the massive expansion of education was both socially right and economically imperative, 'we have entered an era of secondary education without fees for all. It is obviously desirable, but less obviously it does involve complications and adjustments' (SCMP, 20/1/78). Facing some queries from the unofficials about the potential threat of falling student standards, Topley defended the policy and argued that it was high time that Hong Kong came into line with the majority of socially advanced and technologically developing societies by providing a sound basic course of education for all children.

> We must remove from our system, too, anything which encourages or can be used to justify under-age children seeking employment ... It is our belief that, to be effective in meeting the needs of our young people and our community, this basic course can be no shorter than nine years ... As the first six years are free, so should the latter three (SCMP, 13/3/78).

In the 1978/79 budget debate, although majority of the LegCo members supported the policy, they did have different views concerning 'free and compulsory'. There were four relatively senior unofficials in LegCo, Chung, John Bremridge,[87] Lee and Mr Hilton Cheong-Leen, who spoke in support of the policy. Cheong-Leen even called it a 'social anomaly' that 16 per cent of 12-14 year olds were still not in full-time education (SCMP, 30/3/78).

On the second day of the debate, several unofficials spoke against the policy. Father McGovern argued that the priority of needs in other areas (such as kindergarten, primary education and more career and personal guidance) were higher than that of this policy and to help those in need, a fee remission scheme could be introduced. He argued that the policy would also encourage parents to give up their responsibilities. Huang still insisted on his standpoint and rejected the policy on the grounds that it provided services free for both the rich and poor and the subsidy should be targeted on the needy. Dunn had reservations about the policy as the government did not explain clearly the rationale for it and the money could be spent on other services to improve their quality (SCMP, 31/3/78).

Topley, in his reply to these comments, argued that it was unfair to ask people to pay fees if the government made the education compulsory. Means-tests and investigations into family's situations would be rejected by the people and eventually, would hamper the whole system. He repeatedly argued that Hong Kong should go at the same pace as the socially and technologically advanced countries, by providing a compulsory and complete basic education (STJP, 13/4/78). Eventually, the budget was passed and in 13 July 1978, the Finance Committee approved the policy to abolish all school fees for Form 1-3. Hong Kong became the second region (after Japan) in Asia which implemented nine-year free and compulsory education.

However, those who moved in to F.2 and F.3 in private schools, did not enjoy these benefits, only those in government and aided schools. In February 1978, the HKPA-CSA launched a campaign for free education for all and tried to pressurise the government by a months-long mass student protest at the ED headquarters (SCMP, 13/2/78 & 18/2/78, STJP, 21/2/78). But the government did not yield to demand (SCMP, 19/2/78) which did not arouse much attention or support.

The policy was implemented but the opposition still existed and gained more support when problems emerged. In the debate on the Education Amendment Bill to empower the DoE to issue attendance orders, Rev Joyce Bennett[88] warned about falling academic standards. In June 1979, the government announced its decision to abolish the 'Tong Fai'[89] from September 1979. Rev Bennett argued again that, 'Chinese people have always valued education. Do you value something you get for free? This is something which only time will tell' (SCMP, 12/5/79).

There was another argument put as well as the principle of compulsion and its relationship to the decline in the quality of education. Dr Kay Barker[90] said that compulsory schooling was basically an excellent idea but what would happen afterwards was both undesirable and unnecessary. 'Compulsory schooling, can, if we are not careful, just be a form of baby-sitting' (HKS, 27/8/79). It might be a wonderful opportunity for some but might be a little more than a destructive period of drudgery for others (SCMP, 27/3/80). In 1981, Father Raphael at the La Salle College Speech Day, spoke against compulsory education and claimed that those who were unwilling to learn were being forced to attend lessons and were being kept in schools rather like prisoners in gaols (SCMP, 29/11/82). Even Topley, in October 1980, admitted that the policy had 'taken certain problems from our streets and transferred them to the classroom'.[91]

The problems reflected the fact that the policy was implemented without thorough preparation, by the schools and teachers. It was not until the end of 1980s that the Education Commission launched a review but it was only limited to the issue of students' behavioural problems. However, the education sectors had a joint effort to evaluate the free and compulsory education policy from 1987 and published their report in 1990. Though having many criticisms of the policy, the principle of free and compulsory nine years education remained intact and was in fact, endorsed by most of these sectors.

Table 8.12
Development of Nine Years Free and Compulsory Education Policy

Year	Historical development
1971	Implementation of free and compulsory primary education.
1972	Announcement of the intention to provide three more years subsidised education in the Governor's Speech to LegCo in October 1972.
1973	Reconstitution of the Board of Education to study the matter in January.
	Board of Education presented its Report in the form of a Green Paper to the government in August and to the LegCo in October. Report called for cautious steps to implement the plan, to provide 80 per cent of places to all P.6 leavers in 1981. It was against 'free' education.
	Green Paper publicised for public consultation.
	MacLehose personally dissatisfied with the slow pace of development.
	LegCo set up an ad hoc group to prepare for the White Paper.
1974	White Paper 'Secondary Education in Hong Kong Over the Next Decade' published in October which called for providing subsidised three years secondary education for all in 1979.
1975	Economic crisis and the slow down of the plan, especially the school construction plan. However, government resisted using a fee increase to create additional resources for the plan. Alternative measures to deploy resources adopted instead.
	Q.W. Lee called for free education but rejected by Topley as resources did not permit thus.
	CIC study on child labour which argued for the relationship between this and the limited supply of junior secondary places.
1976	Economy recovered and the plan revitalised and speeded up.
	MacLehose proposed measures to catch-up with the initial plan.
	MPs from UK condemned child labour in Hong Kong.
1977	Continous debate and negotiation with private sector.
	Government decided to terminate the bought places scheme when the situation allowed.

MacLehose unveiled the plan to provide free and compulsory education services in 1978 in his Speech to LegCo in October. General support from the Councils, the pressure groups, the education sector and the public.

1978 Budget debate in March. LegCo endorsed the policy tc provide free and compulsory education policy. Several members had reservation. Budget finally endorsed by LegCo.

Finance Committee endorsed the detailed budget of the policy in July and policy implemented in September.

1979 Cancellation of the 'Tong Fai' from September.

Continous debate on the issues of 'free and compulsory', and the subsequent problems engendered by the policy, such as declining education quality, problems in implementation, student behavioural problems etc..

1980 Topley admitted the problems caused by the policy.

Observations

By contrast to the housing programme, this policy ended in a greater success. Not only did it meet its initial target, but the government also succeeded in reaching the target one year earlier than the initially planned. The final policy proposal, 'free and compulsory', was more generous than its initial promise. The policy had wide support from the public, the business sector, the education profession, the pressure groups and the Councils. The favourable response from the public and the education sector was understandable though a minority of them were opposed it. The support from the business sector, especially from the manufacturing industries, could be explained by the long term benefits that they would gain from the improvement of the labour force and the subsequent improved competitiveness of Hong Kong's products in the world market, and also by their shared belief in a moral responsibility to prevent child labour, which was no longer acceptable in the 1970s.

The pressure groups, education professionals and unions, shared similar interests with the government and there was little conflict over the general principle and direction of the policy. They criticised aspects of the implementation of the policy, such as its speed in times of recession, the design of the Junior Secondary Examination for the Form 3 leavers, curriculum design, the language issue and the potential threats to the employment of teachers. Among these pressure groups, the PTU and EAG were relatively powerful in bargaining with the government. Yet, they did not have a formal position within the education advisory or planning system. The private sector focused more on its own interests and when their role was increasingly taken over by the subsidised schools, their bargaining power was gradually extinguished. There was little direct participation from the mass public in this issue as compared with the housing policy.

Comparatively speaking, the opposing arguments, mainly from a minority segment of the education sector, were weaker. Reservations were based on the concern for the quality of education, the utilisation of limited resources, and the enforcement of compulsory schooling. Although the government acknowledged these problems, it decided to press ahead with the policy.

The government's determination could be perceived as a result of several factors. The policy was a continuation of previous policy. When the number of primary graduates increased, it was logical to have a corresponding increase of secondary school places for this increasing population, otherwise social problems would occur. The participation of youth in the riots in the late 1960s had demonstrated the potential threat from them if inadequate chances for education persisted.

The need of the economy had an influence on the implementation of the policy as shown in earlier paragraphs. The need to produce more well-educated and trained people certainly met the needs of the business sector and the economy. The economic crisis in 1974 had delayed progress but the problems in the late 1970s did not have any similar effect. In fact, in this time of financial hardship, the government still sought by every means to push the plan ahead. From the officials' viewpoint, the policy was introduced on its 'merit' and for economic reasons. The policy could also prevent any excuse for trade sanctions and protectionism against Hong Kong, as there were pressures from overseas about the child labour problem. Topley had repeatedly suggested that the implementation of the policy could put Hong Kong in step with the developed countries.

The development of the policy, its early implementation in 1978 and the principle of free and compulsory education, can further be explained from the personal interests. Topley expressed his surprise when the FS decided to implement the plan one year early. His interpretation was that the decision was made jointly by the Governor and the FS,[92] ExCo, had not been consulted about this decision. The decision to make the policy compulsory was in order to solve the problem of child labour completely, and the government's argument of 'if you make it compulsory, it must be free' seemed necessary to smooth its implementation. Of course, at that stage, there were adequate resources for the officials to push ahead with the policy.

Certainly, social and economic factors, external pressures and the interests of the officials served to sustain the state's commitment to this policy. The social and economic factors explain the need for such policy. The state played an important role in determining the timing and design of the policy. Perhaps, the over-ambition of the government to have the policy carried out as early as possible, its denial of the limitation in the context of the policy and the lack of preparation for the plan, could be explained by the impact of the officials' determination to push it forward and their influence over its timing.

Notes

1 Within this total, expenditure on social welfare and housing increased by twenty and thirteen-folds respectively over ten years. See Table 8.1.

2 However, in 1981, the number of beds per thousand population was still 4.2. One of reason was the increase of population. The population in 1981 was 4,987,000 compared with 3,937,000 in 1971, i.e. an increase of 26.7 per cent.

3 The revision called for an increase of 5,000 beds, 5 clinics, 3 polyclinics, 1 health centre, an additional medical school and 1 dental school within 8 years, i.e. 1976-1984. The plan was largely followed with minor modifications.

4 Another regional hospital, apart from Queen Mary Hospital (regional hospital for Hong Kong island and teaching hospital of Hong Kong University) and Queen Elizabeth Hospital (regional hospital for Kowloon), the Princess Margaret Hospital started to operate in 1975 serving the Kowloon West and New Territories residents.

5 Though the percentage increase was drastic, the actual increase, if compared with the increase of incomes, was only notional. The charge for specialist out-patient consultation was the same as for general consultation.

6 Figures calculated by United Nations for Hong Kong in 1980 was 10 per thousand births (the figure compiled by CSD was 11.8). Singapore and Australia had the same rate. Japan (7), Sweden (7), Netherlands (8), Canada (9) and France (9) were lower than Hong Kong. UK (11), USA (11), Austria (12) and New Zealand (12) were all higher than Hong Kong. See United Nations, 1991, Table 15.

7 Though the causes of such improvements cannot be directly attributed to the improvement of medical services, once cannot neglect this contribution.

8 The rest of the pupils were in private schools without any government subsidy.

9 Technical Institutes offer courses leading to technical qualification from certificates to diplomas, for the post-Form 3 students. The first Technical Institute was the Morrison Hill Technical Institute which opened in 1969. The next four were Kwun Tong (1975), Kwai Chung (1975), HaKing Wong (1977) and Li Wai Lee (1979). The intake of technical institutes increased from 13,387 in 1974 to 29,857 in 1981, an increase of 123 per cent in 7 years. See CSD, 1985, Table 13.2.

10 The number of enrollments for post-secondary college, polytechnic and university in 1974 and 1981 were 8,248 and 12,206; 17,363 and 25,037; 7,021 and 9,908 respectively. The growth rates were 48.0 per cent, 44.2 per cent and 41.1 per cent respectively in 7 years. See CSD, 1985, Table 13.2.

11 The Papers included:

1973 Report of the Board of Education on the Proposed Expansion of Secondary Education over the Next Decade (Green Paper)

1974 Secondary Education in Hong Kong over the Next Decade (White Paper)

1977 Senior Secondary and Tertiary Education: A Development Programme for Hong Kong over the Next Decade (Green Paper)

1978 The Development of Senior and Tertiary Education (White Paper)

1981 The Hong Kong Education System (overall review of the Hong Kong education system)

12 In the 1973 current prices, the cost would be HK$ 3,000 million . See HKAR, 1973, p.5.

13 The main difference between HOS and PSPS is that the latter scheme has participation from the private sector. The government prepares land and the building contract for the estate, and invite tenders from the private sector. After the completion of the project, the Authority is responsible for all the selling arrangements and the private company is guaranteed an agreed level of return.

14 There were different opinions on the result of the programme. Generally speaking, the programme could not accommodated the number of people that it has promised. However, Sir Ian Lightbody and Mr Bernard Williams, both argue that the plan did meet its original target if calculated by the space allocation standard per person in 1973. As the allocation ratio increased in that period and hence, the programme could not accommodate 1.8 million people though it has produced the floor space adequate to accommodate the population in 1973 space allocation standard.

15 In 1980, the percentage of household expense for housing for public rental housing (Group A/Group B), HOS flats and private self-contained

flats were 6.43 per cent/2.87 per cent, 5.4 per cent and 27.44 per cent. Group A rental housing refers to those built by the new HA after 1973 and Group B rental housing are those built before 1973.

16 This was the second White Paper concerning social welfare. The first one was published in 1965. See chapter 6.

17 A joint organisation established by the NGOs in 1950 to coordinate their efforts and represent their interests.

18 The recommendation was made by the 'Report of the Working Group on Provision of Social Welfare Services and Subvention Administration' in 1980. Category 1 services, such as outreaching and school social work services to youth, receive a full subsidy from the government whereas Category 2, such as elderly services, only receive a lump-sum or a fixed percentage of subsidy which could only cover part of the operational cost of the services.

19 These included 'Working Party on the Future Needs of the Elderly, Care in the Community: The Right Basis for Services to the Elderly' published in 1973; 'A Programme of Social Security Development: Help for Those Least Able to Help Themselves'; 'Development of Social Work Among Young People in Hong Kong, a Green Paper' and 'Services for the Elderly, a Green Paper'. All were published in 1977.

20 For example, the increase in the youth and elderly population and the problem of delinquency.

21 This was the first systematic elaboration of the government's response to the needs of disabled.

22 It was still not an institutional type.

23 He estimates that the income gained by the lowest decile was 515.68 per cent while the figure for the next 10 per cent was 69.68 per cent. The figure for the middle income groups (the fourth to seventh decile counting from the lowest income group) were 11.27 per cent, 6.06 per cent, 5.43 per cent and 4.74 per cent respectively. The figures for the highest decile was 0.83 per cent. Hence, the welfare state programme did have progressive redistributive effect on income distribution. See Ho, 1979.

24 Yet, as reflected by the Gini Coefficients in 1971 and 1981, which were 0.41 and 0.43 respectively, the gap between the rich and poor had not been reduced.

25 He was the Commissioner of Resettlement and first Secretary for Housing (1973 to 1977).

26 He was the Assistant and later the Director of Housing in the 1970s to the early 1980s.

27 To repeat the history, before the 1970s, there were the Housing Authority (at that time, under the domain of the Urban Council), the Housing Society and small building cooperatives. All of them received different types of subsidies from the government, in the forms of reduction of land costs and interest-free loans. The government also built public housing through Public Works Department and managed this by its Resettlement Department. The Housing Board was the highest advisory body on housing matters to the government.

28 From a personal interview.

29 The management duties were scattered and shared by the old Housing Authority, Resettlement Department, Housing Board and Urban Council.

30 The terms of reference of the new HA were,

1. To manage existing public housing estates of all kinds, and all future public housing estates as well as Cottage Areas and Licensed Areas;
2. To plan and build public housing estates 'for such kinds or classes of persons as the Authority may, subject to the approval of the Governor determine;
3. To be an Authority for the clearance of land for development, subject to such directions as the Governor may give;
4. To be the Authority for the prevention and control of squatting and;
5. To advise the Governor on all housing policy matters (Star, 16/4/75).

31 He was the last Commissioner for Resettlement and the administrative head of the old Housing Authority.

32 Mr Lightbody described the situation of the resettlement estates in his early days of being the Commissioner for Resettlement as thus, 'I remember when I first took over the resettlement in 1971, I took a trip ... from the top of this resettlement estate. I looked down between blocks of this estate. You couldn't see the courtyard. It was covered wall by wall with illegal stores selling all sorts of things'. From a personal interview. The first professionally trained housing manager was employed by the RD as late as in 1971 (SCMP, 21/5/71).

33 From a personal interview and also a report of an interview with Mr Williams when he retired in 1983 in SCMP. The exact date of the report could not be identified.

34 The implication was that the task of building the blocks was removed from the PWD to the HA.

35 From a personal interview with Lightbody.

36 At that time, he was the Principal Assistant Colonial Secretary in charge of land issues. Later, to facilitate the development of new towns in the

New Territories, the major sources of land for the plan, a new branch within the PWD, the New Territories Development Department, was created and he was made the Director of it. Later, to coordinate the development of new towns, a new administrative structure in New Territories, the New Territories Administration and a Secretary for New Territories were created. Akers-Jones was then transferred to be the first Secretary for New Territories.

37 From a personal interview.

38 Williams said that the CSD has been consulted and he, as the head of the Department, had argued that the target should be in the unit of 'family in flat' rather than in 35 sq.ft. per person. The cost might be higher than that estimation. However, he argued that the PWD and Finance Secretary did not accepted his suggestion and therefore, his idea was neglected. From a personal interview.

39 This coincided with the warning from Williams when he served in the CSD as a member of the planning group of the TYHCP. See the previous footnote.

40 At that time, he has joined the Housing Department as Assistant Director.

41 From a personal interview with Mr Bernard Williams.

42 Such a consideration had been expressed by Haddon-Cave and Lightbody during 1975/76 debate on the budget. See Hong Kong Hansard, 1975/76, p.37 & p.763.

43 From a questionnaire completed by Lord MacLehose. He wrote that, 'The Home Ownership Scheme was agreed in principle between the Financial Secretary and myself at a time that additional housing was needed beyond what the budget provided for, or whose economic effect would have been imprudent in macro-economic terms'.

44 Lightbody disagreed with this term as he argued that the HA still received 'land' as a form of subsidy from the government. And, without that, the housing programme and HA could not survive. The point was made in a personal interview.

45 MacLehose, in his speech to LegCo in October 1977, said that 'it is the later [rent increase] that has attracted criticism, most of it misguided. I wished to assure public housing tenants and the public that the Housing Authority accepts its obligation to provide decent housing for low income groups at rent they can afford' (SCMP, 6/10/77). Although MacLehose was not apparently moved by the appeal but this response shows that such a scale of public outcry did have an impact in engendering a response, though not a concession, from the chief of the civil service.

46 Their argument was that the government should not include the rates of the blocks and interest paid back to the government in the calculation of the HA's budget as it would 'exaggerate' and distort the real financial situation of HA in which 'deficit' would be the possible outcome. Therefore, if rates was excluded from it, there would be little or no 'deficit' and therefore, no need to increase rent. 'Indeed, rents could be lowered and the public housing would really be the social services as the Government has claimed to be' (HKS, 10/10/77).

47 The relative value of the estate was determined by comparison with other estates, taking into account factors such as location, amenities, environment and services provided.

48 The progress of this was also very fast. Almost at the same time, Haddon-Cave disclosed that three sites were set for tender and two of them would be offered in April 1978 and another in October 1978 (HKS, 11/10/77). The first lot of PSPS flats was sold in 1979.

49 The proportion of HOS/PSPS flats was gradually increased compared with rental flats, though the latter still had a larger percentage. The HA also designed a new type of housing block, the 'Y' design, which had a better layout and thus was, 'flexible' enough to be converted for sale. One example was the Fung Shing Court in Shatin, sold in 1983.

50 He argued that 'the first priority has for many years been the provision of subsidised rented housing for the lowest income group, and it must so continue. The second, relatively new priority, is the HOS' (SCMP, 16/11/78).

51 The official was Dr E.G. Pryor, the Assistant Director of Planning and Research of Housing Department spoken in the Asian Regional Meeting of the Commonwealth Association of Surveying and Land Economy in 26 February 1979 held at Hong Kong.

52 An appointed Unofficials member of LegCo and the ExCo. She has been the senior member of LegCo and the senior member of the ExCo until July 1995. A prominent political figure in Hong Kong.

53 In the LegCo debate, she argued that 'the poor should be housed at a subsidy and that the rich should pay full market value is indisputable. But between these two extremes is a growing number of would-be home owners in the middle income range who are excluded from public rented housing because their incomes are in excess of the limits of eligibility, but private sector accommodation is beyond their reach' (SCMP, 22/10/81).

54 To avoid abuse of the new policy, the limit for reselling in the market was set at ten years (previously, it was five years) and after ten years,

the owners has to pay a cost to cover the land premium to the government for the land cost before selling it in the market.

55 Note that, in my interviews with Lightbody and Williams, they repeatedly argued that the government was successful in building adequate floor space for 1.8 million people based on 35 sq.ft. per person. The policy did not fail in this aspect but only failed to provide housing for 1.8 million according to the 50 sq.ft allocation standard. That is why Williams repeatedly criticised the planning method of the TYHCP based on floor space instead of 'family' in unit of flat.

56 Mr Lam Wong, Mr Allen Lee and Dr Rayson Huang expressed their regrets about the decision. This shows that the LegCo councillors also endorsed the 'realistic' decision and the need to protect the economy.

57 It suffered from the Oil Crisis and recession in 1973 and 1974 and then the overheated economy in 1978 and 1979. This was admitted by Liao, who replaced Scott as Secretary for Housing in 1980 in an interview with SCMP in 5 April 1980.

58 He was the Secretary for Home Affairs in the 1970s.

59 From a questionnaire completed by Lord MacLehose.

60 From personal interviews with them.

61 Although the idea of home ownership and encouragment of private sector participation were pushed by the LegCo Unofficials, their effect was rather limited. The final decisions and choices were made by the officials.

62 Such as Lightbody, Williams, Akers-Jones and S.Y. Chung. All from personal interviews.

63 Mr Ho-lap Fung was the former Director of Society for Community Organisation, a social action-oriented NGO in Hong Kong. From a personal interview.

64 The intervention of government in assisting this middle class group did not affect the market at that time, as they were no longer able to afford the market prices of private sector housing.

65 In the 1965 White paper on education, the government planned to provide places for 15 to 20 per cent of the total number of students completing the primary education. See HKG, 1965.

66 An interim target was set to provide 50 per cent of the 12-14 age-group with aided places by 1976, and within this 50 per cent, 18-20 per cent of the 12-16 age-group would be able to proceed to aided 5-year courses. Plan approved by Finance Committee of LegCo in August 1971.

67 Other proposals included in the Paper:

1. A new examination for the junior form (Form 3) graduates to assess their ability for promotion to senior form;

2. When adequate places for all Primary 6 leavers existed, the Secondary School Entrance Examination (SSEE) examination would end;
3. To increase the proportion of technical subjects to 25 to 30 per cent of the total subjects provided in Forms 1 to 3 and the same proportion within the nine years education period;
4. One-third of the Form 4 students to be allocated places for Form 6;
5. The Technical Institute to increase its places for Form 3 leavers;
6. From 1975, all government and aided schools will adopt the 'floating class' system and 'extended day' policy (HKG, 1974b).

68 Mrs Symons was the former headmistress of the Diocesan Girls' College, a grant school with very good reputation in Hong Kong.

69 This argument was later put forward to support the arguments that the nine year education be free and compulsory.

70 Topley has denied the move in the LegCo budget debate in April 1975 (SCMP, 3/4/75). Later, an ED spokesman denied again the intention to increase fee in 1975 though a study done by CDO has shown that the citizens realised that increase was finally inevitable in the future (HKS, 29/4/75).

71 This was suggested by Mr Q.W. Lee, a LegCo councillor.

72 A pressure group focus on education policy set up in 1972 by those people, mainly the education professionals, who concerned on the matters.

73 He is the Board of Chairman of Hang Seng Bank, the second largest bank in Hong Kong.

74 Floating class and extending days policies were aimed at increasing the students intake of a school without providing extra premises. One or more class are designated as 'floating class' and they will have no designated classroom but moving around different classrooms for classes.

75 Note that MacLehose did not mention 'free' education. He used the phrase 'provide nine years of education for all and within the means of all' (HK Hansard, 1976/77, p.13). After this decision, the next step, following the 'step-by-step approach', would be senior secondary education and tertiary education. MacLehose went on to appoint a group to prepare for the Green Papers on these topics.

76 In Hong Kong, all government schools are under the management of the Education Department.

77 For example, the government could only provide subsidised places for 51 per cent of the primary 6 leavers in 1975. To provide another 50 per cent of places, the government had to increase the number of places by

at least 10 per cent to 15 per cent of places every year. It was unrealistic to build sufficient subsidised schools within such a short period of time. Therefore, buying places from the private sector was most probably the faster and more efficient method.

78 The independent schools (private schools) could not increase the fees for the students once they had participated in the bought places scheme. However, the subsidy per head paid by the government to aided schools and the private schools were not equal and the former enjoyed a higher rate. Therefore, the students of these schools did not pay fees, or made just a very low payment, whereas the private school students had to pay much higher fees. The increase of benefit level allow the schools to avoid increase of fees, and to have more resources to hire qualified staff and improve the facilities.

79 A scheme started earlier to convert private non-profit making schools to aided schools.

80 In 1977, Mr Topley restated the government's policy to phase out the bought place scheme for Form 1 to 3 in those private independent schools whose operations did not meet the desired standards and to bring on to fully aided status to those private non-profit making schools which are willing and suitable in fours stages began from September 1979 (SCMP, 19/10/78). Eventually, 57 non-profit-making schools, some of which were originally receiving a per capita grant, included in the scheme of phased conversion to full-aided status and the process ended in September 1982.

81 The overwhelming majority of the population in Sau Mau Ping were lower class.

82 Cheng argued that only a very few people were involved in the decision and the ED certainly did not know about it. This was agreed to be so by Topley, Mr Wah Szeto, Mr Man-ho Ha, Rev Joyce Bennett, Dr Kay Barker and Mrs Catherine Symons. From personal interviews.

83 He was the Head of the Department of Psychology of the University of Hong Kong.

84 He was the Vice-chancellor of the University of Hong Kong.

85 Mr Wu, who had a business background, was the appointed unofficial member of LegCo at that time.

86 An association formed by a group of Chinese industrialists In Hong Kong.

87 John Bremridge became the Financial Secretary after Sir Philip Haddon-Cave in 1983.

88 She was a LegCo member and had been a headmistress of an aided-school before her retirement.

89 This type of fees is primarily collected for paying the teaching materials in classes (tong).

90 The headmistress of St. Stephen Girls' College and later, a member of the Education Commission.

91 Quoted from the mimeograph prepared by A.R. Sweeting, 'The Social History of Education in Hong Kong:Notes and Resources'. In fact, Topley expressed his awareness of the potential harm to the quality of education by the policy in a personal interview.

92 Though Topley repeatedly supported the policy in the public. In a personal interview, he also acknowledged the potential difficulties of reaching the target in 1978 which existed at that time. He knew there would be problems but he did not openly talk about them.

9 Theories of the welfare state for the 1970s: a recapitulation

The above analysis has supported several observations. Firstly, the selective and prioritised development of services in the 1970s was largely based on the initial framework set at the earlier stage. The TYHCP was the continuation of the previous housing scheme but in a more systematic and coherent form under an unified structure, the reconstituted HA. The NYFCEP was based on the previous promise to provide more subsidised junior secondary places in the coming years. So the programmes were largely built on the previous foundations with new developments due to the changing context and policy dynamic in the 1970s.

The further development of the local economy required a better-trained labour force to compete with the emergent three 'Little Dragons', South Korea, Singapore and Taiwan in the manufacturing and tertiary sectors. The merging of the local economy into the world economic system had exposed it to potential pressure from trading competitors.

The formation of new intermediary organisations, had higher expectations of the state in relation to social issues, intensified pressure group activities. The emergence of a new middle class which had a similar orientation formed a new grouping which actively participated in the policy process through their appointment into the Councils and the advisory committees or just by their presence as a powerful interest group that had to be taken into account in the policy making process. To some extent, the increasing participation of these organisations and groups in the policy process modified the political power distribution. The advent of a new governor, the changing of the administrative structure as recommended by the McKinsey Report, coupled with the changing contextual factors modified the governing principles of the state. All these contributed to the path, format and timing of welfare state development in the 1970s. In the following paragraphs, different theoretical explanations will be critically examined.

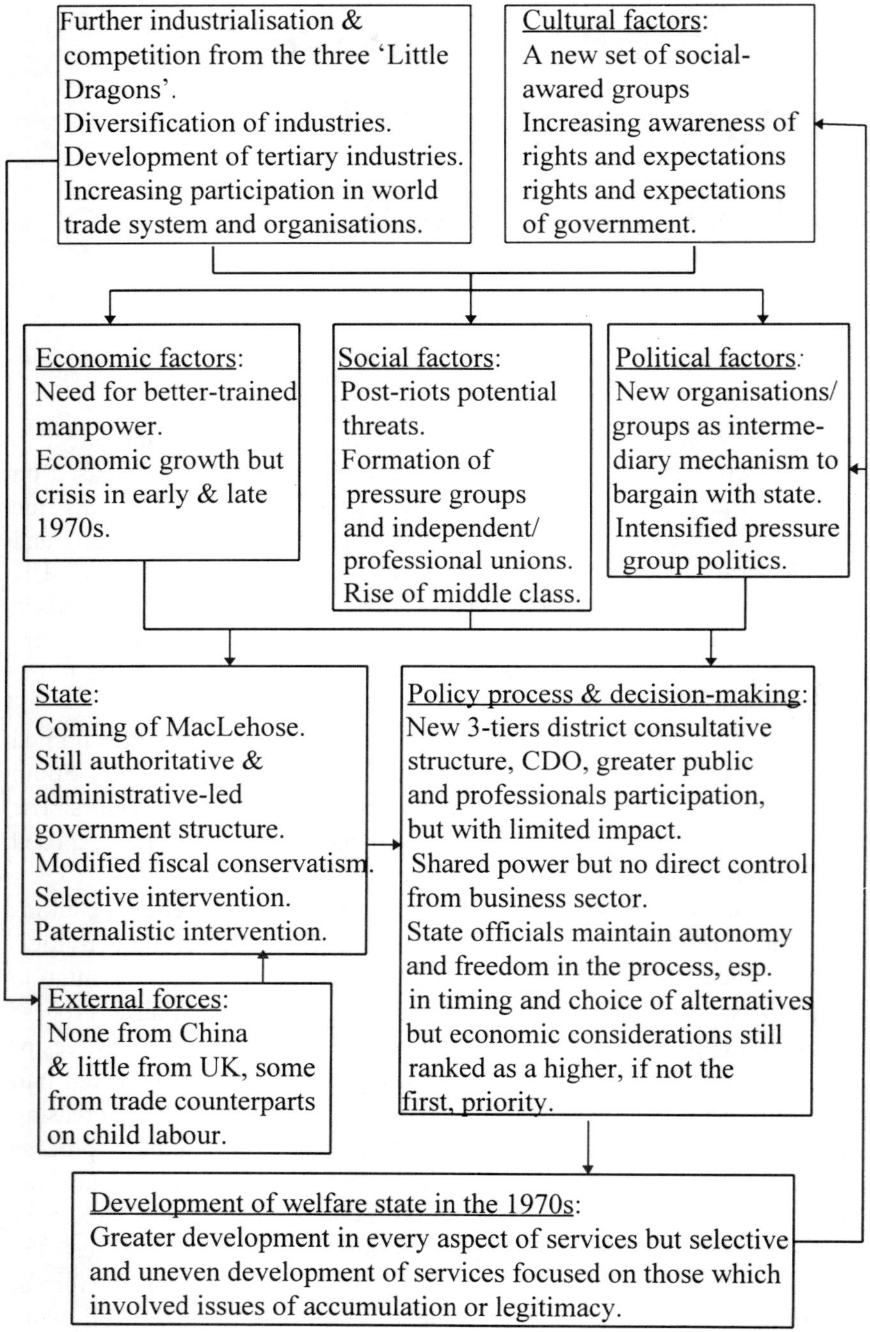

Figure 9.1 General model of theory of the welfare state, 1970s

Assessment of the socio-economic explanation

The previous discussion shows that economic factors played their part in pushing as well as pulling the development of the programme. Generally speaking, there was a positive correlation between the overall economic situation and social services expenditure. When the economy flourished, the expenditure increased and vice versa. Moreover, the growth of social services, such as housing and education, were meeting the changing needs of the economy. Yet, the relationship was by no means, straight forward. We notice that there was variation among the impacts of the economy on individual services. So in between the economy-expenditure relationship, there were intervening factors.

World system theory can also partially explain the development. However, the relationship can not be simply explained, for example, by referring to the co-existence of the merging in the world economy and the growth of education services. The detailed examination of this policy case has revealed that it was probably the increasing 'concern' about local labour conditions, especially child labour, from close trading partners, together with 'concern' from the sovereign state, which formed one of the factors leading to the adoption of the education policy. The government was faced with an embarrassing situation and to release Hong Kong, and probably the officials, from this embarrassment and criticism from overseas and UK, the policy was adopted. Although MacLehose denied that there was any significant pressure from the UK government and the OECD countries,[1] such factors were referred to by several interviewees and perhaps, these differences related to the interpretation of the extent of their influence.

The changes in social structure were also considered by the government in planning social welfare services for families, youth and the elderly. Families had faced changes resulting from industrialisation in the 1960s and had lost part of their functions. This resulted in increasing youth problems. Therefore, family services had to be strengthened to enable the family to function better (a typically traditional belief in the role of informal sector), and youth social work services, including school and outreach social work, were provided.

The growth of the economy also greatly improved the living standards of the Hong Kong people. It was natural that in the 1970s, there were increasing expectations of the government to provide better quality services. At the same time, the locally-born generation had emerged as a distinctive group. The culture and mentality of this group deviated from the traditional ethos. They urged greater state intervention in various social issues and in services provision. The 'refugee mentality' and 'boundary politics' were contested by this new reformist orientation. However, it was not these changing beliefs that directly contributed to the growth in services. Similar to the case of the economic factors, this presence was transmitted through an intermediary factor, politics, to the policy process and the state agenda.

Assessment of the political explanation

In the 1970s, different pressure groups had been formed over various social issues. Housing issues gained the widest public participation. These pressure groups argued with the government (and HA) for alternatives to the government's proposals, and urged it to make concessions and improvements in the operation of the policies, to improve the estates' environment, to admit to the unacceptable standard of the resettlement estates and demonstrate the intention of providing a better living environment. Comparatively speaking, there was less concern over education and the health services where most of discussion was left to the involved professionals.

It is easy to establish a relationship between these social movements and increasing participation from the 'public' in the policy process by formal and informal means and the growth of the welfare state, but it is rather difficult to measure the extent of their influence or their actual achievements. Due to their limited membership and resources, and their ad hoc structure, the pressure groups' influence was restricted to certain specific issues and areas, it did not affect the overall policy direction. The increased social action in the 1970s was still far from being a massive social democratic movement aiming at taking power and changing the government's policy direction. Instead, it was a watchdog to monitor policy and suggested the agendas and alternatives to the government using a confrontational strategy. Social pressure, from these grassroots sources and the pressure groups, did have some influence on government policies but they were never powerful enough to have overall control of the process, the structure and the policy output.[2]

Compared with this grassroots mobilisation, the medical professionals in medical policy planning, educationalists in education policy planning, social workers in preparation of the Five Year Plan and policy papers, all had more participation and opportunities for influencing the agenda and had greater direct contact with the officials.

Comparatively speaking, the traditionally strongest group in the formal structure, the businessmen, large corporations and their associates still occupied a significant share of seats in these formal bodies. Davies's study of the composition of the various committees and Councils has clearly indicated this (1977). They were, probably, the most successful 'pressure group' functioning in Hong Kong in the 1970s. Yet such a significant share of seats still could not guarantee that their suggestions would be accepted by government. This could be partly explained by the limited constitutional power of LegCo and partly by lack of strong follow-up pressure on the state. At the same time, the expanded welfare programme also served the key interest of the business sector and this group was in support of the programmes. Though in the mid-1970s, facing the economic crisis, the government had to impose an additional profit tax on the companies, the welfare programmes received little objection from them.[3]

Anyway, there were no great differences between the interest groups, grassroots pressure groups and professional unions, and the government on the overall policy direction. All these parties had a consensus (though based on different rationales) on the need to improve services, with better education and increased subsidised housing. The support for nine years education did not only come from the education sector but also from the business sector.

For example, Lightbody suggested that while there were some demands from the pressure groups, there had been no major arguments about the provision of public housing just many minor disagreements concerning the implementation of the policies. He argued that there was 'universal approval' for the housing building programme and so did the pressure groups.[4] While the traditional business sector largely maintained its power, and there was increasing participation from the professionals, the grassroots pressure groups, none of them could control the government's agenda completely, so, as before, it could maintain its own initiative and final power over policies making. There was no drastic shift of power from the business sector, the professionals and the officials to the grassroots pressure groups though, certainly, the public pressure became one of the contextual factors that the officials and the elite could not neglect in forming their course of action.

Assessment of the state-centered explanation

The state's power was based on several factors, including the constitutional arrangements, the possession of professional and expert knowledge, and success in managing the economy. One of the strategies of the government was to 'administer without politicising' the society and social issues. State decisions, it was argued, were based on the comprehensive, rational and technical considerations of various factors and the policy was impartial with respect to every sectoral interest.

However, the state's action was not free from external influences. The social, economic and political factors created an objective policy context, and needs and demands that the state had to deal with. The state could not neglect matters, such as the housing needs of the lower and middle classes and the need for better-trained manpower, in pursuance of their own course of action. If the state failed to meet such needs and demands, it might risk its own existence.

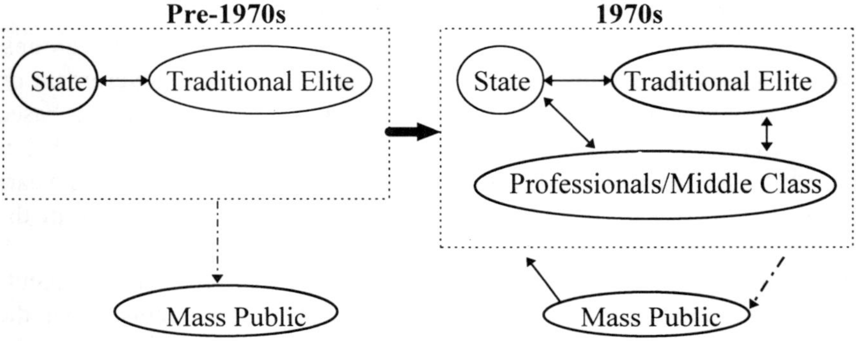

Explanations: -·-·-·-·-→ reaction to demands according to their own perceptions
←——→ direct interest negotiation
——→ assertion of demands

Figure 9.2 Power relationship of the state and society, pre-1970s and 1970s

The government's need for legitimation and accumulation put the state in a position where it had to consider the needs and demands of the other parties. For the business sector, the government gained legitimation by successfully clearing land for development and infrastructural provisions, by socialising production costs by the provision of various social services and the provision of a stable, secure and facilitative environment for investment, and doing all this within the capacity of the economy and the public finances. For the public, the government gained legitimation by providing them with cheap and affordable services which improved their living standards. In turn, the programmes did generate a social stabilisation effect.

Such a need for legitimation was more imminent in the 1970s, after the riots in 1966 and 1967. In this context, the government had a special concern to expand and consolidate its acceptance, or at least to prevent its rejection, by the ruled. Hence, when there was a crisis, with or without support from other groups, the government was ready to intervene in a more active manner.

It was the success of achieving these two tasks which enabled the state to gain great autonomy in planning policies which followed own governing principle and its interpretation of the context. Although the governing principle was still fiscal conservatism and Haddon-Cave still repeatedly argued for 'positive non-interventionism', in many cases the government deviated from this. The government was willing to intervene if it considered that it was necessary to do so on pragmatic and utilitarian grounds and if resources allowed.

The 'resources consideration' was a key constraint on government action. MacLehose stated that,

> These are bold plans for the future. But to succeed they must be linked to the economic prosperity of Hong Kong that has provided the resources for all that has been done in the past and must provide for everything in the future. Continued economic growth is one of the prerequisites for the well-being of the community (HKAR, 1973, p.8).

Basically, to maintain a budget surplus was not only a strategy but a dogma of the Finance Branch.[5] However, as shown by figures for the overall revenue and the social services expenditure, while the government would slow down expansion when facing a decrease of income due to economic recession, the growth of social services expenditure and public expenditure continued.[6] The resources consideration was only one of the conditions that can be traded-off by some other factors.

Developments could also be explained by the personal interests of individual officials apart from those of the 'abstract' state. The most popular argument referred to the personal charisma and attitude of MacLehose. Scott argues that 'it is unlikely that social policy outputs would have expanded so quickly if MacLehose had not directly and personally accelerated the delivery of such services and harried the bureaucracy into the achieving specific targets' (1989, p.165). To certain extent, it is valid to argue that the persistence of MacLehose had the effect of pushing forward reforms which might otherwise, have been implemented at a slower pace, and counteracted the conservative orientation within the bureaucracy. The disagreement between the Governor and senior officers was quite clear over the areas such as the TYHCP (ibid, ch.4).[7] MacLehose's personal concern for the housing programme gave it a high position, if not the highest, on the government's agenda. It was he who 'pushed' the officials to prepare the plans, as well as the NYFCEP, in a great hurry.[8] According to Topley, it was the firm stand of the Governor and the availability of resources that made the decision to have the NYFCEP implemented one year earlier successfully go through the bureaucratic structure and the Finance Branch without much discussion or consultation within the government, the Councils and the public.[9]

Scott has commented that the achievement of MacLehose was to modify 'the extreme conservative fiscal policies of the 1950s and 1960s, which had failed to deliver those goods and services in the quantity which the population demanded' and 'purse-strings were loosened but prudent housekeeping remained a central tenet of administration' (ibid, p.128). When, in times of economic prosperity, and the resources allowed this, those projects which received great support from the Governor easily got through without much debate. Of course, MacLehose's personal support could not completely override the financial constraints on the government particularly during the economic recession, in which fiscal conservatism was strongly defended by the FS and shared by the officials in-charge of the housing programme.

Apart from MacLehose himself, other officials also played a part in the policy process. Within the government, the policy had to go through debate and planning by various Branches and Departments. Of course, their personal judgements, and orientations had an impact on the planning of the policy. But the technical constraints imposed by resource availability and their reactions to the public demands, were more significant in influencing their decisions.

For example, the technical considerations concerning land, infrastructural development and financial resources had impacts on the housing programme. Several interviewees stressed the limitation of land availability on the development of the public housing programme. When the majority of the land was located in the new towns, such as Shatin and Tuen Mun, a longer time to develop the infrastructure was required before the building could actually start.[10] Concerning the NYFCEP, there was no significant division among the officials on the principle of the policy but only on the schedule and timing. Technical considerations related to the availability of adequate subsidised school places for all at acceptable standards, instead of providing these in a substandard private schools through the bought places scheme.

Conclusion

The above discussion shows that no single factor can explain the adoption and implementation of the welfare policies of the 1970s. Various background factors formed a context in which various problems and needs emerged, and demands were made. These demands were formulated and argued for by different interest groups within the policy process, either through the formal structure or through 'street politics'. Within the policy process, various interests were represented by social activists, the business sector and the officials interacted.

Having a strong social movement was not a sufficient condition for the success of any demand though certainly this was one of the factors that the state had to consider. Rather, the orientation and position of those who held the decision-making power were more important. The rationale for the overall policy direction, expansion, improvement and further development, can be understood through an analysis of the macro socio-economic context but the choice of action, detailed planning, schedule and implementation were better explained by focusing on the state and its response to the external pressures. As there were few disagreements over the overall policy direction and the state's great degree of control over the process of planning and implementation, it enjoyed high autonomy in the course. The state autonomy lay within the broad category of 'Type III autonomy' that Nordlinger proposed 'in which state-society preferences are non-divergent and the state acts upon its preferences' (1981, p.29; ch.3). In this condition, 'public officials invariably translate their own preferences into authoritative actions, and there preferences have at least as much explanatory importance as societal preferences' (ibid, p.80).

Notes

1 From a questionnaire completed by Lord MacLehose.
2 This view was shared by Sir David Akers-Jones, Mr Bernard Williams and Sir Ian Lightbody in the interviews with them concerning housing policy and by Mrs Catherine Symons on education policy. However, Rev Mary Bennett held a different opinion. She was more positive about the influence of pressure groups on government policy.
3 In 1975/76, there was a 1.5 per cent additional profit tax imposed and in the next fiscal year, the rate was further increased for another 2 per cent until 1980/81 fiscal year. See Tang, 1992, Table 2.4.
4 From a personal interview.

5 Except for the financial year 1974/75, the government maintained a surplus in every financial year and accumulated considerable reserves by the end of the 1980/81 financial year. See Table 7.2.

6 One of the reasons was probably the tree-branch effect in which once you start a programme, you have to maintain it on a scale comparable to the previous year. In fact, it was rather difficult for the government to cut programmes but instead, the most viable alternative was to slow down the growth of expenditure.

7 This verifies the claim that the 'abstract' state can has internal interests/ideas conflict and reminds us not to treat the state as a monolith.

8 This impression was formed, supported and agreed to in interviews with Lightbody and Williams.

9 From a personal interview.

10 Sir David Akers-Jones, Mr Bernard Williams and Sir Ian Lightbody expressed the same opinion in their interviews.

Part Four
DEVELOPMENT OF THE WELFARE STATE, 1982-1992

10 The context: 1982 to 1992

In previous chapter, the development of the welfare state was perceived as a dependent variable of the contextual factors, the state and the policy process. In the 1980s, all these contextual factors were undergoing rapid change and there were changes in the power distribution and, subsequently, in the formal structure and the power of the state. Following the MacLehose's visit to Beijing in 1979; with the coming of a new Governor, Sir Edward Youde in 1982 and the visit of Margaret Thatcher in the same year to Beijing, negotiations between Britain and China on the future of Hong Kong formally started. This was another watershed in Hong Kong's history and far more significant, of course, than the 1966-67 Riots in having comprehensive and far-reaching impacts on Hong Kong's society, economy and politics.

Economic context

The '1997' issue had engendered a crisis in the local economy whose performance was closely tied to the progress of the negotiations and the subsequent transitional arrangements. To the mid-1980s, many companies and capital withdrew from Hong Kong due to uncertainties over its future and a lack of confidence in the Communist Party and the Chinese government. Although the future of Hong Kong was settled after the signing of the Joint Declaration in 1986, some businesses which still had doubts proceeded with their withdrawal from Hong Kong.[1] This withdrawal of old British capital and corporations from Hong Kong made way for the local Chinese capital and enterprises from China whose influence grew.[2] The uncertainty intensified economic problems in the early 1980s. Affected by the world recession also, Hong Kong underwent several years of recession until the mid-1980s.

The government suffered from unprecedented successive budget deficits from 1982/83 to 1984/85, so, the growth of public expenditure at that time was restricted to a modest level.[3] Moreover, as required in the Joint Declaration, the government had to put half of its land sales revenue into the Land Fund as a reserve for the future SAR government. As land sales were one of the major sources of revenue, this limited the disposable resources of the government.

Table 10.1
Surplus/deficit for the budget and accumulated fiscal reserve 1982/83 to 1991/92 (HK$m)

Financial year	Actual deficit/surplus of consolidated account[a]	Accumulated fiscal reserve[b]	Accumulated reserve balance[c]
1982/83	37	19,071	--
1983/84	(2,123)	16,077	--
1984/85	2,901	15,518	--
1985/86	4,506	16,961	--
1986/87	670	20,003	32,950
1987/88	7,240	32,522	45,450
1988/89	7,860	--	61,510
1989/90	480	--	72,580
1990/91	(5,680)	--	76,540
1991/92	6,280	--	99,050

Notes:

a. Expenditure includes General Revenue Account, Capital Works Reserve Fund, Development Loan Fund, Home Ownership Fund, Lotteries Fund, Student Loan Fund, HA and UC accounts and expenditure on public works funded from the Asian Development Bank. For data of 1988/89 onwards, revenues exclude the income of HA, UC & RC and expenditure exclude the Funds (except Lotteries Fund) and project funded by Asian Development Bank.
b. Include accumulated balance in General Revenue Account only.
c. Include the General Revenue Account and the Funds Accounts (Capital Works Reserve Fund, Loan Fund and Capital Investment Fund).

Sources: HKAR, various years
CSD, 1989, Table 11.1; 1991, Table 11.1 & 1993, Table 11.1

Nevertheless, the potential of the Chinese market and the even worse economic conditions in many other countries induced some companies and migrants back to Hong Kong. China's open door policy allowed more of its corporations and capital to invest in Hong Kong. With the tremendous development of trade opportunities in China, the growing export from China through Hong Kong to overseas, and the supply of cheap means of production from China,[4] the economy of Hong Kong settled down and it achieved a better growth rate in the late 1980s and early 1990s.[5]

Table 10.2
Growth of GDP, 1982 - 1992 (1980 market price)

Year	GDP (HK$m)	Change (+/-%)
1982	153,560	2.7
1983	163,260	6.3
1984	179,238	9.8
1985	179,580	0.2
1986	199,498	11.1
1987	228,483	14.5
1988	247,415	8.3
1989	254,434	2.8
1990	262,189	3.0
1991	273,434	3.9
1992	288,053	5.4

Sources: Mok, 1993, Table 2.3
HKAR, 1994, p.400

With a prosperous economy but with an uncertain future and an unexpected economic and fiscal crisis, the government had to be more careful in managing the budget. Though it had a large fiscal reserve, the government was more cautious in spending money, setting priorities and was very eager to gain cost-efficiency.

Another significant change within this period was the continuing restructuring of industries and labour market. The tertiary and services sector continued to grow at the expense of the manufacturing sector. The changing needs for manpower and the problems of unemployment resulting from this had to be catered for.

Table 10.3
Employment in selected industry sectors, 1982-1992 (in thousands)

Year	Manufacturing	Wholesales, retail, import/export, hotel & restaurant	Financing, insurance, real estate & business services
1982	847.2	517.7	166.1
1983	855.4	532.0	161.7
1984	898.9	573.8	169.5
1985	847.6	600.4	180.9
1986	865.6	620.1	194.3
1987	867.9	657.9	212.2
1988	837.1	711.3	235.5
1989	791.5	774.0	254.8
1990	715.6	829.6	276.6
1991	654.7	880.2	289.1
1992	571.2	906.9	307.5
(+/-%)	- 32.6	+ 75.2	+ 85.1

* All figures except 1991 and 1992 (September of the year) are refer to the 4th quarter of each year.

Sources: CSD, 1987, Table 2.4; 1991, Table 2.4
HKAR, 1994, Appendix 18

Social context

'1997' also destabilised the sense of belongingness of the people of Hong Kong. The future uncertainties re-created the 'refugee mentality', but this time for the locally born generation. The most pressing problem was migration, especially among the highly educated, professionals and wealthy people, to other countries. Hong Kong had a continuous history of migration since the Second World War and in crisis situations, such as in the riots in the late 1960s, the trend would be intensified suddenly. In the 1980s, the figures were kept at approximately 20,000 per year. But when the negotiations over Hong Kong's future started, the trend intensified and reached about 30,000 per year. The trend accelerated after the June 4th

Incident in 1989 and continued for several years. In the year of 1990, the outflow reached a peak of 62,000 (Wong, 1992, p.918).

This alerted the government and policies were introduced to encourage those people who had higher potential to migrate not to do so and these policies also aimed at alleviating the problems brought about by the migration of this group of people. Massive investment in infrastructural projects[6] occurred to increase the confidence of people about Hong Kong's future. The British Nationality Selection Scheme was another strategy to keep this group of people in Hong Kong.[7] Another measure was to expand the higher education sector on an unprecedented scale from 1990 in order to replace those who had migrated to other countries.[8]

The further changes in employment and the growing affluence added to the number of the middle class. This middle class also became a pillar of the social and political movements of the 1980s. In terms of participation and attitudes towards the current system, they had two rather contrasting attitudes. The first type was a rather positive, participatory and progressive attitude. This section formed various political groups and actively pushed for various reforms. They were the backbone of the 'democracy camp' (Cheung et al, 1988). The second attitude was rather negative, withdrawn and conservative. This group of people might choose to emigrate to other countries or urged for the maintenance of the existing social, economic and political systems in order to minimise the instability arising from the transition to 1997. No matter which orientation they had, either pushing for changes or maintaining the status quo, this social class was a new and one of the significant forces in the policy process. They were the people that different political groups and government to appeal to and their interests had to be protected.

Apart from this social change, the population structure also changed with more and more elderly people. The increasing number of the elderly not only increased the pressure on existing services but also created new problems of caring for them after they retired from work.

Cultural context

Continued the cultural change in the 1970s, it seemed that the social consciousness and expectations of the government was further increased. The government faced with increasing demands from the public who were more aware of their rights and more articulate and skillful in expressing their arguments and demands. Of course, the mass media and the political groups also played a significant part in formulating and presenting these demands and monitoring the policy of the government.

Table 10.4
Growth of population aged 65 and above, 1982-1992 (in thousands)

Year	Population ≥ 65 (mid-year estimation)	% of ≥ 65 of total population	Dependency ratio (per ,000)
1982	359	6.8	99
1983	375	7.0	102
1984	390	7.2	105
1985	406	7.4	108
1986	425	7.7	111
1987	447	8.0	114
1988	469	8.3	116
1989	470	8.3	119
1990	483	8.5	122
1991	501	8.7	124
1992	520	8.9	127
Increase	44.8%	30.9%	28.3%

Sources: CSD, 1989, Table1.3; 1991, Table 1.8, 1992b, Table 2.10; 1993, Table 1.5

In 1986, Lau and Kuan researched perceptions of the function of the government. They found that the majority of respondents were very clear about the government's role in social provision, such as alleviating unemployment, providing housing and resolving social problems (Lau & Kuan, 1988, p.89) (Table 10.5).

In social indicator research conducted in 1988, Lau et al also discovered a similar situation (Table 10.6). This shows that the public had increasing expectations regarding the functions of the government and its role in the various social services. That was clearly different from the construct of the 'minimally integrated socio-political system' of the socio-political and cultural system in the 1970s.

Table 10.5
Perception of the functions of government (percentage)

Statement	Very much agree	Agree	Dis-agree	Very much disagree	Don't know/no answer
Government is primarily responsible for resolving social problems.	9.0	80.2	6.0	0	4.8
Government should find a job for everyone, so that no one will be unemployed.	9.0	67.3	18.6	1.0	4.0
Government should provide a place to live for all the people of HK.	17.9	75.1	4.8	0.5	1.7

Source: Lau & Kuan, 1988, Table 3.9

Table 10.6
Perceived functions of government (percentage)

Statement	Strongly disagree	Disagree	Agree	Strongly agree	Don't know
Provide social service even at the expense of economic growth.	0	19.7	67.7	3.8	8.8
Set up a central provident fund run by the government.	0	7.6	71.5	8.8	12.1
Impose heavier tax on the rich to reduce income inequality.	0.3	15.9	57.8	16.9	9.1
Provide unemployment relief for the unemployed.	0.5	18.2	64.6	9.6	7.1

Source: Lau et al (eds), 1991, Table 8.13

However, there were also some differences between different sectors of society, as in the 1970s. The 1988 research on social indicators showed that there were different value beliefs across different age groups and different educational levels. In asking about their satisfaction with the present political situation,[9] those younger people and those with a higher educational status were comparatively less satisfied (Table 10.7). In this research, respondents were also asked for their comments on the statement of 'Hong Kong's political system is the best under existing circumstances' and there were also similar findings (Table 10.8). It was clear that the younger and the better-educated people were more inclined to disagree with the existing political system. They were also less satisfied with the performance of the government and had a lower level of trust in it (Lau et al, 1991, pp.186-187; p.199). Moreover, they had an increasing interest in politics and a higher propensity to participate in political action (ibid, pp.195-197).

Perhaps the overwhelming belief in the 1980s was to be found in the slogan of 'prosperity and stability'. There was a general consensus over the belief that Hong Kong's prosperity depended heavily on its stability and these two beliefs were also essential to maintain its status after the unification with China. These were the guiding principles of political discourse in Hong Kong and these two beliefs were prioritised above all other values and, even, that of democracy on certain occasions.[10] So pro-democratic groups were often attacked for their urge for wider democracy which would 'rock the boat'.[11]

Political context

In the 1980s, we can also observe the increasing participation of the public, through various channels, in the policy process and in changes in the formal structure. These changes were stimulated by the increasing pressure for participation, the issues of '1997', and the government's preparation for withdrawal.

The promise of 'Hong Kong ruled by Hong Kongese' after 1997 stimulated much enthusiasm from the activists, most of them middle class. Different 'policy discussion groups'[12] were formed from the early 1980s. In the mid-1980s, these small groups formed coalitions and they were the foundation stones for the Democratic Party.[13] The formerly fragmented non-associational groups and pressure groups formed larger alliances and became unified. The traditional elites, appointed members of the Councils and the committees, and the business sectors[14] also organised themselves to fight for influence over policy making.

Table 10.7
Degree of satisfaction with political situation in 1988 (percentage)

	Dissatisfied	Average	Satisfied	Don't know	(N)
Total	17.7	25.8	26.3	30.2	(1662)
Age					
below 30	27.8	34.6	20.8	16.8	(457)
30-54	15.7	23.9	28.1	32.3	(898)
over 54	8.9	18.1	28.9	44.1	(304)
Education level					
low	9.7	18.2	26.4	45.8	(660)
middle	21.2	29.6	27.3	22.0	(822)
high	31.4	36.7	21.9	10.1	(169)

Source: Lau et al (eds), 1991, Table 8.1

Table 10.8
Agreement with 'Hong Kong's political system is the best under existing circumstances'

	Disagreed	Agreed	Don't know	(N)
Total	21.7	70.5	7.8	(396)
Age				
below 30	35.3	61.8	2.9	(102)
30-54	19.4	73.0	7.6	(211)
over 54	11.1	75.3	13.6	(81)
Educational level				
low	12.4	75.1	12.4	(169)
middle	26.5	70.3	3.2	(185)
high	35.9	53.8	10.3	(39)

Source: Lau et al (eds), 1991, Table 8.8

The need to restructure the policy process and the consultative and representative structure of the state was also due to the preparations for the post-1997 administration and the recognition of the inadequacy of the current system. The British and the Hong Kong governments recognised the need to develop an experienced group of people who could run Hong Kong after 1997. It has been noted that it was Britain's usual practice to prepare for a democratic structure in its former colonies before its withdrawal and Hong Kong was just another such case. Some conspiracy theorists perceived the democratic reforms in the 1980s as a mean to counteract the China and pro-China's power.

The need to reform the structure was also due to the increasing inadequacy of the consultative system and 'government by consensus'. Throughout the 1980s, demands were made for wider dissemination of information and consultation as well as direct participation in the decision-making process, both at the district and central levels. The former CDO and UMELCO system were inadequate to accommodate such ever-increasing demands (Lau, 1981). In fact, Lau argued that this old system would only serve to arouse even stronger social movements,

> Administrative penetration in Hong Kong, while not going far enough, does have the 'negative' effect of bringing the government and the people closer to each other, thus further politicizing the latter. The presence of government representatives in the localities provides convenient targets for political demand-making. And the denial of discretionary power to local representatives will very easily transform local issues into global political disputes. (ibid, p.884).

In turn, the opening up of the formal structure had the effect of further intensifying the formation of political parties and demands for more participation.

In fact, the government changed its attitude towards the non-associational pressure groups. In a confidential SCOPG report published in 1979, just one year after its establishment, it said, 'pressure groups may well bring about desirable changes in the community, provided they work within the law' (FEER, 17/3/83). In 1980, the Home Affairs Branch also suggested that,

> At times, it is possible to divert some of the group's effort into more useful channels by bringing active members into contact with or even directly on existing boards and committees. This brings the individual and the group into the established systems, helps them to obtain a more

balanced picture of the Government and its policies and can remove them from extremist influence. (1980, p.10)

The strategy was from exclusion and rejection to one of inclusion in the formal structure though still mixed with a suspicious feeling.

The newly formed groups had different opinions and orientations. Their divisions were not concerned with social policies, but were also based on two additional issues. Firstly, the reaction to China, 1997, the Basic Law and the June 4th Incidents and secondly, the attitude towards democratic reform. There were broadly speaking, two different set of attitudes in the 1980s. The first type of response to China was deep fear and distrust towards the Communist government and Party. These groups also insisted on condemning the June 4th Incidents and supporting the pro-democratic movement in China. This group included the United Democrats of Hong Kong (UDHK), Hong Kong Alliance for Patriotic Support of the Democratic Movement in China[15] and Hong Kong Association for Democracy and People's Livelihood (HKADPL).[16] They were also actively involved in pushing for democratic reforms in Hong Kong.

The second group's attitude towards China and 1997 was that of welcome and support. They agreed that the crackdown on June 4th was necessary. They were also highly suspicious of the pace of democratic reform but they still participated in elections for fear of losing an advantageous position in the post-1997 government. Examples were the FTU, Heung Yee Kuk, Democratic Alliance for the Betterment of Hong Kong (DAB), Cooperative Resource Society (CRC) and Association for Stabilising Hong Kong.

The rise of the pro-China Left groups was largely due to the fact that China would take over the city in 1997. It was obvious that these pro-China groups would enjoy better positions immediately and after 1997 but they were not very popular among the voters in the elections.[17] The NCNA had gradually become another source of power in Hong Kong, frequently expressing its opinions on government policies. For the trade unions, the FTU became more active in community affairs, labour disputes and elections. Comparatively speaking, the pro-Taiwan TUC further declined in the 1980s. This was partly due to the aging of its leadership and the retreat of Taiwan from Hong Kong affairs.[18] The professional unions still played an active role in respective policy areas. Most of these groups were chaired and led by the 'middle class', professionals and business elites (for the business groups) (Tam, 1989, Cheung et al, 1988).

These different groups did not necessarily take a totally different approach to social policy. The Left and the pro-democracy camps shared a general consensus over the positive role of social services and argued for a better system. The business sector was more cautious about investment in social services. However, they all agreed over the supremacy of the market economy and that social services expenditure must not ruin the prosperity. However, the earlier mentioned divisions and the electoral competition did prevented them forming an united front to bargain with the state.

To accommodate the increasing demands for participation and involvement in the policy process, changes were enacted in the formal structure. The three-tiers district consultative system gradually gave way to a new three-tiers council system. The CDC was abolished while MAC and AC were retained but their significance was gradually reduced by a new DB. In 1981, the government had published a White Paper on District Administration in Hong Kong. This proposed the creation of a Board, with elected members who would be responsible for advising government on policies and vested with certain powers to manage district affairs.[19] In 1982, DBs were formed in 18 districts throughout Hong Kong.[20] In 1982-1985, DBs consisted of ex-officio and officials members, appointed unofficials and elected members.[21]

Table 10.9
Expansion of elected memberships in DBs, UC and RC

Year	District Boards	Urban Council	Regional Council
1982	132(489[a])		
1983		15(30)	
1985	237(369[a])		
1986		15(30)	21[c](36)
1988	264(432[a])		
1989		25[b](40)	21[c](36)
1991	274(441[a])	25[b](40)	21[c](36)

Notes:

a. Figures include 27 ex-officio members from the Rural Committees in New Territories.
b. Figures include 10 indirect elected members by the 10 DBs within the UC's geographical boundary.
c. Figures include 9 indirect elected members by the 9 DBs within the RC's geographical boundary.
d. Figures in brackets represent the total number of seats.

Sources: Association for a Better Hong Kong, 1991; Louie & Sham, 1995

In 1984, the Hong Kong government published the White Paper on the Development of Representative Government in Hong Kong, and promised to ‘develop a progressive system of government, the authority for which is able to represent authoritatively the views of the people of Hong Kong’ (HKG, 1984b, p.8). For the DB, this involved the expansion of elected members at the expense of both official and appointed members. From 1985, the official members only attended meeting and had no voting power and the elected members had a majority of approximately two-thirds in the Board.[22] In 1992, Patten suggested that all members of DBs should be directly elected by the voters.[23]

The middle tier was formed by the UC[24] and Regional Council (RC). The RC was made responsible for the management of sanitation, hygiene, hawkers and markets, and recreational facilities in the New Territories and was set up in 1985. Both councils were served by appointed and elected members with a majority of the latter.[25] Disregarding the limited domain of the Councils, these councillors were always using their status to comment on other government policies.

The top tier of the system was the LegCo. Here the trend was for an increase of elected members at the expense of official and appointed members.[26] Following the suggestion in the 1984 White Paper, there were 24 elected members, 12 from functional constituencies, 10 from an electoral college formed by DB members and 2 from an electoral college formed by the UC and RC. With the ex-officio and appointed members the total number of was set at 57, the number of official members had dropped from 19 in 1983, to 11 in 1985 and in 1991, further decreased to 3.

The government unilaterally designated certain occupational sectors as significant to Hong Kong and therefore, these could have seat(s) in LegCo to represent their interests. This was a form of corporatism. As most of the functional constituencies were based on the business and commercial sectors, it was clear that this system would give legitimate power, through election, to these groups in the government structure, while previously it had been exercised through informal channels and by appointment. The other constituencies mainly involved professionals, such as doctors, health professions, teachers and social workers, which were the rising social groups from the 1970s plus two representatives from the labour constituency (Table 10.11). These arrangements reflected the relative power of these sectors and also the government’s dependency on their support and co-operation when it was facing increasing attack and interference from China and the newly formed political groups, such as UDHK, in Hong Kong from the mid-1980s (Scott, 1989, ch.7).

Table 10.10
Composition of the Legislative Council, 1980-1992

Year	Official (incl. president)	Appointed unofficial	Indirect elected[b]	Direct elected	Total
1980	23(27)[a]	26(27)[a]	-	-	49(54)[a]
1983	19(29)[a]	29(29)[a]	-	-	48(58)[a]
1985	11	22	24	-	57
1988	11	20	26	-	57
1991	3	18	21[c]	18	60

Notes:

a. Figures in brackets show the maximum possible membership when this differs from the actual membership.

b. Figures include functional constituencies and electoral colleges.

c. The seats from the DB electoral college were abolished but the UC & RC's seats were retained as part of the functional constituency election.

Sources: Miners, 1989, Table 7 & p.124; HKAR, 1989 & 1991

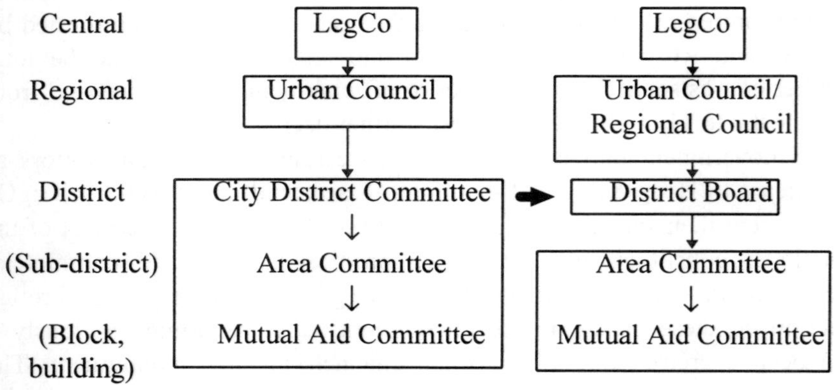

Figure 10.1 New three-tiers system in the 1980s

Within the Councils and DBs, 'party' (group) formation among the members was increasingly common. The desire to form groupings was increased by the need to secure success in elections as well as to seek allies within the Council. Party politics firstly appeared in the DB election in 1988 and were further consolidated in the 1991 LegCo direct election.

Table 10.11
Changes of designated functional constituencies in LegCo

Functional Constituencies	LegCo Session 1985-88	1988-91	1991-95
Business	Commercial (2) Industrial (2) Financial (bank) (1)	Accountancy (1) Health care (1)	Tourism (1) Real estate & construction (1) Financial service (1)
Sub-total	(5)	(7)	(10)
Professionals	Social services (1) Medical (1) Teaching (1) Legal (1) Engineering, architecture, surveying & planning (1)		Engineering (1) renamed as Architecture, surveying & town planning (1)
Sub-total	(5)	(5)	(6)
Unions	Labour (2)		
Sub-total	(2)	(2)	(2)
Others			UC (1); RC (1); Rural (1)
Sub-total			(3)
Total	12	14	21

* Data for 1988-91 & 91-95 indicate the constituencies added to the lists.

Source: *Louie & Sham, 1995*

The direct election in 1991 for LegCo led to the creation of the two largest political groupings, the UDHK, and the CRC.[27] CRC is formed by several appointed and elected members, most of them with business background.

They became the second force in the Council. From then, the coordinated and harmonious relationships within the LegCo were replaced by party political divisions.[28] In view of these changes, the government also opened-up the membership of ExCo,[29] the HA and HoA and many other advisory committees.

Within the civil service, the dual centre of power formed by the Governor and the FS, gradually changed once Youde arrived in 1982. His appointment was primarily for the purpose of the negotiation over Hong Kong with China and as he was preoccupied with such affairs, he had less time for internal affairs. A suitable senior official, the Chief Secretary (CS), was given a greater share of these duties. Haddon-Cave served in the post from 1981 to 1984, Akers-Jones until 1986 and Sir David Ford from 1987 to early 1994. The CS became the chief of the entire civil service next in rank to the Governor. He had to defend government policies and argued over public demands. Although the power and role of the FS did not reduce rapidly, it gradually below that of the CS. The orientation of the CS therefore becomes another focal point for study in the thesis.

So the changes in the economic and social context led to structural changes and an altered distribution of power among the various groups. British capital interests had gradually declined and the space left was filled by local Chinese enterprises. The relative power shift was also reflected in the composition of the Councils. The harmonious relationship between business interests and the government was shaken, partly by the changing political structures and partly by the increasing influence of China.

Impacts from external forces: United Kingdom and China

Impacts from United Kingdom

It is rather difficult to verify or falsify any relationship between the UK government and domestic policies due to lack of data and documents. Certainly, we can find many similarities in welfare provisions and policies, such as the 'privatisation' of medical and housing system in the 1980s. Ever since the commencement of the negotiation over Hong Kong's future in 1982, there was increasing intervention from the UK in local affairs, but this was largely confined to the appointment of Governors, foreign affairs, Hong Kong's democratic reform, defence and the relationship with China. Such intervention did not aim to disable the Hong Kong government but instead to uphold its authority and maintain its efficiency, which were always the major concerns of the 1980s' Conservative governments. There was hardly any significant interference in local social policies.

So there are some similarities between the UK's recent experience of privatisation of social services and developments in Hong Kong. However, we cannot conclude that Hong Kong's recent changes are especially influenced by the British experience. For example, the consultant who recommended the setting up of HoA was from Australia.[30] The panel working on the comprehensive review of the education system was composed of experts not solely from Britain. While it might be incorrect to say that the UK had no influence on local policies, it is fairer to say that the Hong Kong government was increasingly exposed to international experiences and policy discourses, instead of solely relying on the UK's advice.

Impacts from China

China's influence in local politics was kept at a minimal level from after the 1967 riots until the early 1980s when the Left and pro-China groups started to participate again. They were actively involved in local affairs, participating and winning seats in the elections. They also had more involvement in welfare policies such as in debating the proposal for Central Provident Fund. The pro-Left private secondary schools also joined the Direct Subsidy Scheme and started to receive government grants.

The Left groups had their own representatives in all three tiers of the councils either by appointment or by election. Though it was a long-standing ideological belief of the Left to condemn capitalism and colonialism, these Left representatives did not advocate many radical reforms in welfare policies based on the dogmatic beliefs, as compared to their enthusiasm for criticising the Hong Kong government over the democratic reforms and the China-Hong Kong-Britain relationship.

Though the Chinese government increased its influence on Hong Kong affairs and steadily built up its own power circles by co-opting local elites,[31] it seldom intervened in welfare policies. The Basic Law stated that the existing structure of the welfare system would be maintained.[32] Obviously, they were more interested in other issues such as those had been tabled for discussion in the Sino-British Joint Liaison Group.

Generally speaking, the Chinese government, either itself or through its 'agents', had power to intervene and they did intervene in some areas. However, we can see little interference in local welfare policies and their impact on the overall development of welfare state was very limited. In fact, popular resentment of over-intervention before 1997 still had the effect of alerting the Left not to go beyond certain limits. Moreover, the fragile but smooth cooperative relationship between the Chinese and British governments during the governorship of Wilson prevented open confrontation with and intervention from China.[33] Generally speaking, the welfare agenda was not a top priority for the Chinese and British governments until 1992. However, China's intervention did begin to gradually extend to important social policy areas after 1992.[34]

Impacts on the policy making process

If we approach the issue from the formal basis of the Royal Instruction and Letters Patent, the statue for LegCo and the administrative rules of the bureaucrats, there was no significant change and it seemed that the government could still maintain its authority and its 'administrative-led' position as guaranteed in the constitutional structure. It was quite obvious that in the 1970s and first half of the 1980s, the government bureaucrats still enjoyed a high degree of autonomy (Gould, 1992). The 'administrative state' thesis proposed by Harris (1978) and Lau (1982, 1985) was applicable to the situation before the mid-1980s. As concluded by Scott,

> This was enhanced by the absence of pressure on the policy-making process from China and Britain; by the continuing weakness of organized groups (except for business groups); by a still largely unformed public opinion; and by a complaisant and generally uncritical Legislative Council. The Hong Kong government appeared to be purposive and in control. It was relatively autonomous -- and was permitted to be so by China and Britain and by business interests -- because it received credit for the success of the economy and because it was seen to be in command of the local situation (1986, p.459).

However, the situation did gradually change from the mid-1980s when the social, cultural and political context also changed and the state lost its dominant position. Then the government was frequently attacked and criticised by interest groups both inside and outside the formal political structure. There were more articulate and experienced 'political entrepreneurs' (the politicians) and more well-organised groups to serve as the new intermediary agents to articulate or even exaggerate the demands of the public. Further more, interference from China also seriously undermined the government's authority. For a period of time, the Hong Kong government was criticised as a 'lame-duck'.[35]

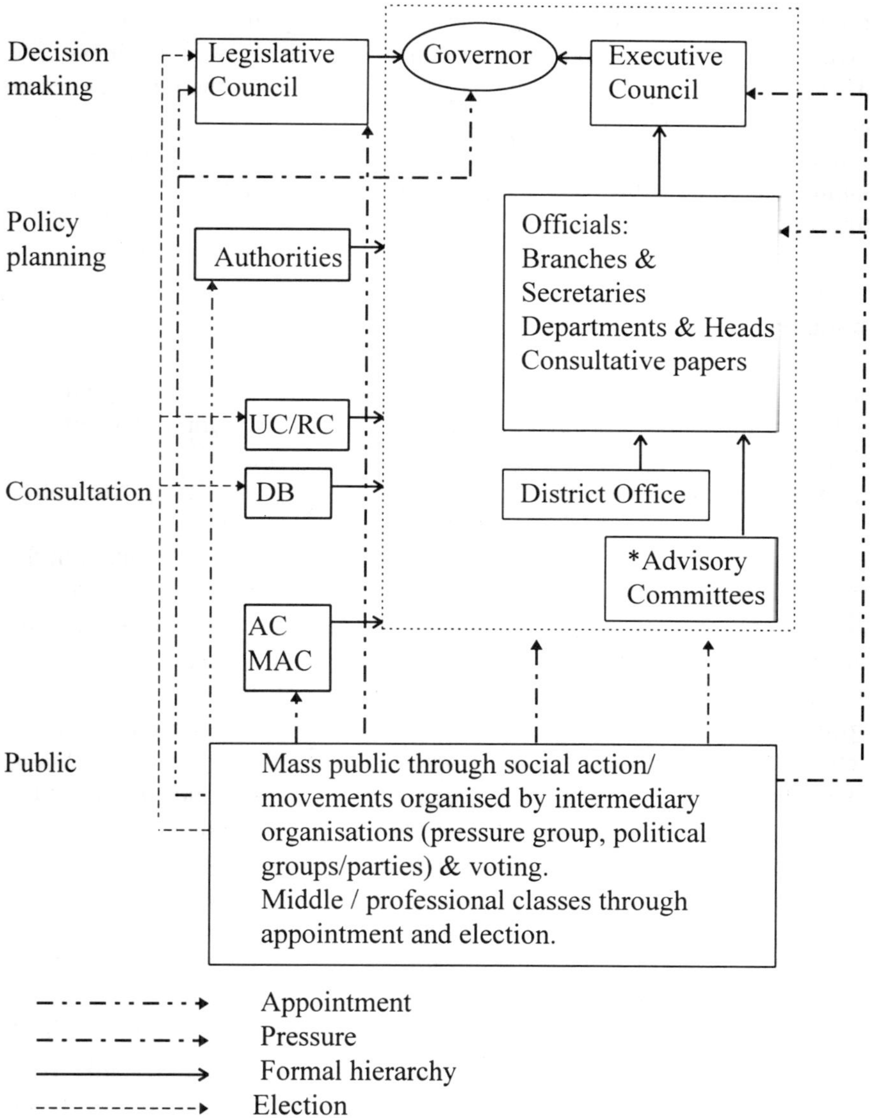

* Similar to those in the 1970s and in education, Education Commission replaced the Board of Education as the highest advisory body to the government.

Figure 10.2 Policy making process, 1980s

Obviously, the newly formed political groups, especially the pro-China groups and the so-called 'democracy' camp had gained increased power. Government had lost support from a considerable part of the business elite who were, previously, their prime target for co-option[36]. The business sector had organised itself to participate in politics directly. So the government, especially from the mid-1980s, lost its 'dominant' position in decision-making, in controlling the policy agendas and influence over public attitudes.

Summary

The Hong Kong government's authority and autonomy was gradually eroded in the 1980s. However, its autonomy was not completely stripped away. To a certain extent, it still enjoyed freedom to make its own judgments and decisions on various policies after considering the policy context and negotiating with the interest and political groups.

The rapidly changing political, social, economic and cultural context in the 1980s required the government to introduce new measures, such as structural reforms, in response to these changes. Such reforms were no longer piecemeal and incremental (Gould, 1992). Perhaps the greatest challenge to the government in the 1980s was not the concern for legitimacy, as the end date of 1997 was already known and there was no such challenge even from the most outspoken middle class (Lui & Wong, 1992), but instead, it was the concern to maintain and improve the accountability and efficiency of the machinery of government. These were also the concerns of the interest and political groups.

Notes

1 The most notable examples were Jardine, Swire and the Hong Kong & Shanghai Bank Corporation, also known as the Hong Kong Bank. They were the most powerful long-standing British corporations in Hong Kong.

2 One of the manifestations of this change was the inclusion of more business interests in the formal structure.

3 The deficits, shown in the General Revenue Account, were HK$3,500m, HK$2,993m and HK$1,563m for 1982/83, 1983/84 and 1984/85 fiscal years respectively (HKAR, 1983, 1984 & 1985, chapter on economy). Noted that due to the differences in the accounting method between the

General Revenue Account (showing the expenditure of the government) and the Consolidated Account (showing the public sector -- government plus the funds and the subsidised sectors), there were differences in the size of deficit for these three fiscal years.

4 Such as the provision of low cost land and labour in the nearby Pearl River Delta area.

5 Though the inflation rate was high, the economy still had reasonable real growth. For example, the inflation rates, from 1981 to 1984, were 15.4 per cent, 10.5 per cent, 9.9 per cent & 8.1 per cent respectively. Then, the rates were kept at a lower level of 3.2 per cent, 2.8 per cent & 5.5 per cent for the following three years. Then, they went up to 7.5 per cent, 10.1 per cent, 9.8 per cent, 12.0 per cent & 9.5 per cent from 1988 to 1992. See Tang, 1992, Table 10.1.

6 Hence, the new Airport project was started even with no commitment from private capital and an agreement from China. The row over the new Airport project and its impact on public finance continued for several years. Another example was the new Port project, resulting from large scale reclamation in the urban area, on the west of the Hong Kong harbour. Several transport improvement projects to build trunk roads and railway were also introduced.

7 The Scheme was introduced after the June 4th Incident. After rejecting the call for granting a right of abode in the United Kingdom to all Hong Kong British Passport (BDTC & BNO) holders, the British government announced a scheme which would give a full British passport and right of abode to 45,000 selected families. According to the point system, the people who benefited most were those who had a higher education level, were wealthier, were professionals and young people.

8 Details will be provided in the chapter 11.

9 At that time, there was no direct election to LegCo. In 1988, there was a heated debate in the further development of representative government but the idea of expanded direct election was dropped after opposition from pro-China groups and the China government.

10 As shown in the 1980s, in economic crises engendered by the political controversies between Britain, China and Hong Kong, so were cries for maintaining stability and prosperity at all costs. In the debate over introducing direct election to the LegCo in 1988, the pro-Left group has argued that 'meal voucher' was more important than a ballot paper. Also, in the social indicator research done in 1988, 58.6 per cent of the respondents stated that stability and prosperity were more important than democracy and only 17.2 per cent considered the reverse to be the case. See Lau et al (eds), 1991, p.183.

11 However, the discourse changed dramatically after the June 4th Incident when the Hong Kong people came to a general consensus on the positive value of democracy. After that, democracy was no longer attacked as potentially rocking the boat. The differences between different groups were only on the pace of democratic reform. By the 1990s, every political party included democracy as part of its political platform.

12 Their major strategies were to discuss and comment on government policies. They had no intention of participating in elections. However, some of them changed their position and did participate in elections. Examples are Meeting Point and the Hong Kong Affairs Society.

13 The core members of the HK Affairs Society, Meeting Point and the HK Association for Democracy and Peoples Livelihood came together to form the United Democrats of HK in 1990. The Hong Kong Affairs Society was disbanded at that time. In 1994, Meeting Points was merged with the United Democrats and formed the Democratic Party.

14 Example of these new organisations is the Business and Professional Federation (1991). It is a group of members of the Consultative Committee of Basic Law (who from the business sector) which organised themselves to express views on the future political arrangements. They were also actively involved in the elections. For a description of the alignments among the groups, see Lam & Lee, 1993, chapter 4.

15 This organisation only focused on democratic reform in China and not on local social policies. However, there were an overlapping of members between it and the UDHK.

16 The HKADPL condemned June 4th but they were more welcoming to a dialogue with China. Meeting Point also held a welcoming attitude to China and 1997 and also supported a wider democracy. However, they differed from the UDHK in that they held a more cautious approach in handing the June 4th Incident.

17 For example, the pro-Left candidates for 1991 LegCo election all lost, the seats were all taken by the pro-democracy groups, the UDHK.

18 They only had one representative in LegCo through indirect election in the labour functional constituency. There were two seats in the constituency and usually, the FTU took one and the other was taken by the TUC. Independent candidates could not win a seat here because the nominations and voting are by unions as single units.

19 These included a small annual budget to carry out or subsidise the environmental improvement projects, welfare services and recreational

activities within the district. The actual functions of each Board were varied according to the directions set by each of them.

20 From 1985, there were 19 districts, as Tsuen Wan and Kwai Chung were split into two districts.

21 The elected members occupied one-third of the seats. Ex-officio and official members also have voting powers.

22 The ratios between elected and appointed members of DB were 1.87:1 and 1.96:1 in 1988 and 1991 respectively.

23 In the latest election in 1994, except for the 27 ex-officio members from the Rural Committees, all the 346 seats were directly elected.

24 The UC was set up in 1936 replaced the Sanitary Board to manage these affairs in Hong Kong Island and the Kowloon peninsular.

25 The RC's composition was different from the UC in having representatives from the Rural Committees and the Heung Yee Kuk which represented the interests of the descendants of the 'indigenous people' (those who resided in the New Territories before 1898).

26 This was also coincide with the agreement stated in the Joint Declaration and the Basic Law.

27 CRC was transformed into the Liberal Party in 1993.

28 This was formally declared the end of the 'government by consensus'. The system of having a 'senior member', as a leader of all the members in LegCo was abolished in 1992. The changes also broke up the cooperation between the LegCo and ExCo.

29 After the 1985 LegCo election and the introduction of elected members into it, the Governor started to appoint some of them to the de facto cabinet of Hong Kong, the ExCo. After the 1991 LegCo election when the UDHK won a landslide victory (gaining 14 out of 18 direct elected seats), they demanded that the Governor appoint the elected members, disregarding of their political stand, to ExCo. This posed a very difficult situation for the Governor as the UDHK members promised to reveal the secrets of ExCo meetings to the public in order to be accountable to the public. The situation rapidly changed as Chris Patten took over the office of Governor in July 1992. He dismissed all the ExCo members who had political party backgrounds and stated that those who wanted to be appointed must abandon their membership of political parties and their seats in LegCo, and thus defeated the UDHK's demand as their members in LegCo would not surrender their posts in it.

30 Details of the case will be provided in chapter 11.

31 In this aspect, they received a far more popular response than the Hong Kong government. They successfully lobbied the most wealthy entrepreneurs, such as Mr Li Ka-shing and even former government

officials and councillors into their establishment. Examples were Sir David Akers-Jones, Sir S.Y. Chung, Mrs Rita Fan and Miss Maria W.C. Tam.

32 See Chapter Six of the Basic Law.

33 Under the governorship of Chris Patten, the relationship broke down and China was more skeptical about major policy changes which might have effects after 1997. The retirement protection scheme announced in 1994 was one of these examples.

34 Such as those that would have significant financial implications for the future SAR government, e.g. the retirement protection scheme.

35 This term was initiated by former Governor, Sir Edward Youde in an opening ceremony of a secondary school in 7 May 1983.

36 There were unconfirmed rumours that, Sir David Wilson, left the position as Governor of Hong Kong, because he could not get the support of the traditional British business corporations, such as Swire and Jardine, as he was accused of giving too many concessions to the pressure groups and parties while neglecting the business interest. This opinion was also expressed by an ex-Executive Councillor, Mrs Rita Fan in a personal interview.

11 Development of the welfare state, 1982-1992

This chapter will describe the general development of the social services from 1982 to 1992. This decade signified another turning point in the welfare state history of Hong Kong. The services continued to expand in quantity, though at a modest rate compared to the 1970s'. However, the most significant developments were the 'marketisation' reforms.

General development of the welfare state in the 1980s

Development in the 1980s could be broadly characterised by the term 'marketisation'. This form of privatisation was not merely a copy of similar reforms overseas. The changes had two characteristics, the scale of the welfare state was not reduced but growth was limited to a modest rate and, there was the intrusion of market values and operations. The share of social services expenditure remained at around 45 per cent of total government expenditure and 7 to 8 per cent of GDP in this period (Table 11.1).

The growth of social service expenditure was comparable to the GDP growth (Table 11.2 & 11.3) and slightly higher than the growth rate of government total public expenditure. In this sense, the welfare state did not receive a setback due to the marketisation reforms. However, when compared with the growth rate in the 1970s, the speed of development was scaled down.

Table 11.1
Social service expenditure as percentage of total expenditure, 1982/83 to 1991/92

Fiscal year	Percentage of government total expenditure	Fiscal year	Percentage of government total expenditure
1982/83	31.8	1987/88	44.8
1983/84	35.4	1988/89	47.2
1984/85	44.6	1989/90	45.0
1985/86	44.5	1990/91	45.8
1986/87	45.3	1991/92	45.7

Sources: HKAR, various years

Table 11.2
Public expenditure on social services (current price and consolidated account), 1982/83 -1991/92

Fiscal year	Expenditure on social services (HK$m)			
	Education	Medical	Housing	Social welfare
1982/83	5,105	2,665	4,919	1,710
1983/84	5,758	2,956	5,609	1,938
1984/85	6,951	3,312	5,293	2,232
1985/86	7,558	3,767	5,516	2,469
1986/87	8,410	4,370	5,780	2,780
1987/88	9,190	4,980	7,030	3,140
1988/89	11,360	5,670	9,750	3,810
1989/90	13,030	7,310	11,570	4,760
1990/91	16,070	9,290	12,420	5,810
1991/92	18,890	11,170	12,580	6,910
Increase				
82-92	270%	319%	156%	304%
71-81	572%	548%	1323%	2074%

Sources: CSD, 1987, Table 11.1; 1991, Table11.1; 1993, Table 11.3

Table 11.3
Comparison of growth rate of GDP, public expenditure and social service expenditure, 1982/83 - 1991/92 (current price -- HK$m)

Fiscal year	GDP (%)	Public exp. (%)	Social services expenditure (%)				
			Ed	Med	Hou	Soc Wel	Total
1982/83	12.9	17.6	22.4	23.4	26.3	40.2	25.8
1983/84	11.4	8.2	12.8	10.9	14.0	13.3	12.9
1984/85	19.8	3.2	20.7	12.0	(-5.6)	15.2	9.4
1985/86	5.0	8.9	8.7	13.7	4.2	10.6	8.6
1986/87	15.2	10.3	11.3	16.0	4.8	12.6	10.5
1987/88	23.1	11.9	9.3	14.0	21.6	12.9	14.1
1988/89	18.0	20.8	23.6	13.9	38.7	21.3	25.7
1989/90	15.1	26.5	14.7	28.9	18.7	24.9	19.9
1990/91	12.0	16.2	23.3	27.1	7.4	22.1	18.9
1991/92	15.1	13.9	17.5	20.2	1.3	18.9	13.7

Notes:
a. All GDP figures are calculated by calendar year from 1982 to 1991.
b. All expenditure items are taken from the Consolidated Account.
c. Ed: education; Med: medical; Hou: housing; Soc Wel: social welfare.

Sources: CSD, 1987, Table 3.1; 1989, Table 3.1; 1991, Table 3.1; 1993, Table 3.1
HKAR, various years

Health services

Generally speaking, health conditions in Hong Kong continued to improve in the 1980s.[1] The infant mortality rate reduced and the life expectancy rate increased.[2] However, the expansion of health services in the 1980s was less than in the 1970s. There were construction plans for hospitals but few of them could be completed on time.[3] The increase in hospital beds was very modest compared with the previous decade (Table 11.4). The increase in government hospital beds was only 17.5 per cent, compared with the 50 per cent in the 1970s. The total growth rate was 11.4 per cent, compared with nearly 30 per cent in the 1970s.

Table 11.4
Increase of hospital beds in Hong Kong, 1982-1992

Year	Government[a]	Assisted	Private[b]	Total
1982	10,743	9,222	2,725	22,690
1983	10,881	9,336	2,718	22,935
1984	11,759	9,578	2,736	24,073
1985	12,288	9,622	2,728	24,683
1986	12,285	9,601	2,664	24,550
1987	12,631	9,540	2,725	24,896
1988	12,687	9,577	2,793	25,057
1989	12,715	9,537	2,807	25,059
1990	13,008	9,440	2,834	25,282
1991	12,625	9,766	2,886	25,277
1992	23,386[c]		2,999	26,385
Increase	17.1%		10.1%	16.3%

Notes:

a. Including beds in government hospitals and dispensaries. Figures for 1989 and after have been adjusted to include beds in government hospitals, maternity homes and clinics following the establishment of the Provisional Hospital Authority in 1988.

b. Including beds in private hospitals, maternity and nursing homes. All private maternity homes were closed down from 1985.

c. All government and assisted hospitals were merged under the management of Hospital Authority.

Sources: HKAR, various years

Development in this stage was dominated by the establishment of the Hospital Authority in 1992. The objective for setting up such an administrative mechanism was made clear by the government,

> The lesson of public health services all over the world is that increased expenditure does not necessarily translate into higher standards. What is really important is the way the money is used and how well the facilities are managed (HKAR, 1989, p.14).

The major emphasis of the Authority is on 'quality of management' and through this it believes, without ever-increasing state investment, the hospital services can be maintained and improved. Another significant change was the fee charging policy. Medical charges remained at a 'low' level but the percentage increase, was very high. The increases for fees for out-patient consultations and general ward admittance were 600 per cent and 760 per cent respectively.[4] Following suggestion by the review in the mid-1980s and subsequent reports produced by Hospital Authority and the Health & Welfare Branch,[5] the charges for hospital beds could be further increased.

As the state was still shouldering almost all the medical expenditure, we cannot argue that the state had retreated from its commitment to the health services. However, there was an increasing financial contribution from the users to the budget. Moreover, greater 'cost-consciousness' and 'value for money' were installed in managerial practices. The whole hospital sector was managed by a private-enterprise style Authority, led by managers and administrators. The consumption of services was more 'commercialised' and 'commodified'.

Education services

After reviews of the education services which took place step by step in the 1970s,[6] upon the recommendation of the Board of Education, the government sought advice from the OECD and invited four renowned overseas educationists[7] to form a panel to conduct a thorough review of the education services in Hong Kong. The panel prepared a report, 'A Perspective on Education in Hong Kong', which recognised the needs of the economy and the effects of education in promoting social upward mobility, on pushing the rapid development of the education services (HKG, 1982). Following the recommendations of the report, the Education Commission (EC) was set up in 1984 as the highest advisory body for the government which had the task of monitoring the whole education system.[8] By 1992, five reports had been published, covering education from pre-primary to post-graduate levels.

In the 1980s, the education services continued to develop at every level except primary education.[9] Enrollment in primary education decreased by 6.8 per cent within the period of 1982 - 1992 (CSD, 1993, Table 13.3). Enrollment in secondary education also decreased by 2.6 per cent within the same period, as the population decreased (ibid, Table 13.4). Following the nine years free education, the provision of free but not compulsory senior secondary education places for all in grammar and technical schools,[10] was achieved in 1992. The continual expansion of subsidised schools showed that the trend towards the socialisation of education provision was maintained in the 1980s.

The most significant expansion was in the tertiary sector. According to the 1982 plan, the student population of the two existing universities,[11] would be increased by 30 per cent and the places for undergraduate degrees would also be increased by 35 per cent. The second polytechnic, the City Polytechnic of Hong Kong, was established in 1984. The third university, the Hong Kong University of Science and Technology, admitted its first students in 1991. The private post-secondary college, the Hong Kong Baptist College, received full financial support from the government.[12] The Open Learning Institute had an enrollment of approximately 15,500 undergraduate students in 1992 (HKAR, 1993).

Wilson announced a plan for the further expansion of the sector in 1989 in which the undergraduate intake would be increased to 15,000 in 1995, which was twice the student intake in 1989. Then, 13 per cent of the age group would be admitted compared to 7 per cent in 1989. If the targets were achieved, there would be 67,000 places in 1995, which was 25 per cent of the age group when compared with 14 per cent in 1989.

Accompanying all these developments, there were changes which amounted to a reversal of the socialisation of education. The Direct Subsidy Scheme enabled the aided and assisted private schools to opt-out from the control of ED.[13] The rapid increase of post-secondary tuition fees, from HK$ 6,200 in the 1988/89 academic year to HK$ 11,600 in the 1992/93 academic year, represented an increase of 87.1 per cent within five years, and meant that the users had a greater share in financing the expansion of the sector.[14] The Open Learning Institute was also expected to operate on a self-financing basis after the first few years of its life.

Housing services

There were three significant developments in the housing services in the 1980s. Firstly, there was the shift from social rented housing to owner-occupation as the dominant mode of public housing provision.[15] As lain down in the 'Long Term Housing Strategy'[16] (LTHS) published in 1987, there would be a change in the ratio of provision between PRH and home ownership flats with a preference for the latter.

> Housing policy should be sensitive to changing needs and aspirations and should not lose sight of the need to give priority to those most in need. In the 1950's, 60's and early 70's, the greatest need was for low rental housing and production was concentrated on public rental housing project. Improved economic conditions in Hong Kong have brought with them rising expectations and there is a demand for improvements in

living conditions, including a growing aspiration to own rather than to rent (HKG, 1987a, p.1).

> Home ownership promotes stability in the community. It brings with it a sense of pride as well as commitment to the community. There is a growing desire for home ownership in Hong Kong. It is demonstrated by the enthusiastic response to the HOS sales ... increase in owner occupation in the territory in previous years (HKHA, 1990, p.7)

With the Home Purchase Loan Scheme (HPLS) started in 1988, applicants in the long waiting list for rental housing were encouraged to transfer to private housing. The scheme was also opened to sitting tenants with no means-test mechanism.[17] The experimental sale of rental housing to the tenants, though it failed in 1991 and was shelved, was one of the series of policies aimed at transforming the nature of housing consumption. The policy was particularly targeted on those better-off tenants in PRH who were considered suitable for home ownership.

> The demand for home ownership from sitting tenants in Housing Authority estates is of particular significance because of the large number of potential households involved. This demand is very largely unmet partly because of the high price of private sector property and partly because of the stiff competition of HOS ... The proposal to sell rental flats to sitting tenants is one measure to satisfy demand for assisted home ownership from sitting tenants (HKHA, 1990, p.7).

The second change was the increase of rent of public housing. The first comprehensive review was carried in 1986 and it suggested that the rent be set at 15 per cent of the median income of public housing households (HKHA, 1986).[18] The second review was held in 1991 and the percentage was increased to 18.5 per cent for those who requested a larger floor area. So those who could and were willing to pay higher rents could enjoy better housing, in terms of its size.[19] On the contrary, those who could not afford to pay higher rents had limited choice and had to move to older and/or remote estates.[20] Currently, the rent collected was already adequate to recover the building costs and generate a surplus for a further building programme.[21] To 'encourage' better-off tenants to move out of PRH and to improve equity in the distribution of subsidies, the HA introduced a 'double-rent' policy. By 1992, there were approximately 60,000 households affected by this policy.[22]

The third change was the reformation of the HA in 1987 to encompass all the duties relating to housing policies, including both public and private housing, as recommended by the LTHS. It has the responsibility to implement, review and monitor the LTHS. The new HA maintained its previous form as a semi-governmental organisation but with much greater autonomy in its planning and implementation of policy and its budget management.

All these changes denoted a gradual retreat by the government from the management and financing of the public housing programme and the shift from social rented housing to owner occupation. The provision of public housing was still in the hands of a public body and funded by the collective effort, through rent payments and profits gained by the sale of HOS/PSPS, but consumption was increasingly privatised and commodified.

Table 11.5
No. of permanent dwellings and population accommodated by HKHA, 1982 -1992

Year	Types of dwelling provided		Population accommodated (,000)	
	Rental	HOS/PSPS	Rental	HOS/PSPS
1982	459,300	15,500	1,884	70
1983	475,500	23,000	1,950	92
1984	502,700	35,400	2,010	142
1985	516.500	47,700	2,037	169
1986	526,200	64,900	2,088	222
1987	536,300	72,200	2,208	254
1988	555,300	81,900	2,205	300
1989	583,100	93,500	2,208	338
1990	618,100	112,100	2,244	397
1991	623,700	121,100	2,160	421
1992	641,300	144,700	2,252	511
Increase	39.6%	833.6%	19.5%	630%

Sources: HKAR, various years

Social welfare services

Social welfare received greater attention in the 1980s with a gradual expansion in every aspect of the services. The major foci were the elderly and the rehabilitation services which were both neglected and had had a low priority for many years. 'Social Welfare into the 1980s' was published in 1979, but it was not until the early 1990s that the White Paper on social welfare, 'Social Welfare into the 1990s and Beyond' (HKG, 1991) and a Green Paper on rehabilitation was published (HKG, 1992).[23]

The White Paper reviewed the development of social welfare services in the 1980s and concluded that there were still inadequacies in the provision of basic services. The Paper admitted that the changing demographic trend (ageing population), disintegration of the family, rising expectation of service quality, the crystallisation of demands and needs through the development of representative government together with other social, political and economic factors, had affected the development of services in the 1980s and continue to do so in the future. The Paper concluded that increased resources should used to strengthen the family and care for vulnerable children, marginal youths and elderly (HKG, 1991a). The role of the family and informal networks in providing care to the needy was recognised and stressed in the Paper (ibid, p.18).

While it continued to rely on the informal sector to provide much care, the state also implemented a development plan for the welfare services. Services for different target groups were expanded, new services were added and Public Assistance was improved.[24] Apart from the adjustment of the basic rate[25] of the Public Assistance Scheme and other allowances, eligibility criteria, such as for the Old Age Allowance, were relaxed to allow more people to benefit.[26]

However, parallel with this expansion and improvement, there was another trend. The growth in subsidies was kept at a modest rate, especially from the end of the 1980s to the early 1990s, and this forced the NGOs to find alternative sources of support, such as private donations. Some NGOs sought co-operation with private companies to operate contracted-out services and joint ventures in the redevelopment of their property to gain extra resources.[27] In relation to the utilisation of public funds, the government promoted a vigorous 'value for money evaluation process' to measure 'the effectiveness and efficiency of management in achieving service objectives' (HKG, 1991a, p.41).

There was also a trend to increase the fees charged to the service users. As stated by the government, 'in an increasingly affluent society, the principle of asking those who can afford to pay for the service provided is not unreasonable' (ibid, p.42). The government argued that it was neither reducing the government's commitment nor attempting to recover the full costs but just allowing clients to contribute to the services and discouraging misuse. Also, the measure, it was argued, would generate additional income which the NGOs would have autonomy in using for the improvement and expansion of services (ibid).

The private provision of welfare was also encouraged to play a more important role. The government formally recognised the contribution of the 'non-subsidised and non-profit making organisations, as well as other community or profit-making organisations' in the provision of welfare services (ibid, p.17; p.42).[28] A typical example was the expansion of privately-run hostels for the elderly, the government also bought places from them to accommodate those who could not wait for access to the non-profit making hostels.

Characteristics of the services development in 1980s

This brief review of the developments confirms our observation of the two major characteristics of development in the 1980s, expansion but at a modest rate and a trend to marketisation. The expansion of services was not only in their quantity but also their targets. Among these expanded target groups, we can witness a trend to allocate more resources to the better-off class (or the middle class). The change can be observed in the hospital and the housing services.

We also observe the intrusion of market-type exchange relationships into the social services. Consumption was increasingly selective and based on the ability to pay. The clients and the providers were given the new roles as consumers and producers. Not only did market values intrude into the services but the private sector also gained a greater share in the provision of services, e.g. in housing and hostels for the elderly.

The housing and hospital services were given a new administrative structure, an 'Authority' with greater autonomy to design its policies and flexibility in meeting needs (demands). They had an autonomous status but at the same time, maintained their identity as semi-statal organisations. In this sense, the changes in the organisational structure might not be the most significant ones. Instead, the changes in their operating principles, such as the increasing commodification of services, privatisation of provision and consumption, abandonment of need-based and non-market criteria in distribution (replaced by effective-demand based criteria), and the increasing emphasis on cost-efficiency and cost-conscious in management were what really mattered.

In this period, the housing services were at the forefront of reform, the hospital services were the next major experiment, followed by the education services (especially higher education). Changes in social welfare were not so explicit and dramatic partly due to its relatively small share of resources and also the lack of substitute or alternative sources of services which made it difficult for the government to withdraw from its responsibility.[29]

The Long Term Housing Strategy, 1985-1992[30]

Historical development

While the TYHCP approached its end in the mid-1980s,[31] the government started to design a new housing plan. The document, 'A Review of Public Housing Allocation Policies' was published in 1984. Public opinions were obtained,[32] analysed and the 'Housing Subsidy to Public Housing Tenant' and the 'Rent Policy Review' Green Papers were published in 1985. The results were the 'double-rent' policy for better-off tenants, PRH rents set at 15 per cent of the median PRH household income[33] and an increase in HOS on redevelopment sites. At the same time, the preparation of the LTHS had started but no formal announcement was made of this nor was there open consultation with the public.

It was not until mid-1986 that the Director of Housing (DoH), Mr Freddie Pang, disclosed the government's preparation of a long term strategy and stated that the draft would be ready at the end of 1986 (SCMP, 27/8/86). Then Youde disclosed some information about the strategy in a Speech to LegCo, noted that it would encourage home ownership and the private sector's involvement in building more flats (STJP, 9/10/86). Mr John Todd, the SecH confirmed that the government was meeting the professional and private developers to discuss the strategy (STJP, 30/10/86). Up to that time, neither the public nor the PRH tenants were informed or consulted about the strategy.

In December 1986, Todd revealed another proposal under consideration, to provide low interest rate loans to PRH tenants to buy private flats and vacate their PRH for others in need. Through channelling the housing need to other sources of provision, the total housing demands on the PRH could be decreased. Moreover, the government expected the private developers to be the first line providers in building flats for home ownership with the HOS playing a minor role when the private market could not supply affordable housing (STJP, 17/12/86). The overall aim of the strategy, according to Todd, was to 'promote social stability and maximise opportunities for home ownership' (HKS, 31/12/86).

The strategy was formally published on 27 March 1987. The Housing Panel of LegCo was briefed by the government about the strategy and was assured that the public would be given three months for submission of their views (HKS, 24/1/87). However, when the strategy was tabled in LegCo, Liao[34] argued that there was no need to have any public consultation as the Strategy contained no new direction, just additional improvements to achieve the existing objectives, though the public was welcome to submit their views to the responsible departments. Furthermore, 'its implementation will not adversely affect those who are eligible for public housing under present policies' and 'it is for this reason that the Government has decided not to publish a consultative document' (SCMP, 9/4/87). Instead, a 'statement' was distributed to the public, primarily to explain the objectives and course of action that had been decided upon.

The strategy was devised to fulfil two principles,

1. to promote an equitable and efficient use of scarce resources in satisfying housing demands from all income groups; and
2. to promote social stability and a sense of belonging to Hong Kong by securing better living conditions for the needy and maximising the opportunity for home purchase (HKG, 1987b, p.8).

These two fundamental principles were translated into strategic aims. Among them, the idea of home purchase and owner occupation was emphasised the most.[35] Efforts must be paid 'to secure the most efficient use of the Territory's resources by maximising the private sector's contribution to housing production, thereby freeing Government funds for other public purposes' (ibid, p.9).

Based on these strategic aims, the government considered three strategies, the Rental Led Strategy, HOS/PSPS Led Strategy and the Private Sector Priority Strategy. In the light of the forecast housing demand, with the increasing desire of home ownership, the government came to the conclusion that the Private Sector Priority Strategy was the best choice to fulfil housing needs (ibid, Section 7). Its argument was that to fulfil this objective, 'the greater the contribution of the private sector, the less will be required of Government resources to support the public housing programme. Such resources can therefore be released for other public purposes' (ibid, p.37).[36] The strategy recommended an increase in the supply of ownership flats by the public and private sectors[37] and the new HPLS.

Though there was no formal consultation, pressure groups still took every chance to express their views. The debate focused on the choice of the Private Sector Priority Strategy and the introduction of the HPLS. The private developers were in favour of the scheme[38] though they also doubted the government's projection of a possible surplus of private flats as the market would adjust automatically (STJP, 3/5/87). The Hong Kong Institute of Surveyors and the Royal Institute of Chartered Surveyors (Hong Kong Branch) were also in support of the scheme(HKS, 9/5/87).[39]

However, some pressure groups and several LegCo members were against the plan. Mr Yin-fat Hui, the representative of social welfare constituency in LegCo, criticised the loan plan as a 'camouflage' for the government to render assistance to the real estate developers. The HKPCPHP also criticised the plan as a step backward (SCMP, 9/4/87) and stated that HPLS would only push up private flat prices. The Social Affairs Committee of the FTU was strongly against the strategy and called for the reinstatement of the PRH-led strategy (HKS, 16/4/87). Generally speaking, the pressure groups and their representatives in the representative structure were not in favour of the strategy. They were worried about the decrease of PRH supply and its adverse effect on waiting lists and tenants affected by the redevelopment plan.

The informal public consultation from April to June ended with no change to the overall direction and proposals of the strategy, and minor amendments to the HPLS policy.[40] In the face of strong disagreement from the pressure groups and some DB members, LegCo finally endorsed the strategy, the HPLS and the idea of promoting home ownership on 8 July 1987. During the debate, all except one of those who spoke expressed their support for the strategy. However, they showed their disappointment in the lack of provision for the 'sandwich class' (HK Hansard, 1986/87, pp.2000-2025).

The proposal to reorganise the HA was announced by Todd. He argued that the move was not privatising the service but that a more integrated authority was needed to satisfy the LTHS's aim to provide housing for various target groups (HKS, 24/7/87). The proposal was adopted by the HA in July 1987 (HKS, 24/7/87). ExCo agreed to reorganise the HA (from April 1988) in the following month. The reorganisation would include the scrapping of the post of Secretary for Housing and of the Housing Branch, part of their duties would be transferred to the Secretary for Lands and Works and the rest would be given to the HA (SCMP, 3/9/87). The chairman of the new HA would be an unofficial appointed by the governor (HKS, 18/9/87).[41] The pressure groups worried that the reformed HA would be too independent to be monitored by the government, the LegCo or the public (HKS, 18/9/87; 7/12/87) but the proposal went ahead.

The government also planned a new financial arrangement between itself and the HA. The HOS Fund would be transferred to the HA[42] and 'government permanent capital', which was composed of government loans and land costs not to be repaid, would be created in the accounts.[43] This arrangement was severely criticised by the pressure groups and some academics but the government and the HA did not yield to these criticisms and proceeded with the proposal (STJP, 22/1/88). The Housing (Amendment) Ordinance was gazetted in February 1988 and was passed in LegCo in March.[44] The only complaint from LegCo members was the announcement that Sir David Akers-Jones would be the first chairman of the HA (SCMP, 17/3/88).[45]

The implementation of the strategy was not smooth. The HA encountered several problems in the initial period, concerning land supply, finance resources and the unpredictable fluctuation in the private housing market which led to a housing crisis for middle class. Land was traditionally the major problem for the construction programme. Akers-Jones, on his first day as chairman of the HA, had mentioned that this was his biggest worry (SCMP, 7/4/88) and he admitted again that this was a real issue after the first meeting with the HA's Development Committee (STJP, 27/4/88). The shortage of land resulted from the keen competition from the private sector for a scarce supply of land especially in the urban areas.[46] The building target of 53,000 per year from 1985 to 1991 was reached, though with difficulty,[47] (MP, 26/1/91) but Akers-Jones was pessimistic about the possible achievement of the target in future years (MP, 29/7/91).

Another problem was the financial deficit of the HA especially in its first few years. The government agreed to inject HK$ 8.6 billion plus the HOS Fund from 1988 to 1990. However, in the HA's 1990/91 budget, it was forecast that there would be a deficit of HK$ 3.7 billion in that year and in the following budget. Moreover, the HA had been asked to pay for the land development costs for Tseung Kwan O and Tung Chung[48] which were previously paid by the government (HKEJ, 11/12/91). However, the government had to reserve resources for other policies and decided not to inject additional money. In February 1992, the HA predicted that it would face a deficit of HK$ 9 billion in the 1992 to 1996 financial years, unless the government agreed not to charge the HA full land development costs in future and not to ask for the HK$ 2 billion land development cost that the HA owed the government for past years (MP, 29/2/92).[49]

Akers-Jones said, due to the deficit, the HA would defer several policies such as the study of sandwich class housing and the extension of the HPLS (SCMP, 28/9/90).[50] Moreover, with approval from the FS, HA went to the banks for a HK$ 1.2 billion loan but no further loans were allowed from the 1992/93 financial year (MP, SCMP, 6/12/90). Rents were also raised to increase the revenue. The rents for newly built estates were set at higher levels and the price for HOS/PSPS flats was also increased, as private flat prices increased, to generate more surplus. A new policy, the sale of PRH, was also proposed for discussion. This idea had been rejected in the mid-1970s and repeatedly rejected later by the HA and government for different reasons. Even during the preparation of the LTHS, Liao had again rejected the option.[51] However, in October 1989, the HA changed its decision and decided to have a trial exercise to sell PRH to sitting tenants. Akers-Jones explained that selling PRH was one strategy to generate resources to support the future building programme (HKEJ, 3/10/90).

Without interference from government, the HA established a study group to examine the details of the scheme. The HA estimated that if the plan succeeded, it would gain HK$ 2.4 billion extra income in the 1992 to 1996 financial years (MP, 29/2/92). The HA also argued that owning a flat would certainly increase peoples' self-confidence, social belongingness and responsibility as well as their commitment to Hong Kong, so it was wise to promote home ownership by every means (HKEJ, 5/6/91). Mr Tung Fung, the current DoH, also stated that,

> We want to increase the ratio of home ownership. If we can sell the unit to you, on one hand, we can achieve the idea of home ownership and on the other hand, we can decrease the burden of subsidy to these flats.[52]

The HA was quite confident that they would get a favourable response as they repeatedly argued that the price, which was set at about 40 per cent of market price, was reasonable, affordable and attractive. However, this view was not shared by the tenants[53] and pressure groups. The pressure groups organised action against this proposal and it then failed.[54] Their major disagreement, was not on the principle of promotion of home ownership by PRH sales but on the price. The majority of the residents considered the proposed selling prices were too high and that it was not worthwhile paying monthly mortgages which were estimated to be two to three times greater than the rents. Akers-Jones did not terminate the scheme, but said that they would reconsider it, probably with reduced prices. The scheme was tabled at ExCo for discussion and was eventually rejected in 1992.

Another issue concerned the housing needs of the 'sandwich class'. The sandwich class was defined, arbitrarily, as those who had incomes above the eligible limit for HOS but who found great difficulty in purchasing a private flat in the market. They were in fact, a segment of the middle class. The idea of providing assistance to this class of people was not a planned strategy in the LTHS. When the government prepared the LTHS, Sir David Ford, the CS, had made it clear that due to inadequate resources, the government could not take care of the housing needs, of the sandwich class (STJP, 9/7/87). Mr Tung Fung[55] also explained that it was impossible for the government to help the sandwich class to purchase a flat at that time. The HA's HOS and Management Committees had agreed that the top priority of the HA was to look after the interests of low income groups. The Assistant DoH (Policy), Mr Kai-fat Lee also argued that if the HA helped the sandwich class now, it would depart from the approved long-term housing strategy to satisfy identified housing demand by 2001 (SCMP, 17/3/89).

At that time, private property prices risen rapidly[56] and there were calls, though by no means strong or co-ordinate ones, from the public urging the government to intervene in the housing market. The HA set up a group to study the sandwich class housing needs in June, shortly after Fung and Lee's announcement (MP, 26/12/89). The working group was chaired by Akers-

Jones. The progress of the working group, however, was slow and in mid-1990 and due to the predicted deficit of the HA, it was decided to shelve the proposal to assist the sandwich class until 1994.

However, the situation changed dramatically later. After the June 4th Incident in 1989, the private flat prices rocketed up again and increased two-fold within two years. The situation of the sandwich class became worse and worse. Although no major social action was launched by this group,[57] at that time, the editorials in the mass media expressed the public concern over soaring private flat prices and the inability of the HOS scheme to take care of the sandwich class. In the 1992/93 Budget, the FS, Hamish McLeod, stated that the government must do something to help the middle class housing problem. During that budget debate, the CRC and the UDHK, agreed strongly with the government's view and urged it to find a solution as quickly as possible (SCMP, 26/3/92; HKEJ, 20/9/92). The government set up a special working group under the chairmanship of the Secretary for Planning, Environment & Land, Eason, to review the housing situation of those families with an monthly income of HK$ 18,000[58] to HK$ 40,000 but the impact of any new policy on the private market must be evaluated at the same time (HKEJ, 2/4/92). In a debate reviewing the LTHS in that year, the CRC put an amendment motion, which was passed by the LegCo, to urge the government to provide assisted housing to families with incomes ranging from HK$ 18,000 to HK$ 40,000.[59] At the same time, the HA decided to re-activate the shelved sandwich class proposal but withdrew from making any immediate commitment in view of the limited resources that they possessed.[60]

The government decided to intervene. Patten announced a new scheme in his first speech in LegCo to 7 October. 1992, to provide 13,000 flats to eligible families by 1997. The eligible income limit was initially set in the range HK$ 18,000 to $ 40,000 per month and the first batch of units would be completed and sold in 1996.[61] As an interim measure, the government would buy 1,000 flats from the private sector and sell them at a subsidised price to the families in need.[62]

1993 was a turbulent year for the HA. Apart from severe protests from the residents and the LegCo councillors over the 'better-off tenant' issue, Akers-Jones suddenly resigned from the Chairmanship and the appointment of a current ExCo member, Rosanna Wong, as the new chairman paved the way for changes. As a response to pressure group criticisms of the HA's independence and the lack of monitoring from the government, the government reformed the Planning, Environment & Land Branch to re-establish a department responsible for housing policy. With the re-establishment of the Housing Branch in 1994, the HA was made more accountable to the government.[63]

Table 11.6
Historical development of the Long Term Housing Strategy

Year	Historical development
1984	'A Review of Housing Allocation Policies' published.
1985	Rent policy review started.
	'Housing Subsidy to Public Housing Tenants' published.
1986	Disclosure of the preparation of LTHS.
1987	Announcement of LTHS & informal consultation.
	LegCo debate in July and endorsed the strategy.
	Proposal of sale of PRH rejected by Liao.
	Proposal of sandwich class housing rejected by Ford.
1988	Housing (amendment) Ordinance passed.
	HA reorganisation and new financial arrangements completed.
	Appointment of Akers-Jones as the Chairman.
	Problem of limited land supply recognised.
	Injection of capital from government.
1989	Formal commencement of HPLS.
	Announcement of the intention to sell the PRH.
	Proposal of sandwich class housing rejected by Assistant DoH in March but the position changed in June when a working group was established which was chaired by Akers-Jones.
1990	Predicted deficit of LTHS.
	Working group on sale of PRH established and publication of the proposal. Faced with unfavourable response from the residents, proposals failed and halted.
	HA's attempt of sandwich class housing shelved due to predicted finance deficit.
1991	Loan from bank to relieve finance pressure.
1992	Rent review held.
	Reactivated the sandwich class housing proposal but shelved again due to financial deficit.
	Government intervened in the sandwich class housing issue.
	HA's deficit problem solved.
	Sale of PRH formally rejected by ExCo.
1993	Resignation of Akers-Jones & appointment of Rosanna Wong as new chairman of HA.
1994	Re-establishment of Housing Branch.

Observations

The formulation of the LTHS and the sale of PRH clearly indicate the impact of the logic of capitalism and the influence of business interests. The private developers and the associated professionals were consulted over the preparation of the strategy but not the public nor the Council although they were given a chance to express their views on the strategy at a later stage. The Private Sector-Priority Strategy shows the influence of the business interest and the associated professions and, also the orientation of the officials, that is the reliance on the private sector in meeting housing needs, as compared with the previous rental-led strategy. The HPLS and the sale of PRH were implemented but would have no adverse effect on the private market. In explaining the new sandwich class housing policy, the officials also made it clear that this would not interfere with the market and none adverse effects on it.[64] The business interests were taken into account and protected, whether there was explicit participation of the private property sector in the decision-making process or not. Their interests were safeguarded, implicitly, by the shared economic logic of the officials.

It was clear that the officials had two basic beliefs. Firstly, the market would be the major provider of housing in the future, and must not be adversely affected by any government policy.[65] Secondly, it was better to run the housing service through a non-governmental structure, borrowing management ideas from private sector.

The idea of home ownership, a form of private consumption of heavily subsidised public services, was adopted and shared by almost every sector of society, irrespective of their class position. 'Targeting' policy, in relation to housing allocation and the better-off tenant policy, aimed at a better and fairer distribution of resources were held by the officials to be measures to divert those who were not considered to be deserving target for public housing to home ownership either in the public or, better still, in the private sector.

These policies, except the better-off tenants policy,[66] received a favourable response from most sectors of the public. It showed shared orientation between the officials, the business interests, the middle class, the political parties, the pressure groups and the mass public. Of course, it is difficult to judge whether the public attitude resulted from manipulation and intervention by the officials and it is true that Chinese culture values property ownership. Nevertheless, this certainly enhanced the legitimacy of the policy, resistance to implementing the overall strategy was never strong and the autonomy of the state's decision making was not challenged.

In contrast to the situation in other areas, HA had played a prominent role in the process. When the HA was reorganised, it had gained autonomy from the government in deciding policy. This was ensured by the structural arrangements between the HA and the government, the attitude of the state and the powerful status of its first chairman, Akers-Jones. The structural reform gave the HA a nearly complete autonomy in planning and implementing housing policy, based on the LTHS. The government had transferred all housing duties to it and was left with no monitoring mechanism to oversee the policy. Even LegCo has no such power to control its policy.

Nevertheless, the HA was not entirely free to pursue its own courses of action. The LTHS set an overall framework and the HA was not allowed to deviate from it. It was also constrained by the logic of capitalism.[67] Moreover, the first few years of the HA also showed that it was constrained by technical factors, such as land supply, finance, and to a lesser extent, public opposition on detailed issues. Facing these technical constraints and unexpected crisis situations, such as the sandwich class housing crisis and the budget deficit, the HA was forced to react. However, how it reacted was largely defined by the HA itself.

Relatively speaking, the impact of the pressure groups and political parties were weak in the formation of LTHS. However, their impact was increasingly significant later, for example in relation to the sale of PRH, the sandwich class housing problem and the issue of 'better-off' tenants. The opening up of LegCo to direct election in 1991 increased the pressure groups' and parties' influence on housing policy. This became a significant way for the opposition to set an alternative agenda. The impact was not through direct control but through pressure on the HA or via the government.

The impact of the parties was greatest in the debate on the sandwich class policy.[68] With their representatives in the LegCo, the parties actively exerted pressure on the government to assist the sandwich class even though this meant going beyond the traditional non-intervention in the property market. Because of the politicisation of the formerly disorganised interest group politics, with the abolition of all appointed seats in all councils and district boards, those groups strove to consolidate their public support through voting and hence, their position in the formal structure. Although there was no strong protest from the middle class itself, the parties spoke on their behalf. There was a consensus among all the political parties on the issue and when this consensus was formed, the government could hardly neglect such a demand.

The issue of '1997' may also have had an impact on the 'marketisation' of housing policy. The government's actions aimed at freeing a major policy sector from China's political interference in the future SAR. In fact, China had not shown much interest in the public housing issue but, it had a greater interest in the allocation of land and the private housing market. Britain had no obvious influence on local housing issues though there were similarities between the plan to sell PRH in Hong Kong and the 'right to buy' in Britain.

The Hospital Authority and the fee charging policy

Historical development

This section will provide a historical account of the development of the Hospital Authority (HoA) and the fee charging policy. The two policies are interrelated and were the two most controversial suggestions contained in the Scott Report published in 1985 (W.D. Scott Pty. Co, 1985) and the subsequent debate. The HoA debate focused on administrative structural reform while the fee charging issue focused on a consumption principle that would have a far-reaching impact on the Authority's finances. The debate on the HoA occupied most attention before 1990, then the fee charging issue occupied the centre stage.

The 1974 White Paper had laid down the development policy for the medical services for ten years from 1975 to 1984. Near the end of this period, in October 1983, in the Governor Speech's debate in LegCo, several members voiced their concerns about the future development and called for a review and a new plan.

In reply, the SecHW announced that a review would be launched. In the 1984/85 Budget debate held in March 1984, LegCo members further expressed their views on medical reforms. Dr Harry Fang suggested the 'privatisation' of the medical services. He called for greater freedom and power in staff recruitment and determining salaries be given to individual hospitals (HKS, 16/4/85). Dr Henrietta Ip suggested a medical insurance scheme in which these 'able-bodied' should pay a minimum premium and questioned the current subsidy policy to hospitals which should be modified to achieve 'value for money' (HKS, 29/3/85).

The Governor and ExCo formally endorsed the review proposal in May 1984. An Australian consultant, W.D. Scott Pty Company (henceforth 'Scott Consultant' in this thesis) was commissioned to carry out the job.[69] The SecHW also appointed a Steering Committee to provide 'overall guidance' (W.D. Scott Pty Co, 1985, pp.1-4) to the consultants. This Committee consisted of the two medical professions in the LegCo, Fang and Ip, who had expressed support for 'privatisation'. The review ran from February to November 1985. It focused on reviewing 'the organisational structure for managing government and subvented [subsidised] hospitals, with the aim of assessing the potential for achieving better integration between these hospitals on a functional basis and to advise whether this aim should be met through the establishment of autonomous authorities for managing government and subvented [subsidised] hospitals'. It also included the utilisation and control of resources; the staffing of hospitals; fee charging and co-ordination between government and assisted hospitals (W.D. Scott Pty Co, 1985, para.1A-1).

During the preparation of the report, Dr Peter Lee, president of the Hong Kong College of General Practitioners, criticised the existing system which did not allow those who could afford to paying more for better services. He suggested setting up a scale of charges and allowing the well-off to pay more and reducing wastage of subsidy by making someone responsible for the utilisation. Moreover, the 14 government hospitals could be given autonomy under their own Boards and they could receive a lump sum from the government every year (HKS, 23/9/85). This was similar to the idea proposed by Fang to 'privatise' the hospital administration.

The report, 'The Delivery of Medical Services in Hospitals' (the Scott Report) was completed and submitted to the government in December 1985. The administration studied the proposals and considered that the major proposal to set up an independent hospital authority (IHA) must be agreed before implementing any other proposals. ExCo, after discussion, decided to launch a public consultation from March to August 1986 (PHoA Report, 1989, pp.6-7). Other major proposals suggested by the Scott Report included proposals of cost-recovery and cost-containment.

The SecHW, Mr John Chambers set up a working group to study the proposals and the public comments and to make recommendations to the ExCo after the consultation. During the consultation, public comment focused on privatisation issues, the setting up of the IHA and proposals to increase medical charges. However, Chambers argued repeatedly that the government had no intention to 'privatise' the medical services.

In a City Forum[70] held on 6 April 1986, Dr Hin-kwong Chiu[71] supported the idea of the HoA as did Dr Chen-ya Huang, representative of Hong Kong Affairs Society (STJP, 7/4/86). Later, the LegCo's Health Panel endorsed the idea of IHA and called for an unified fee charging policy. However, they argued that the cost-recovery ratio should be set at 3 per cent of the total cost which was roughly equivalent to the present fee level (STJP, 21/5/86, 11/6/86). Another opinion group, the Meeting Point, while agreeing with the idea of the IHA and the plan to recover a part of the medical costs, suggested that the government must consider carefully the issue of ability to pay (STJP, 29/6/86). The Hong Kong Branch of the British Medical Association also offered its support for the IHA as it could 'decentralise the power of a sole department and reduce existing bureaucratic problems' (HKS, 3/11/86).

However, there were other groups opposed to these proposals. An ad hoc pressure group, the Joint Committee on Medical Services Policy disagreed with the idea of an IHA on the grounds that it could not solve the problem of under-supply of services and it stated that the fee charging policy would worsen the living conditions of poor people (STJP, 11/6/86). Another group formed by health personnel, the Medical Services Concern Group representative also opposed the IHA. It argued that the focus should be on the improvement of existing administration and that the IHA might only create adjustment problems for staff and the public (STJP, 28/6/86). The Association of Government Nursing Staffs (AGNS) had a similar argument and position. A survey by the Government Doctors' Association (GDA) showed that 62 per cent of 350 respondents (all doctors) were against the proposal and if the government pressed ahead, it had to guarantee its future financial commitment (STJP, 28/6/86).[72] A group of Catholic organisations objected to idea of cost-recovery in medical services (STJP, 21/7/86).

Generally speaking, the reaction from professionals and the pressure groups to the fee charging policy was not really positive but responses to the idea of IHA were mixed. The professionals, except those currently employed in the sector, agreed with the ideas but the pressure groups and the staff were rather sceptical. The 'Report of the Provisional Hospital Authority' (1989) described the public reaction thus:

> On the whole the general public were enthusiastic about the enhancement of community participation in hospital services as recommended in the Report. The district boards, professional bodies and academic institutes expressed support for the proposal to establish a Hospital Authority provided it was made clear that the Government would not relinquish its responsibility for financing medical services. The proposal was also generally welcomed by staff of subvented [subsidised] hospitals who expected that this development would lead to improved fringe benefit for staff and a more equitable distribution of resources to the subvented [subsidised] sector (1989, para 1.6.1).
>
> However, the staff of the Medical and Health Department were generally opposed to the proposal and considerable anxiety was voiced about the possibility of reduced fringe benefits and loss of their civil service status and job security. The boards of directors of some subvented [subsidised] hospitals also expressed concern that the philosophy, characteristics and traditions of individual [hospital] be handed over to the proposed Hospital Authority. They emphasised the importance of maintaining their autonomy, in particular with regard to

the right to employ and dismiss their own staff and to make use of donations to provide additional services for their patients (ibid, para 1.6.2).

LegCo held a debate on the Scott Report on 15 October 1986 and the majority of members expressed their support for the IHA on the grounds that it could improve management efficiency and equity in the distribution of resources (STJP, 16/10/86). In early 1987, the Principal Assistant SecHW at that time, Mr Wilfred Tsui, said that the MDAC also endorsed the idea of the IHA (HKS, 9/2/87). Finally, the ExCo met on September 1987 and decided to proceed with the IHA (PHoA, 1988, para.1.7).

Wilson, in his Speech to LegCo on 7 October 1987 announced that the government had decided to implement the IHA and a provisional authority (PHoA) would be set up in April 1988. Other changes in the governing structure included the splitting of the Medical & Health Department (MHD) into two departments: a Health Department (HeD) and a Hospital Services Department (HSD) (STJP, 8/10/87). It was now 14 months since the public consultation had ended (i.e. August 1986) and nearly two years since the Scott Report had been finalised (i.e. November 1985).

Chambers explained that some of the officials, especially those from the Finance Branch, held reservations on financial grounds. However, none of them totally rejected the plan.[73] Chambers himself was a major proponent of the new structure and he tried to convince others. The doubts and reservations from the officials might have helped to delay the decision. Moreover, as explained by Mr Michael Ho, the chairman of the AGNS, opposition from the pressure groups and staff unions had also caused a delay.[74]

The Provisional Hospital Authority (PHoA) was to plan for the establishment of the statutory Authority in mid-1988.[75] Even after the government had made the decision, the officials still had to respond to a series of public queries about the policy. The focal point concerned privatisation and staff terms of employment. Just after the Governor's Speech, Chambers again said, in a press conference, that the HoA did not mean privatisation and the Government would still be responsible for the funding of hospital services (STJP, 10/10/87). He argued that, 'there is no intention, and in fact, it was not possible to operate hospital services at the same basis as the Mass Transit Railway or the Kowloon Canton Railway to make a profit or even to break even' (HKS, 10/10/87). Later, he explained again that, 'we do not expect the Authority to be profit-making or even to break even. Nor does the change mean that the policy for the provision of hospital services is no longer a Government responsibility' (SCMP,

26/10/87). He explained that the HoA was meant to improve the management and operation of the hospitals.

After careful consideration, the government selected Sir S.Y. Chung as the chairman. He was not a medical professional but a businessman with proven record serving in public affairs.[76] Moreover, according to Chambers, Chung did not have any vested interest in the medical field and therefore, could be free from any sectional bias. The same logic was also applied in rejecting the appointment of current employees to the board, although some of them could be co-opted to sub-committees at a later stage.[77] However, doctors and the medical professionals who were not current staff were appointed to the Board.

Following the establishment of the PHoA, there were a series of restructuring of posts and organisations.[78] The first dispute that the Authority faced was with staff over employment terms. Tak-hay Chau, Chamber's successor, stayed as SecHW for only a year and was forced to transfer to the Trade Department in late 1989 after intensified conflict with the staff unions.

After fourteen months' work, the PHoA completed its planning and proposals for employment terms in December 1989 and submitted them to the government for consideration. In its Report, the PHoA followed four broad principles in planning,

1. the Hospital Authority should be independently administered, and the present government and subvented [subsidised] hospitals, and their staff, should be fully integrated;
2. there should be greater delegation of authority to the hospital level so that more effective management could be introduced;
3. a separate development function should be established to keep abreast of improvements and innovations in hospital services world-wide, including modern management methods;
4. public participation should be enhanced (PHoA, 1989, ch.3)

Chief executives and managers were established at every level to manage the hospital services, replacing the previous doctor-dominated system.[79] Concerning the integration of the hospitals, the PHoA proposed that a 'formal agreement in respect of each subvented [subsidised] hospital should be signed between its Board of Directors and the Authority, which would set out the arrangements regarding the future management, funding and operation of the hospital concerned' (PHoA, 1989, para 0.9). Concerning financial arrangements with the government, the PHoA proposed that it should have maximum autonomy and flexibility in utilising its resources. The government should provide adequate resources for 'baseline expenditure',[80] funding for new projects and the new employment terms of the staff, initial set-up costs, and service improvements. There would be a Memorandum of Administrative Arrangements between the HoA and the government.

In designing the Authority, Chung, as the chairman and ExCo member, argued in meetings against the adoption of the Housing Authority model[81] for the HoA. He said that this would only cause problems in the implementation of policies by an old-style government bureaucracy. Chambers seemed quite hesitant at first, not about the new model but about the potential difficulty in 'privatising' over 40,000 employees though eventually he agreed.[82]

In relation to the fee charging policy, the PHoA proposed,

> The Authority should be authorised to determine fees and charges within the broad policies laid down by the Government (1989, para 0.11.1).
>
> The Provisional Authority considers that the fees for public wards, currently at about 2.25 per cent of total cost, are too low and should be increased, by phases. However, it is proposed that the initial step should be to change the basis of charging from the cost of food to a percentage of cost recovery, and sharp increases should not be introduced until some improvements in services have been achieved (ibid, para 0.11.3).

The Report proposed that households could afford to pay 15 to 20 per cent of the cost which would be about 2.7 per cent to 3.6 per cent of their annual income (ibid, para 0.11.4).[83]

The proposal for fee charging as well as the new terms of employment caused opposition from the concerned parties. In relation to the terms of employment, the staff were increasingly worried about future arrangements and annoyed by years of waiting for a concrete reply. To show their frustration, they had boycotted meetings with the newly formed HSD on staff terms in March and April 1990 (SCMP, 26/3/90; 25/4/90). The League of the staff unions in the former MHD had walked out of a meeting and a sit-in of 5,500 nurses was also held (SCMP, 7/4/90). When it failed to persuade LegCo to postpone the HoA Ordinance, the League threatened to launch a series of actions (STJP, MP, 17/5/90). Chambers said the dispute would not postpone the take-over of hospitals by January 1991 (SCMP, 20/5/90) but later he was proved to be over-optimistic in the belief.

Surveys of the staff had indicated that majority of them would not opt to transfer to the HoA. A survey by the Joint Council of Subsidised Hospital Doctors revealed that 90 per cent of these doctors did not want to transfer to the HoA as the terms of transfer were far from clear. Another survey done earlier by the GDA showed that 90 per cent of government doctors did not want to transfer to the HoA (STJP, 1/6/90). Chow also publicised the result of his survey which interviewed 3,000 staff, 70 per cent of them said that they would not opt to transfer to the HoA (HKEJ, 10/7/90).

Faced with such strong pressure and the possibility that very few staff would opt to the new HoA, Mrs Elizabeth Wong[84] adopted a softer approach and for the first time, admitted that staff choosing to transfer to the HoA would lose some of their benefits (HKEJ, 21/6/90). Two days later, Chambers also admitted that the calculation of benefits was wrong and a consultant company had been appointed to help to draft new terms. The consultant could not help to resolve the conflict. The PHoA rejected the staff's demand for a cash allowance[85] which was 40 per cent higher than its own proposal (HKEJ, 7/7/90). The government proposed another arrangement and tabled it for ExCo discussion in 10 July (MP, 9/7/90).

The ExCo endorsed this proposal of the PHoA and the Health & Welfare Branch with minor modifications at its meeting. Wong argued that this would be the final proposal (MP, 11/7/90). The GDA rejected the new proposal as the amendments were minor and the staff would still have lost out. The chairman of the GDA pointed out that it was not the amount that mattered but it was the attitude of the administration and the process of consultation for the past three months that had frustrated the staff (SCMP, 11/7/90). However, from then on, the staff gradually divided amongst themselves. The subsidised sector seemed to be satisfied with the new terms offered as they were much better than their existing benefits.

Wong continued her soft approach, admitted that 'the government has done a poor job of selling the proposal' (SCMP, 15/7/90) and appealed to the staff to read and consider the new terms carefully. After a series of discussions between the staff and the Health and Welfare Branch, the Civil Service Branch, the HeD and HSD, their differences were narrowed. The Hong Kong Medical Association issued a statement that they would not support industrial action and the convenor of the League, Mr Po-luk Chan also softened its stand and said that now was not the time for drastic action (SCMP, 24/7/90). The issue was gradually resolved and increasingly staff were willing to opt for the HoA's term of employment.[86]

Regarding to the fee charging policy, the officials had repeatedly denied that either the Authority or the government had arrived at a definite decision after the publication of the PHoA Report. After Wong submitted the Report to LegCo in 4 April 1990, she disclosed that the government agreed, in principle, with the idea of raising the fee to 15 - 20 per cent of the cost, though she explained that there was no plan to increase it immediately when the HoA was established. It would take at least five years to implement the proposal and a waiver system would be provided for those who could not pay (MP, 5/4/90). She used a famous sentence, which was used repeatedly by all the concerned officials to reply to the attack on the fee charging policy, 'no one will be denied adequate medical services because they cannot afford it. This is a policy statement, and policy statements do not change' (HKS, 5/4/90).

Three pressure groups, Meeting Point, HKADPL and the Society for Community Organisation jointly issued a statement indicating that the survey quoted in the PHoA Report was misleading and over-estimated the ability to pay of the public (MP, 7/4/90). A league of trade unions concerned with the medical services rejected to the proposal and the idea of cost-recovery (MP, 8/4/90).

In a meeting with DB members, the Deputy SecHW, Mr Nigel Shipman, stated that the proposal in the PHoA's report must be modified and fee rises would be gradual and only after substantial improvement in the hospital services (MP, 27/4/90). However, that was not enough to pacify the opposition and sixteen RC Councillors, three Tuen Mun DB members and three New Territories resident organisations issued a joint declaration which rejected the proposal to increase fees (STJP, 27/4/90). Another group, the Joint Committee for Concern on Medical Services, mainly composed of labour groups, also rejected the proposal to increase fees (SCMP, 28/4/90).

Responding to all these criticisms, Wong claimed that the public had over-reacted and was over-worried. She explained that the reasons for this proposal were to control costs, improve services and obtain better value for money, not to surrender the government's responsibility for the service. The better-off would have to pay more while those who could not afford to pay would have a waiver system to protect them (MP, 29/4/90). Her assistant, Mr Wing-lap Leung made the same argument again later and disclosed that an inter-departmental working group had been set up to study the waiver system (SCMP, 7/5/90).

However, public opposition persisted. Another concerned group for the medical and health services which was composed of lawyers, social workers and clergyman, demanded that the HoA should stick to the existing system and that any increase should be pegged to the inflation rate (SCMP, 30/4/90). Michael Ho[87] also rejected the idea and argued that a waiver system would not work (SCMP, 7/5/90). The UDHK openly criticised the proposal and demanded that the government scrap the idea of cost-recovery (SCMP, 12/6/90). To counteract the survey done by the PHoA, the GDA had interviewed 497 patients and found that 76 per cent of them opposed a fee charging ratio of 20 per cent of the cost, 59 per cent opposed a ratio of 10 per cent of the cost and only 6 per cent thought that the present system had to be changed (SCMP, 7/11/90). Another survey done by Mei-tak Chow, who interviewed 705 respondents from the lower income group, showed that if the ratio increased to 15-20 per cent, 50 per cent of them said that they could not afford more than 5 days hospitalisation (MP, 21/2/91).

After this strong reaction and opposition from the public, councillors from the Boards and Councils and the HoA, which was formally established on 1 December 1990, did not push rapidly to increase the fee. In mid-November 1991, the HoA informed the government that they had no plan to increase the charges at present (STJP, 29/11/91). The HoA Ordinance was gazetted in 6 April 1990 and passed in LegCo on 25 July. One of the clauses stated that the SecHW had reserved the power to set the fee charging policy and any increases. Now, the fee charging issue was taken up by the HWB. Apart from setting up a task group to study the waiver system, another task group to study the possibility of medical insurance in Hong Kong was set up in December 1990 (STJP, 12/12/90). So government did not give up its intention to establish a new fee charging policy.

Another major task for the HoA was to deal with the transfer of staff,[88] the integration of hospitals and the negotiation of terms of the Memorandum with the government. The HoA was rather successful in negotiating with the subsidised hospitals and eventually all these hospitals were grouped under the HoA in January 1992. Comparatively speaking, the fee charging issue was more difficult to deal with. The working group on the waiver system never published its results. The medical insurance working group completed its task in mid-1991 with several recommendations but no concrete reaction from the government. The HWB was very cautious in handling this issue as it had learnt from the previous negative public response. The government set up another working group on the overall issue of fee charging in January 1992 (MP, 9/1/92; STJP, 20/1/92). Fifteen LegCo members jointly urged the government to issue this working group's recommendations at the end of the year and to consult public opinion (STJP, 30/4/92). Another working group, the Medical and Welfare Services Fees and Waivers Committee,[89] comprised of some directly elected LegCo members, studying fee charging policies for the social services, including hospital services, was set up in February 1992. The working group finished its work in August 1992 and recommended that hospital charges should continue to be based on the catering costs but that the real cost of the treatment should be printed on the bills (SCMP, 24/8 - 25/8/92).[90]

This prolonged discussion since the Scott Report in 1985 had annoyed some of its proponents. Dr Che-hung Leong[91] was one of the chief supporters of revising the fee charging policy. He criticised the present fee charging policy as out-dated and said that the government did not have the courage to admit that they did not have adequate resources to finance the medical services (STJP, 30/4/92). The government, according to Leong, was playing an impossible role in subsidising all patients and pretending that it had adequate resources to do so (MP, 29/4/92). Mr Keith Pearson, member of the working group studying medical insurance, criticised Wong for spending too much time in seeking advice and wasting too much time on consultation (SCMP, 17/8/92), yet without making a final decision.

In July 1993, the Health and Welfare Branch published 'Towards Better Health', a consultative document with a lengthy discussion on possible funding methods. It suggested several alternatives, one was to raise the charge to a highest level of 15-20 per cent. The HWB stressed that this was only a suggestion and that the government would sincerely listen to public opinion. According to Ho, the HoA was more eager to raise the charge for hospital service than was the HWB as it would improve the finances of the Authority.[92] The HWB, though sympathetic to the idea, was very cautious in handling the issue. At this time, the officials put forward arguments about the standardisation of fee charging across institutions and the rationalisation of resources for different types of patients as bases to defend the proposal.[93]

The establishment of the HoA, though encountering many difficulties, was finally achieved in 1990. However, the idea of increasing the fee was once again dropped in 1994. After almost nine years of debate and discussion, and strong opposition from the public, the officials were very cautious in planning and the ways to put forward it in view of the opposition.

Observations

From the review of these two policy issues, their development were constrained by several forces, the staff and the subsidised hospitals, the pressure groups and later the parties and councillors. The staff and subsidised hospitals served primarily to delay the government's establishment of the HoA. The public, pressure groups, parties and the unfavourable response on the fee charging proposal had served to postpone a decision about it for years and led to its final abandonment. The professional bodies and the medical and health professions were very active in the policy process, whether they supported or rejected the proposals.

Staff and their unions were, most probably, the most difficult parties to deal with as they actually delivered the services. Without their support, the structural reform would have had a very slim chance of success. Public opposition to the establishment of HoA, as expressed by intermediary organisations such as pressure groups, professional organisations, parties, ad hoc concern groups (but not mass public mobilisation), was comparatively more effective in the debate on the cost-recovery proposal. Nevertheless, the success of the opposition over this issue was also due to the special nature of hospital services. It was a very expensive service but one of the most decommodified social services, consumed by those who would have nowhere to turn to if they could not afford the new level of charges. In this sense, the denial of access to services by potential consumers if the fees were increased to an unaffordable level would almost certainly engender a massive scale of social unrest. Also, the denial of cheap medical services, that is a decrease in the social wage, would also increase the pressure on wages and threaten the stable environment for investment.

Table 11.7
Historical development of the Hospital Authority and the fee charging policy

Year	Historical development
1984	Announcement of the hospital service review.
	Tender won by W.D. Scott Pty Co. (Australia).
	Suggestions by Harry Fang & Henrietta Ip for 'privatising' the medical services in LegCo.
1985	Review of hospital services conducted and Report completed in November and submitted to government in December.
	Proposed setting of Independent Hospital Authority and increase of hospital charges.
	Report suggested increasing charges to recover a greater portion of the cost.
1986	ExCo decided to have public consultation (March to August).
	Medical professionals supported the idea, but staff and pressure groups doubted the proposal.
	Increase of fee rejected by pressure groups.
1987	MDAC endorsed the idea.
	ExCo endorsed the idea in September.
	Wilson announced the government decision to implement the
1987	IHoA proposal on 7 October.
	LegCo debate and endorsement of the IHoA on 15 October.
1988	Transferral of Chambers to PHoA and succeeded by Tak-hay Chau as Secretary for Health & Welfare.
	Establishment of PHoA (October) and split of MHD.
1989	Transferral of Chau, succeeded by Elizabeth Wong.
	Publication of PHoA Report in December.
	Establishment of a permanent HoA, integration of hospitals and transfer of all staff to it.
	Report suggested the charge could be increased to 15 to 20 per cent of cost (compared to approx. 3 per cent at present) and this level would still be affordable by the users.

1990	Final offer of HoA's terms of employment, with better response from staff especially the subsidised sector. Staff disputes gradually resolved.
	HoA Ordinance passed in July.
	HoA formally established in December.
	Strong public, party and LegCo rejection of the proposal to increase fee. Repeated denial by officials to implement the proposal of fee increase and reassurance of 'no one will be denied medical services because they cannot afford' then.
	HoA Ordinance reserved the power to change the fee charging policy to the HWB.
	Inter-departmental working groups to study waiver system and the possibility of a medical insurance scheme.
1991	HoA informed the government that it had no plan to increase the fee in November.
	Working group under the HWB to study policy for different services.
1992	Merging of subsidised and government hospitals.
	Fee Charging working group decided to retain the existing hospital fee charging system.
	Prolonged discussion without decision annoyed its proponents such as Che-hung Leong.
1993	'Towards Better Health' consultative paper proposed again the possibility of increase the fees and a cost-recovery policy.

However, the argument for increasing charges was not without support among other than officials. The argument that 'those who could pay should pay' did receive support especially as the overall income level in Hong Kong increased. Hence, the proposal to improve and expand the Class B hospital beds[94] was agreed by all parties, was implemented and received a favourable response. Though there was no mobilisation on the issue, the middle class demand for a better service in the public sector was supported by the government and other parties.

The reforms were not entirely the construction of the officials and it has been shown that they were also argued for by some medical professionals[95] in LegCo. In fact, the reform could be perceived as a response to criticisms especially from the medical professionals. However, in designing the details of the HoA, official views and the concerns of the PHoA were important. The reasons for setting up the HoA, according to the official explanation, were to improve efficiency and flexibility in the utilisation of resources, management and public participation. These would result from being free of bureaucratic control. In this sense, a conspiracy theory, relating the reforms to a desire to shed responsibility and to de-politicise the services and eventually free them from the control of a future SAR government or from the growing social pressures and party politics, has little validity. In fact, the reforms did not free the government from the responsibility of intervening in and financing the hospital services and or reduce the public pressure on the officials and the Authority.

It is true to say that the government's concern was over an administrative reform and the possibility of saving resources by striving for 'value for money' in view of the ever-increasing hospital budget. Such a concern was certainly a high priority on the state's agenda in the 1980s. Although the economic situation was generally positive, there was no imminent fiscal problem and the potential danger from the ever-increasing cost of running the services was far from real at that time, such situation was not impossible at a later time.[96] This was probably the strongest reason why the government attempted repeatedly to revise and push forward with the fee charging policy.

There was no evidence to show that China had exerted any influence on the reform.[97] In commenting on the influence of the UK, Chambers argued that the government had continuous learnt from all overseas countries, not solely from the UK. 'Privatisation' was a world-wide trend and Hong Kong was just considering all these experiences in order to improve the efficiency of the medical services.[98] Mr Selwyn Alleyne, the Deputy FS in the late 1980s, also put forward this argument.[99] Relevant and similar experiences from the UK as well as other overseas countries served as a reference point for the changes in Hong Kong.

Notes

1 For example, the life expectancy rates for males and females had increased from 72.6 to 74.8 and 78.4 to 80.5 respectively between 1982 to 1992. The infant mortality rate dropped from 9.9 to 4.8 per thousand births from 1982 to 1992. See CSD, 1993, Table 1.4.

2 As argued in chapter 8, the improvement might not be entirely due to the improvement of services but its potential contribution cannot be neglected.

3 It was planned that five general hospitals would be built in the 1980s but, in fact, only the Prince of Wales and Tuen Mun Hospital were completed.

4 The charge for out-patient services and hospital general wards per day were HK$ 21 and HK$ 43 in 1992 compared to HK$ 3 and HK$ 5 in 1982.

5 See 'Report of the Provisional Hospital Authority' (December 1989) and 'Towards Better Health -- a consultation document' (June 1993). For details of the recommendations, please refer to the case study in this chapter.

6 The last step was a review of primary and pre-primary education in 1981.

7 The chairman was from the UK and the other three members were from Australia, USA and West Germany.

8 Although tertiary education was beyond its major domain, it could still make suggestions about it. For example, the Commission discussed the length of undergraduate study.

9 The major reasons were: 1) universal education had been achieved long ago and there was not much room to do to expand the system and, 2) the population of those aged 15 and below decreased from 1,282,000 to 1,194,000 between 1982 and 1992, a decrease of 7.4 per cent. The percentage share of the total population of this group also decreased from 24.3 per cent to 20.6 per cent. As the population decreased, the need for the service also decreased. See CSD, 1993, Table 1.5.

10 Compulsory education stopped at Form 3 and the state considered that further education was only for those who had the ability and the interest to do it. Therefore, the enrollment rate is approximately 90 per cent of those Form 3 school leavers. After Form 3, students can choose to study in a grammar school or in the technical institutes.

11 The University of Hong Kong and the Chinese University of Hong Kong.

12 The funding system for post-secondary institution is similar to the UK system. There is a semi-governmental organization, the University & Polytechnic Grants Committee (renamed as UGC in 1995), responsible for the funding of all recognised post-secondary institutions (except the Shue Yan College).

13 However, the scheme received a poor response from the schools and only few joined the scheme.

14 The fee continuously increased to HK$17,000 and HK$24,000 in 1993/94 and 1994/95 and it will be HK$34,000 in the 1995/96 academic year.

15 Although in numbers, the production of rental housing was still outnumbered the production of sale flats. However, the HA agreed that the promotion of home ownership was the major theme in housing provision and had to be encouraged.

16 The details of the Statement are discussed in the later paragraphs.

17 The initial aid was an interest-free loan of HK$ 70,000 to assist them in buying a flat in the private sector. The loan is repayable over 20 years.

The amount was subsequently adjusted in accordance with the increase of private sector flats. From 1991, the loan could be withdrawn in the form of a monthly subsidy to cover the mortgage. Applicants living in the private flats were not allowed to have any property but the same criteria did not apply to sitting tenants. This is an measure to encourage them to move out of rental housing. The loan was further increased to HK$ 400,000 and HK$ 600,000 (for sitting PRH tenants) in 1995 in order to increase the attractiveness of the scheme and in view of the rise of private flats' price.

18 That means, the rent for different size units was set at the 15 per cent of the median income of the household at its maximum.

19 The standard floor space allocation standard is 5.5 sq.m and the rent was set at 15 per cent of median rent-to-income ratio at the maximum. While for those with $7m^2$, the ratio was set at 18.5 per cent of the ratio at the maximum.

20 The situation was not uncommon for those lower income families affected by the redevelopment scheme. There is an assistance scheme for those who could not afford the rent. However, after two years of assistance, they have to move to other cheaper flats if they want to continue to receive the benefit.

21 Note that there was always a deficit on the former resettlement estates and low-cost housing as the maintenance costs were higher than the new estates and the rent was much lower. However, the HA obtained a surplus from the new estates and more significantly, a huge income gained from selling HOS/PSPS flats.

22 The policy was introduced in 1987. Those households who had resided in rental housing for ten years or more have a means-test for their family income. If it exceeds twice the income eligibility limit for applying for rental housing, the household has to pay 'double rent'. The policy underwent another review in 1992 and was modified in 1993 in respect to the calculations of the income and rent to be paid.

23 A White Paper on rehabilitation published in 1995.

24 Renamed as the Comprehensive Social Security Assistance scheme in 1992.

25 Although the rate was kept under constant review, Mok found that the adjustments did not keep up with inflation in the 1980s. The main reason was the failure to adjust the rate from 1985 to 1987 due to the stringent public finances resulting from uncertain economic condition. See Mok, Henry T K, 1993, p.86.

26 For the Old Age Allowance, the eligibility criteria was lowered from the age of 70 to 67 in 1989 and to 65 in 1991. See HKG, 1991b, p.151.

27 Examples of contracted-out services were the operation of a nursery for a bank and community development services for the Land Development Corporation. Examples of joint redevelopment projects were most common in the property booms of recent years.

28 As recommended by the White Paper, the term 'voluntary agencies', which has been used as to refer to the subsidised and non-profit making sector, was changed to 'NGO'. See HKG, 1991a, p.17.

29 In fact, the private sector was not interested in this low (or no) profit business.

30 The Long Term Housing Strategy (LTHS) was an overall strategy guiding housing policy from 1985 to 2001. However, as this research's period is only up to 1992, the development after 1992 is not be discussed though some of the policy changes are referred to.

31 The programme was initially planned end in 1982/83 but it was extended for two more years to 1984/85.

32 All the major proposals in the paper were well-received except the issue of 'better-off tenants'. A private market research company was commissioned by the government to conduct an opinion survey on the proposals and found that 50 per cent of sitting tenants and 69 per cent of private flat residents agreed with fixed-term tenancies and periodic means-testing for tenants. For those no longer eligible for public rental housing, eviction or the alternative of buying HOS flats were favoured.

33 The same market research found that, 40 per cent of PRH respondents considered it reasonable or very reasonable to increase the PRH rent every two years in line with inflation. Two out of three respondent from both groups thought that a reasonable PRH rent should not exceed 15 per cent of family income (SCMP, 13/7/84). The HA was very cautious in handling this issue. Public opinion was divided as expected. There were widespread protests from PRH tenants on the grounds that the new policy interfered with family life, intruded on family privacy (by testing their income) and that it was difficult to define what 'income' should be included. However, it seemed that the HA was quite determined to proceed with the proposal and was only prepared to discuss the detail calculations of the 'income'.

34 Donald Liao transferred to become the Secretary for District Administration in 1985 and Mr John Todd succeeded him as Secretary for Housing.

35 Of course, the government also restated the importance of providing PRH and of the redevelopment of sub-standard housing.

36 The government assumed that the private sector could produce a constant number of flats. If the HA continued to produce so much PRH, there would be surplus of it because people has increasing need of home

ownership. If the supply was heavily dependent on HOS, there would be a danger that private production would not be fully utilised and therefore a wastage of private sector resources and, moreover, HA itself, could not satisfy all the demand for home ownership.

37 It was planned that the production of PRH would reach peak of 38,500 in 1988/89 and then decrease to 8,500 in 1997/98 while in the same period, the production of HOS/PSPS would increase to an average range of 15,000 to 16,000 and then rise to 16,500 in 1997/98. The production of the private sector would average of 30,000 per year with approximately 30 per cent purchased through the HPLS. See HKG, 1987b, Appendix 12.

38 The two major private developers. Sun Hung Kei and Henderson, expressed their welcome to the strategy (HKEJ, 9/4/87).

39 But they disagreed about the rather small amount of the loan which was proposed to be HK$50,000. The Administrative Secretary of the Real Estate Developers' Association, Mr Anthony Chan doubted the attractiveness of the scheme based on this reason (HKS, 9/4/87).

40 Such as an increase of the loan amount and the inclusion of contract and legal fees to make it more attractive.

41 Since 1973, the chairman of the Authority was the Secretary for Housing.

42 Previously it was administered by the Finance Branch.

43 Under this new arrangement, the HA did not need to repay the premium but had to pay 5 per cent interest on the premium to the government each year. Moreover, 50 per cent of the profit from commercial letting had to be transferred to the government Treasury annually.

44 Several suggestions and amendments were included in the Ordinance: the vice-chairman of HA would be the Director of Housing, the official members were reduced from maximum of 6 to 3 and the FS could order the HA to transfer the total or a percentage of the HA's surplus to the Treasury.

45 The appointment of Akers-Jones as the chairman was made in 22 February 1988 earlier than the LegCo debate. This was a surprise to most of the people as he has no strong relationship and involvement in the HA's operation, though he has been the official member of the Authority from 1973 to 1985. HKPCPHP has commented that it was inappropriate to appoint a former senior government official (he has been the Chief Secretary and then Acting Governor from December 1986 to May 1987 before the arrival of Wilson) to be the chairman of the supposed independent HA (SCMP, 10/3/88).

46 One of the solution was to develop new sites for construction in remote locations, such as Tin Shui Wai, Ma On Shan and Tseung Kwan O.

47 Of course, within the amount, there were more HOS/PSPS flats than PRH.

48 It is another new town to inhabitate residents to support the new airport in Chap Lap Kok developed in late 90s.

49 In fact, one reason that contributed to the deficit was that according to the financial arrangements, the HA had already transferred HK$ 1.6 billion as interest and HK$ 0.8 billion as surplus from commercial letting to the government in the 1988 to 1990 financial years (MP, 2/11/90).

50 The HPLS was not affected but the proposal to assist the sandwich class was shelved.

51 Liao argued that the idea was impractical as 'it would not solve Hongkong's housing problem'. It might be better to consider it again in the mid-1990s, only when 'the bulk of those awaiting public accommodation will have been suitably housed'. In his reply to Dr Conrad Lam, a LegCo member, he argued that 'purchasing the flats in which they reside will only mean that they increase their financial burden without much added advantage over their neighbours, who will continue to pay low rents and enjoy the same level of amenities and identical standard of accommodation'. (HKS, 8/1/87).

52 From a personal interview.

53 The HA selected a list of blocks and sent invitation letters to the tenants to indicate their intention to buy or remain with their current status as tenants.

54 When the deadline for indication of intention ended on 21 October 1991, less than 10 per cent of the selected families indicated their interest (HKEJ, 29/10/91).

55 He was the Deputy Director of Housing at that time and later succeeded Mr Freddie Pang as Director of Housing.

56 The price of private flat remained relatively stable and increased steadily until mid-1989. The June 4th Incident has led to a short crash but recovered in the end of 1989. Then, the price gone up rapidly thereafter. The soaring of price was a mixed effect of intense demand (increasing number of nuclear family and increasing population), favourable mortgage terms (10 per cent first installment) and low interest rate (as HK dollar was packed with US dollar and when US interest rate dropped, HK has to followed). Moreover, housing was traditionally the most reliable investment in Hong Kong and in times of high inflation rate as in late 1980s and early 1990s (and low saving interest rate), more people invested in property. When the demand increased, the price kept going up. The situation was relieved in mid-1994 when the government imposed strict regulations on the property market. The price went down but the economy was also in trouble.

57 The only social action was a small scale launched by several professional unions, such as the Social Workers General Union, an overnight sit-in protest.

58 The upper income eligibility limit for HOS flats at that time.

59 The motion asked the government to lease 5 acres of land each year to construct 5,000 flats of 800 sq.ft. and sell them at 50 per cent of the market price.

60 Nevertheless, the 'predicted' deficit suddenly disappeared in late 1992 and was reported to has modest surplus from that year. The situation, as explained by Akers-Jones in the personal interview, was resulted from incorrect estimation of the budget from the finance section of HD and as the profit generated from HOS was greater than estimated. However, the sandwich class proposal was terminated and the impact of the 'financial constraint' did affected the HA's decision in the process of discussion.

61 The first batch was sold in early 1994. The estate was located in Tsing Yi island.

62 The proposal was never been realised, however.

63 It seemed that the HA was downgraded but, according to an interviewee, it was a strategy to protect the chairman from direct confrontation with the opposition groups as in the days of Akers-Jones. Opinion collected from a personal interview with Miss Virginia Ip. She stated that she was told this by Miss Rosanna Wong.

64 The Deputy Director of Planning, Environment and Lands, Mr Bowen Leung, made this point at a press conference immediately after the Governor's Speech to LegCo on 7 October 1992.

65 Apart from the arguments cited here, such an attitude was also repeatedly revealed by senior housing officials in various occasions. For example, in preparing the LTHS, the Director of Housing at that time, Freddie Pang said that 'such proposal has to be considered carefully so private sector housing development won't be affected' (SCMP, 27/8/86). In explaining the quota of HPLS for the first year, John Todd, explained that 'we don't want to upset either the property of financial market, which is why we are limiting it initially to such a small number' (SCMP, 8/3/87). Deputy Director of Housing, Derek Messling, said that the public sector would 'complement, not compete with the private sector' (HKS, 23/11/89). In an interview with Tung Fung, the current Director of Housing, he also put forward the same argument.

66 In fact, there were much opinion still supported a 'targeting' policy.

67 This occurred through 1) the appointment of those who had a strong business (even property) background and associated professionals to the Authority. Moreover, the Authority is also influenced by those officials

who shared the values as the Chairman had served in the government for very long time and the HD which was, in fact, a government department.

68 This contribution of the parties to the sandwich class issue was highlighted by Mr Frederick Fung, chairman of HKADPL, Miss Virginia Ip of HKPCPHP and Mr Tung Fung, DoH in personal interviews.

69 According to the late Secretary General of the HoA, Mr John Chambers (who was the Secretary for Health & Welfare before joining the HoA), there was no particular reason for using the Scott Consultant just because Australia had similar health reforms at that period, as has been sometimes suggested. Nevertheless, it is notable that UK's experts were no longer automatically preferred.

70 City Forum is a weekly open debate held in Victoria Park on Sunday. Different personnel representing different viewpoints are invited to debate social issues.

71 Representative of the medical constituency in the LegCo and chairman of the Health Panel of LegCo.

72 Other demands were made, most related to staff employment conditions, freedom to opt for new terms of employment, maintaining existing staff ratios and the profession's participation in the Hospital Authority.

73 From a personal interview.

74 From a personal interview. This continued before the setting up of the Hospital Authority. Ho was elected as the representative of health constituency on LegCo from 1991.

75 The members were appointed in March to October 1988.

76 Sir Chung was a prominent political figure in Hong Kong and served on the Councils for over twenty years. He was due to retire from the ExCo in August 1988.

77 The GDA, the Nursing Branch of Hong Kong Chinese Civil Servants' Association, and the two newly elected LegCo members, Dr Che-hung Leong (representing the medical constituency) and Mr Mei-tak Chow (representing the health constituency) requested a staff representative on the Authority (SCMP, 11/9/88; STJP, 1/10/88). Mr Tak-hay Chau and Mr Jack Chan (Deputy Chief Secretary) explained the government position for not appointing staff representatives for different reasons. Mr Chau said that 'there are so many categories of medical staff that if each sector is represented on the authority it will become unbalanced and too unwieldy to operate properly' (HKS, 1/10/88). Mr Chau argued that the Authority needed to have other professions on it and therefore could not entertain their request (STJP, 1/10/88). Sir S.Y. Chung explained that having staff representatives would make the PHoA staff committee a negotiating body for employees which should not be the case (SCMP, 30/10/88).

78 Such as the transfer of Chambers to PHoA as Secretary General and the split of MHD.

79 Though the Chief Executive in the central level and in individual hospitals were still doctors, the participation from non-medical profession in the management at other levels and in particular areas, such as managing the budget, served to balance the influence of the doctors.

80 This included the operational cost of the hospital services and the salaries of the staff according to the civil service terms of employment.

81 The HA model involved the creation of an appointed decision making authority but the retention of a government department, filled with civil servants, to implement the decision.

82 From personal interview with Chung and Chambers.

83 The data was from a household expenditure survey.

84 Replaced Mr Tak-hay Chau as the Secretary for Health and Welfare when he was forced to stepped down.

85 Which was used to compensate the benefit lost by the staff in surrendering their civil servant status.

86 The initial response was still not that favourable. Only 20 per cent of the staff have opt for HoA and within these 6,400 staff, only 500 were from the former MHD (STJP, 4/10/91). The HoA has to delay the deadline for transferral. The initial response from subvented sector was far better than civil servants. By November 1991, 86 per cent of the former subvented staff have opt for HoA compared with only 16 per cent in the public sector (HKS, 9/11/91). Nevertheless, the situation improved as staff were more clear about the new terms and in February 1992, 51 per cent of the existing staff have opt for HoA.

87 At that time, he was the chairman of the AGNS and later replaced Mr Mei-tak Chow as the representative of the health constituency on the LegCo from September 1991.

88 The staff unions reorganised themselves to form new unions, i.e. the Association for Hong Kong Nursing Staff and the Hong Kong Public Doctors Association, in 1991.

89 The Primary Health Care Report (1991) and the Social Welfare into the 90s & Beyond White Paper (1991) mentioned the possible revision of the fee charging policy. So, this committee's terms of reference covered the medical services (preventive, primary, out-patient and hospital services) and the social welfare services.

90 Other recommendations included, 1) preventive services should be free; 2) charges for special services should be continued; 3) a voluntary medical insurance scheme would be introduced under the supervision of an independent regulatory body; 4) first day admission charges and charges for registration would be introduced; 5) a pilot scheme to charge

for drugs; 6) accident and emergency services would be charged at the rate of special clinics; 7) the existing waiver system for the poor and disabled, would be continued; 8) welfare services would be free of charge.

91 The representative of the medical constituency in LegCo from 1988.

92 According to the Administrative Memorandum, the HoA could retain 50 per cent of the financial surplus from raising charges.

93 From a interview with Mrs Shelley Lau and Mr Clement Cheung. However, the fee charging policy was dropped once again in 1994. Nevertheless, the HWB has looked for other ways to increase the sources of income from fee charging such as charging for equipment.

94 This is a class of hospital bed with better environment than the general ward beds, usually semi-private room is provided.

95 Including appointed LegCo members Dr Harry Fang and Dr Henrietta Ip and elected medical constituency representatives, Dr Hin-kwong Chiu and Dr Che-hung Leong.

96 Such as Mr Selwyn Alleyne, who was the Deputy Financial Secretary in the late 1980s, Mr John Chambers, Sir S.Y. Chung, Mrs Shelley Lau and Mr Clement Cheung (Principal Assistant SecHW) etc. Data gathered by personal interviews with them.

97 Except some pro-China trade unions (and parties at a later stage) rejected the cost-recovery policy.

98 From a personal interview.

99 From a personal interview.

12 Theories of the welfare state for the 1980s: a recapitulation

There were rapid changes in every aspects of the welfare state in the 1980s. The shift in employment structure signified the emergence of a new social class, the middle class and professionals. The growing size of this class reflected the overall affluence of the society. This resulted from a continually prosperous economy though future development was always in doubt, partly due to the '1997' issue. In this transitional period, part of the middle class actively participated in the politics, and elections were now the channel for them to gain representation in the formal structure. They acted as the spokespersons of underprivileged and vulnerable groups, such as the lower class and the social service users. The business class also organised to fight for their own interests. There were alignments and mergers among these groups and political parties were formed.

This active participation demonstrated that the past apathetic, and 'refugee mentality' had been given up by a sector of population. The Hong Kong people had greater expectations of government intervention and involvement in providing social services and solving social problems than before. They also believed in citizen entitlements and rights more and a better quality services.

The coming of '1997', the changes in the power structure of society, the loss of 'loyalty' and co-operation from the business sector, the increasing public participation in public affairs, together with a different perception of the role of state and the eroding authority of the state all modified the power relationship between the various social groups and the state. State decisions were increasingly attacked and though the administrative-led structure did not disappear, the leading position of the state was gradually eroded. All these changes modified the policy context and process and the applicability of various perspectives in explaining the development of the welfare state from 1982 to 1992.

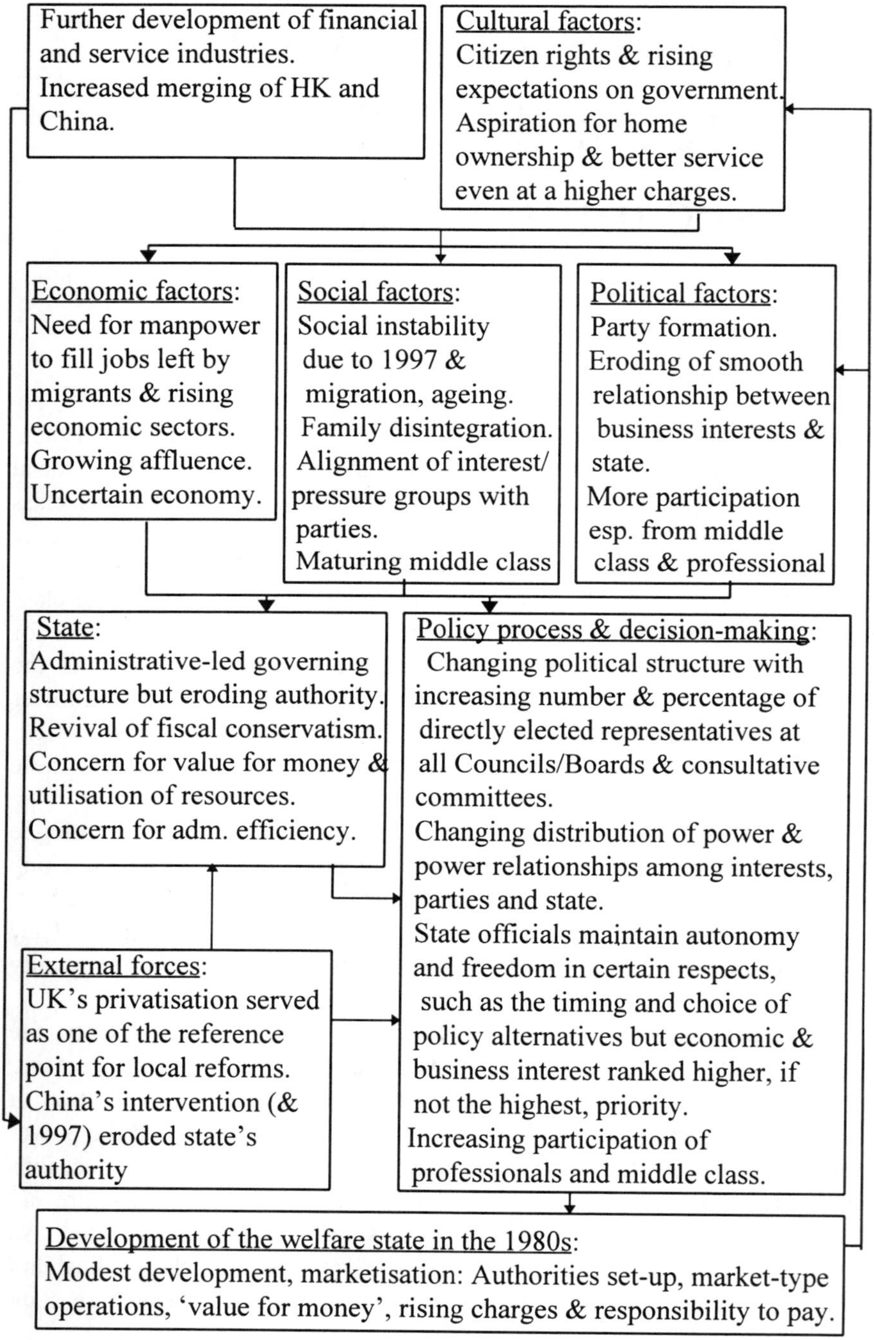

Figure 12.1 General model of theory of the welfare state, 1980s

Assessment of the socio-economic explanation

A cursory review of overall economic conditions and expenditure on social services would show a positive correlation between them, during the mid-1980s economic recession. However, the relationship between economic conditions and the marketisation reforms requires further discussion. The relationship can be explained in terms of a resurgence of a conservative fiscal policy by the government. Facing uncertain economic conditions, the state adopted a more cautious approach to the control of public expenditure aimed at preventing a deficit. The expansionist policy in the 1970s was reassessed by the state and by concerned interest groups.[1] However, it was rather difficult to cut expenditure once the services had been established.[2]

One of the alternatives to control the growth was to prioritise the items of expenditure and design monitoring structures and principles for the utilisation of resources. The government put heavy emphasis on the quest for 'value for money' and on increasing the contribution from consumers and other possible sources.[3] The establishment of the HoA and the reconstitution of the HA were the strategies adopted to monitor the utilisation and rationalisation of resources by private enterprise type operations.

The changing policies were also a response to the changing needs of the society, especially the rising middle class. The growing affluence of the population had changed expectations about the quality of social services. Those who could afford it, usually the middle class, were more willing to pay for better services. The argument of 'users pay' and 'more money for better services' fitted with a capitalist consumption relationship, commonly held beliefs of the Hong Kong people and the arguments for marketisation.

The promotion of home ownership was also a response to continuously rising aspirations. To own a house has long been an aspiration embedded within Chinese culture. Social indicator research done in 1990, showed that, given the chance and ability, the majority of the respondents preferred home ownership.[4] The level of the demand to own a house was further raised by the increase in small nuclear families[5] and the improved incomes of the people. To meet such demands, the government expanded the opportunities for those who wanted to own a flat and could afford to do so, either in the private sector or the public sector (HOS/PSPS). Therefore, the government implemented the HPLS and increased the supply of HOS/PSPS at the expense of PRH.

Apart from the changing culture, social instability in the 1980s forced the government to look for policies which would pacify potentially disruptive forces in order to maintain social stability. A response to the changing needs occurring because of the disintegration of families, the ageing population and the new middle class, though it might be at the expense of other groups, was considered essential. Moreover, a belief that home ownership would promote a sense of belongingness and social stability also supported the government's policies in this transitional period.

However, the existence of these socio-economic factors did not guarantee corresponding response from the state. There were delayed responses or even no responses from the state on some issues. For example, a response to the ageing population, especially in relation to post-retirement protection, was delayed and is still pending a decision. Assistance to the middle class in home ownership was also delayed for several years before concrete action was finally adopted. It was not the existence of socio-cultural situations which directly pushed for the reforms but instead, these served as the indicators of changing demands and also the justification employed by government and parties' debates in the policy process.

Assessment of the political explanation

These changes in context engendered corresponding changes in the power distribution among the social interests. The traditionally powerful business sector gradually declined in the 1980s. Their share of the seats in the formal structure was decreased and they were replaced by the professionals and middle class, on an individual basis or as representatives of groups or parties, through appointment or election. So their influence on the policy process was no longer as absolute and dominant as in the past and they had to compete with other interests in pursuing their own courses of action. The rising power of alternative groups, the parties, made it impossible for the government to ignore their demands, especially when its rule was increasingly dependent on their co-operation. Moreover, the coming of 1997 had divisive effects. All these factors made the previous smooth and mutually-dependent relationship between the state and the business sector gradually break up and business had to organise itself to directly participate in politics to protect its own interests.

Nevertheless, the business interest was not only safeguarded by its presence in the formal structure. Their interest was largely safeguarded by the nature of Hong Kong as a market economy. The level of services in this typically liberal market economy was inevitably restricted by this general limitation. The flexibility of this boundary was dependent on the closeness of the services to the core principles of the market. For example, property trading was at the core of the market economy and therefore the business sector was particularly concerned over housing policy, while the situation in medical and social welfare was different.

Moreover, even the business sector did not directly decide on policies, the state had to consider their interests on their behalf. The concern for accumulation was always a top priority on the state's agenda and any policies which would disrupt the economy were rejected. Such a phenomenon could be observed in the formulation of the LTHS, HPLS and the sandwich class housing issues. Capitalist interests did not directly dominate the government agenda and decision making but the general concern for economic prosperity of the state served to safeguard the business interest.

The shift of power in society and in the formal structure modified the boundaries of the capitalist, and the state and business sector's power to assert their own agenda. The middle class increasingly participated in the formal structure and gained greater benefits in this period. Professional groups actively participated in the discussion of every aspect of the services, especially in hospital and education policies. However, there was no organised effort nor mobilisation from this class but instead, their interests were strongly advocated and defended by all political groups (and the business sector) in LegCo. This was due to their voting power which meant that their demands could not be ignored by the political parties.

So pressure group politics was transformed into party politics and its influence increased from the late 1980s. Their power increased as their resources, in terms of the occupancy of seats in the formal structure, finance, manpower and organisation, strengthened. They developed from an ad hoc structure into a better-organised force, with wider agendas than the previous pressure groups. They had actively expressed opinions on the various social services and argued for a continuous expansion of services. They were against the 'privatisation' of services, such as the increase in fees and the sale of public housing but were not against the principles of 'value for money' and 'cost-efficiency'. Although they were not very successful in the policy debates on the LTHS and HoA, they were successful in postponing the decision to increase fees for hospital services.

Compared with the 'capitalist' and middle classes, the working class's mobilisation was still restricted. Apart from the professional unions, and the staff unions in the HoA case, the trade unions were still fragmented and divided. These divisions were strengthened by the increasing presence of the China factor. So policies were not the outcome of the pressure, either manifest or latent, from the unions. Their impact on the welfare state was still far from that suggested by the social democratic thesis.

Though different groups had different agendas, they shared a broad consensus on the marketisation[6] reform. The debate among the parties, the business sector and the government was not over fundamental ideology and assumptions of the market. Though the democratic camp did repeatedly condemn the market, they also shared a faith in its distributive function and contribution of the capitalist system to the Hong Kong economy. They argued for greater intervention to moderate the market process and to provide better protection for those who were vulnerable and deserving.[7] Policies to preserve a prosperous economy, to rationalise the use of limited resources,[8] to provide a better quality of services, to take care of middle class needs, to improve 'cost-efficiency', and to decrease bureaucratic control over the Authorities, were also supported by them. There was no unbridgeable gap between these rising groups, the business interest and the state. Differences related to the degree of 'marketisation' and aspects of the services to which it should be applied.

Generally speaking, the distribution of power gradually shifted from the business sectors and the traditional elite to the parties led by the middle class and professionals which operated on a 'mass line'.[9] Certainly, the political process was more complicated than it has been in the 1970s and a more careful examination was required of the power relations between them.

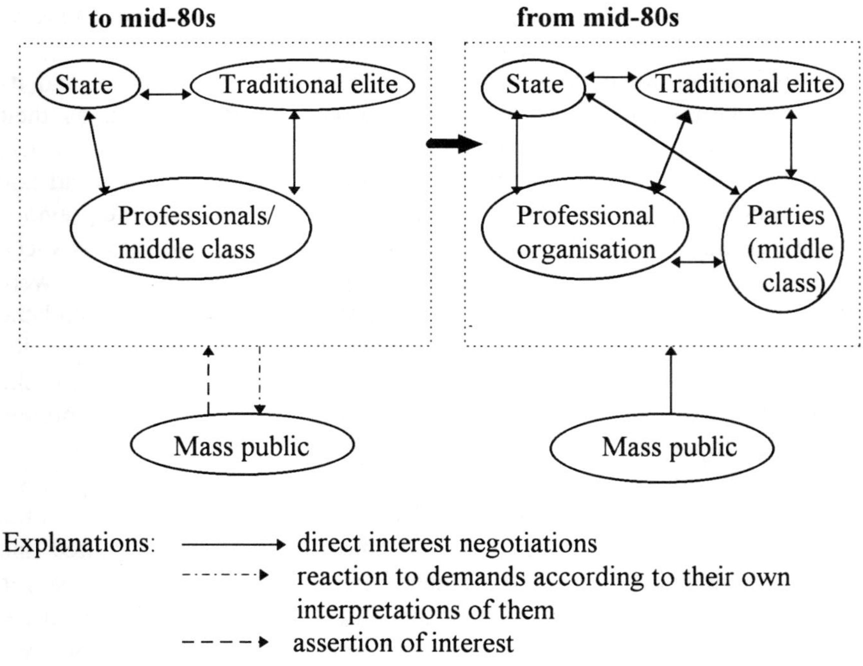

Figure 12.2 Power relationship between the state and society (to mid-1980s and after)

Assessment of the state-centered explanation

Facing greater challenges from new social forces and losing the support of the business sector, the state was increasingly in a dilemma. Generally speaking, the state maintained its relatively high degree of power until the mid-1980s but gradually lost control thereafter.

The government's concerns in pushing the marketisation reforms were, as stated above, to gain efficiency by more vigorous cost-controls, the rationalisation of resources and the introduction of market-type operations to curb bureaucratic red-tape. Such motives could be related to the changing economic, social and political situation. The return to a more conservative fiscal policy was necessary in view of the economic uncertainties and the successive deficit budgets in the mid-1980s. To maintain social stability, policies such as the expansion of tertiary education, the development of elderly and family services, the middle income housing policy and the postponement of fee-charging policy for hospital services, were adopted though they might contradict the cautious and conservative fiscal policy.

Legitimacy was continually one of the basic concerns of the government but ways to sustain it now differed. As the British rule over Hong Kong would end in 1997, 'legitimation' was no longer restricted to mere survival. Apart from the traditional means of maintaining a prosperous economy (accumulation), the officials needed to create an effective and efficient administrative machinery which could cope with the increasing demands for participation in and expectation about the public policy. The creation of autonomous bodies, the Authorities, but still under some control from the government was an attempt to 'de-politicise' policy areas, to provide a channel for public participation as well as a buffer to counteract public pressure and prevent direct confrontation with government (Cheung, 1989; 1991a).

The officials still tried to pursue their own course of action. However, facing the loss of authority and power, they had to be very cautious in dealing with different demands and opposing opinion to press forward their own proposals. The government had to argue for the limited credibility of proposals suggested by the groups and parties. They argued that low turn-out rates for the elections of Councillors weakened the claims of groups and elected councillors that they had public support and suggested their views were 'parochial' and without adequate public mandate. The lack of consistent, coherent and concerted efforts by the political groups further legitimised the government's claim that they were lacking in concern for the overall public interest, which the bureaucrats tried to serve (Chow, 1985a, pp.480-484).

The presence of a general consensus over and support for government proposals also served to strengthen its power.[10] The previous paragraphs argue that although the Hong Kong people made more requests to the government to provide collective welfare, they did not deny individual responsibility in taking care of themselves and their families. Chow argues that the Hong Kongese have little vision of or support for the more comprehensive Western type of welfare state. This is why, he argues, Hong Kong, having all the necessary qualities to be a welfare state, has not developed one (1985a, pp.485-487). The presence of a general consensus over the major policy direction across the interest groups and the state, with only a limited segment of opposition which totally rejected the marketisation reforms, gave the state a strong advantage. Therefore, while there were some differences over the overall policy direction, the government was left with some room, though it was increasingly small, to assert its opinions and plans.

Whenever the state met with strong opposition, it adjusted to accommodate to it. Unlike in the 1960s and 1970s, the officials expected to receive increasing challenges by and questioning from the politicians and the public. They had to pay more attention to public relations and to promoting their proposals. Conventional tactics, such as the use of experts to give advice, as in the cases of the Scott consultants and the OECD education review panel, co-optation of the opposition to the formal structure in order to legitimise a decision but not necessarily to accept the opposition's ideas, were employed.[11]

When the opposition was too strong to be manoeuvred, the state chose to procrastinate over the adoption and implementation of reforms, hoping that the politicians' attention would not last too long and the public attitude would change. After the heated debates were over, the policy would again be put forward but in a modified format. One example of this was the fee charging policy for hospital services. By using such tactics, the government could still preserve some influence over the policy process and decision making.

Conclusion

The overall social, economic and political changes in the 1980s contributed to shaping the context for the reforms, in terms of new needs and demands, the power distribution and its interplay within the modified structure of the policy process. The changes in the relative power of the groups and the state modified their respective ability to further their needs and demands, and their argument over the priorities, the timing and the forms of state intervention.

As debates among the groups intensified, the policy process became more complicated and state officials were caught in a dilemma.[12]

In this new policy process, the officials still maintained a certain power to decide the course of action and decision, but lost their overall control over the interpretation of needs and demands, decision making and other details that they had enjoyed previously. The state had to be more responsive to social demands and more flexible in the policy process. The state's interest was only one of the interests to be considered and could no longer dominate the process. Some degree of state autonomy still existed but it was diminishing as time went by. If the state-centered thesis could be applied to explain the situation in the 1970s, then, 'politics did matter' in the 1980s.

Notes

1 The issue was raised in the process of drafting the Basic Law by representatives with a business background. They argued for putting a ceiling (as a percentage of GDP) in the Basic Law. The proposal was rejected as both impractical and unnecessary.

2 This is known as the 'tree-branch' effect. See Macarov, D. (1978), *The Design of Social Welfare*, Holt, Rhinehart & Winston: New York.

3 Especially when society and the service users were more wealthy and more able to pay for services, especially when they could enjoy better services by doing so.

4 The research found that 65.9 per cent and 12.0 per cent of the respondents would choose owner occupation in private and HOS flats respectively. Only 2.8 per cent and 8.3 per cent chose to rent flats in the private and public sectors respectively. See Lau et al (eds), 1992, Table 3.6; p.61.

5 The percentage of nuclear families increased from 54.4 per cent in 1981 to 61.6 per cent in 1991. See CSD, 1993, Table 1.10.

6 Or 'privatisation', the common terms used in the policy debate in Hong Kong

7 For example, in an interview with the press, Mr Sum Yeung, Deputy Chairman of the Democratic Party describe the platform for the Party as in-between the Neo-Conservatism and welfare statism. The Party will only support for those realistic and pragmatic welfare policies and in against of the Western welfare state system (HKEJ, 11/89/95).

8 For example, Mr Wah Szeto, the core member of Democratic Party, also agreed to increase the school fee for University education as they could pay and should pay for part of the cost. Opinion gathered from a personal interview with him. Mr Sum Yeung also argues that the Party

support for a contributory social insurance scheme in which the employer/citizen has to contribute part of it. He argue that if the state has to shoulder all the finances, it has to increase tax rate and hence, affect investment and intention to work (HKEJ, 11/8/95).

9 Although the parties were led by the middle class, they claimed that their political platform was primarily for the mass public with no built-in class bias, but in practice they argued for more protection for the lower class and were less sympathetic to the business sector. Their survival depended on continuous support from the mass public, not just the middle class.

10 For example, in the case of the double rent for the 'better-off tenants' in public rental housing, establishment of HoA, increase supply of HOS/PSPS.

11 But as they have participated in the process, they have to share the responsibility for the decisions and to be blamed for any wrong judgement.

12 The dilemma in resolving the conflicts between various demands from the opposition and its own, but at the same time, to satisfy as much as it can.

Part Five
THE CONSTRUCTION OF THE WELFARE STATE IN HONG KONG

13 Conclusion

This final chapter returns to the task of examining contribution of various factors to the development of the welfare state. The analysis moves from the detail of individual cases and general developments to the theoretical debate over the applicability of , 'Western' theories to an unique local context. The conclusion suggests that the explanation within the period of study, i.e. 1971 to 1992, generally speaking, shifted gradually from a state-centered perspective to a society-centered perspective. The applicability of Western theories in Hong Kong depends on the 'boundary' of economic superstructure's control, specific socio-economic-political context, the power relationship between different 'actors' and the interests of those in control, as well as the methodological design of the study.

Characteristics of the welfare state development in Hong Kong

Within the period of study of this thesis, the welfare state in Hong Kong gradually expanded in terms of its size, its target groups, its range of services and its coverage of protection. The welfare system developed from a 'minimal-residual' to an 'optimal-institutional' one. The system is 'optimal' in the sense that the scale of provision and range of protection is adequate to prevent and relieve absolute poverty and that those who are in need of basic services and protection have appropriate sources of help, either from the NGOs or the state. The system is 'institutional' in the sense that social services provision has been recognised as a primary responsibility of the state and which has been heavily involved in the production, provision and regulation of these services. Services, such as education and health care, are provided, with no means-tested mechanism, for all who request them.[1] Almost half of the population live in PRH or own HOS/PSPS flats.

Not only minimal standards or mere survival of the human beings have been achieved but services have stretched beyond this to meet other human developmental needs by better quality services.[2] The expansion was largely financed by the rising tax revenues resulting from a prosperous economy, but the scale of provision did not engender an excessive financial burden on the state.

Although the state and the majority of policy analysts are reluctant to use the term 'welfare state', this is, in fact, a welfare state but with some unique characteristics as compared to others. The purpose of the system is not solely individually-orientated, it is also expected to serve society as a whole, by contributing to economic prosperity and social stability. Such functions are either stated clearly in policy documents and/or are realised as by-products of their implementation. However, there has been no vision of creating a socialist ideal version of the welfare state[3] nor radical modification to the primary distribution of income and wealth (or life chances) defined by the market.

During the 1970s, the major characteristic of welfare state development was expansion, though there were differences among services in terms of their priority and the input of resources. At this time, housing and the education service had the highest priority while social welfare received least attention. In the 1980s, the priority shifted to the social welfare services and with less investment in the housing services. The overall expansion of the welfare state was scaled down in the 1980s and growth was kept at a modest rate. At the same time, marketisation reforms were adopted, especially in housing and the hospital services. Efforts made to streamline the distribution of services to different groups according to the principle of eligibility measured by the 'consumers' income level. The 'consumers' are also expected to take a greater part in financing the services.

Which theories of the welfare state are applicable to the Hong Kong case?

Socio-economic perspectives

Hong Kong has gradually developed from a small fishing village to a cosmopolitan city with growing affluence and its society has undergone a rapid process of industrialisation and urbanisation since the 1960s. The changes in the economic structure were accompanied by a shift in the dominant economic activities, from agricultural and re-exporting in the early days, to manufacturing from the 1950s, and financial and service industries from the late 1970s. The development of the local economy did have the effect of facilitating the development of the welfare state in Hong Kong and there was also evidence that expansion was restricted during economic recession. Yet, this most popular thesis in Hong Kong can only explain the aggregate output of the welfare state but not the differential impact on individual services.

Hong Kong society was increasingly complicated, new problems emerged and hence new needs and demands for corresponding measures from the government. In this sense, the structural functionalism/ industrialism thesis can serve to describe the logic of development. There were increasing social problems, such as family disintegration, youth problems and an increasing crime rate, similar to those Western countries experienced in the process of industrialisation and urbanisation. The population structure also changed from a high child dependency ratio to an ageing population and there were increasing problems in caring for them. Social crises, such as the Riots and the '1997' effects (such as migration and potential social instability) engendered social needs and demands for the state to deal with.

However, the perspective is weak in explaining the reasons why certain needs were neglected and had a lower priority while others were not. It also cannot explain the formulation of the policy details. The existence of the objective context could not guarantee corresponding measures from the state immediately.

Hong Kong's social services provision has gradually caught up with those of the developed countries and UK. The convergence and diffusion thesis seemed have an explanatory power here. Certainly, increasing integration (or inter-dependence), initially by the trading system, placed Hong Kong a position which was more open to international influence and experience. This was one of the factors in the debate over the NYFCEP. Such exposure mitigated the previous dominant influence from the sovereign state, the UK. The overseas experience, in addition to the Britain's experience, diffused to Hong Kong through this intensified interaction. However, these experiences, such as the marketisation reforms, were by no means passively received but were scrutinised through the policy process and adopted to the particular conditions in Hong Kong.

Changing values also have certain explanatory power in accounting for the development. The Hong Kongese have been changed from having a 'refugee mentality' to a more enlightened orientation, in terms of higher expectations for the government intervention in social problems and a greater desire to participate in the policy process, initially by the professionals and middle class but increasingly shared by the general public. This new orientation, together with an increasing sense of belongingness to the city, has grown among Hong Kong's people and especially among the younger generation. Of course, the residue of traditional Chinese values, such as the responsibility for individual and family care, still exist. These contrasting orientations have been repeatedly appealed to by different groups in support of their own proposals.

So the socio-economic factors, instead of being the determinants of the development of the welfare state, served to form a context for policy in which needs and demands persisted and, provided a boundary within which the policy makers had to respond. Whether any corresponding measures emerged and in what format can be better explained by other perspectives.

Society-centered versus state-centered thesis

The socio-economic structure reflected the relative power of different groups and changes in it signified the shifting power of the groups. Of all these groups, the officials and the business sector were the two most dominant. The role of Hong Kong as a place for business, from its first day of British rule until today and, as a colony[4] for more than one hundred years upto 1997, were the two fundamental characteristics which set the basic parameters of the political structure. Due to its colonial nature, the Hong Kong government is not a sovereign political entity.[5] In theory, it is an administrative machine ruling Hong Kong on behalf of the UK government, receiving instructions and influence from the Whitehall. It has no democratic structure to transmit public opinion through elections.

However, no state can survive merely by force[6] and Hong Kong is no exception to that. To maintain its continuous rule, the state had to win a mandate by implementing policies favourable to the significant interests in society. When the public was largely apathetic, given its role as business city from its onset, the business sector had a prominent role. The relationship between the state and the business sector was one of mutual-dependency in which each relied on the other for their own interests -- survival and legitimacy for the state and accumulation for the business sector. There was a certain degree of power sharing between them but there was no evidence to support the classical Marxist nor the instrumentalist argument. While the state could maintain a prosperous economy, the business sector did not push for dominant control of the state's policy and hence, there was great autonomy for the state in relation to any direct control by the business sector. Moreover, the business sector might not have favoured such a direct control of the state.[7] Their interests were automatically taken care of by state officials, not by force but by a sharing of values and orientation.

The outcome of this colonial nature and the autonomy status from the business sector and the public (occasionally by the use of force) was the administrative-led structure of governance. The continuation of this structure, in turn, strengthened the autonomous and leading position of the state in the interpretation of social problems, needs and demands and, in planning and implementing the programmes. While there was little alternative opinion or lack any powerful opposing opinion, the state was able to assert its own courses of action, determining the priorities and timing, and the implementation details. This situation was maintained until the mid-1980s. Of course, the state was not free to do whatever it wished. Yet, when the public was largely apathetic with few expectations of the state, threats to its autonomy were rather rare in Hong Kong before the 1970s.

In this sense, the interests and orientations of the state officials were significant in determining the development of the welfare state. The fundamental concerns of the state were accumulation and legitimation. The officials had a strongly paternalistic style of administration, believing that their choices were the best available alternatives. Hence, in the 1970s and until the mid-1980s, the preferences of the officials, as well as the Governors, had significant impacts on the development of welfare state. The response to the Riots was an expansion of various social services to gain public acceptance, the way to assist in economic development was to improve the education services and to expand public housing programmes. The way to cope with home ownership needs was to expand the home ownership scheme, introduce the HPLS and the trial exercise of sales of PRH.

This political context and power distribution gradually changed after the 1970s. There were growing social actions and movements, first by local resident organisations and concerned groups, then by cross-district coalitions, with merger and alignment among groups and finally by party politics. Power was gradually shifted from a coalition between the state and the business sector to a new context where the state, an increasingly divided business interest and the political groups (later the parties) struggled to exert their own interests, their own interpretation of the needs of society and the corresponding measures.

The power of the business class and middle class changed in this period. There was an increasing involvement of local Chinese capital, investment from China and overseas[8] and hence a decrease in the dominant control of British capital. There were also increasing numbers of the middle class and professionals. The middle class contributed a significant share of tax to finance public expenses and they were increasingly frustrated by the disproportionately low benefits they received from the state. Though no organised actions occurred, such views were effectively transmitted into the policy process, by their significant voting power and the presence of middle class and professionals in the governing structure.

General speaking, societal forces gained a stronger influence over the policy process. The formal structure was also modified to reflect and accommodate the changing political power among the groups. More and more representatives with a middle class and professional background were given positions in the formal structure through direct election. Being more sensitive and responsive to social problems and needs, these new groups of actors put forward alternative agendas to the government, and successfully modified the initial priorities and preferences set by the officials and, perhaps, endorsed by the business sector.

During this process, the trade unions still played a relatively passive role. Except for the independent and the professional unions, the two traditionally largest unions, the TUC and the FTU seldom involved themselves in welfare policy debate. The TUC still remains passive today but the FTU became more active from the mid-1980s. Yet, they were more active in labour disputes and labour welfare policy than in the general social services policy. Similarly, the professional unions have continually played an active part in their respective policy areas. Due to the low rate of unionisation and the limited attention paid to the social services debate, there are inadequate grounds to argue for the significance of the social democracy thesis in the Hong Kong case.

Moreover, not every group involved itself in every social services policy process. The private property developers and associated professionals were, for example, heavily involved in housing policy but less so in the social welfare and hospital services. Different policy areas received attention from and participation in by different interest groups and hence, different policy networks were formed. The participation or non-participation of some groups strengthened the chances of success of others, especially the less powerful groups. Similarly, the non-participation (or low participation) of powerful groups and their lack of co-ordination, cooperation and concerted action also strengthened the autonomy of the state.

Not only did different policy areas attract different groups' involvement but they also involved different considerations in policy planning. In Hong Kong, the capitalist structure had differential impacts on different policies. Of all the policy areas, housing lay closest to the core of the market economy[9] and therefore the boundary set by the logic of capitalism was the strongest and the direct participation of the business sector was the greatest, implying that the autonomy of the state and the power of other interests in promoting alternatives was most limited in comparison with other areas.

In reviewing the debates which occurred over welfare issues, it is difficult to argue that the Hong Kong welfare state represented any particular class's interest. The complex nature of the welfare state could serve the business sector, the officials, the middle class and the rest of the public at the same time. Also, in these debates, there were very few examples dominated by clear conflict between classes. The debate over sandwich class housing might be an exception but the policy was also supported by other parties and groups. The welfare state project in Hong Kong cannot therefore be perceived as a result of a particular class mobilisation. It can only be perceived as the product of shifting alliances among various groups and interests.

Power distribution was more evenly distributed in the 1980s[10] than in the 1970s. The participation of new forces served to assert the new social problems and needs, exert new demands and, through their participation in the policy process, constrain or modify the state's actions. However, due to the internal weaknesses of these opposition groups, the state's cautious and careful use of strategies, and the lack of a democratic structure and hence limited participation in and control by the public over the policy process, the state could still maintain certain degree of autonomy.

In the 1980s, the officials' concerns for accumulation and legitimation still persisted but the means to achieve these differed. To achieve legitimation the state could no longer solely rely on co-operation from the business sector but had to seek acceptance by the mass public and the professionals. State autonomy was no longer guaranteed by the structural arrangement but had to be achieved by being more responsive to societal needs and demands asserted by various social groups and political parties. The state's role and power in the policy process was gradually diminished and shared with other groups.

Of course, as shown in the previous chapters, the state's interests and orientation were not necessarily deviant from those of society. To preserve a prosperous economy and a stable society were a common values shared across the society and seen as the mission of the state. The expansion of the social services also received support from the business sector and, the marketisation reforms, such as the promotion of home ownership, and the principle that those consumers who could pay should pay more for the services, were also supported by the opposition groups, though to a lesser extent. When these societal preferences were similar to the state's preferences, the state's autonomy was strengthened. In the 1980s, when societal preferences differed, became increasingly fragmented and when conflicts were more manifest,[11] the state was in a more difficult position and had to be more cautious and strategic about handling the differences in order to derive a course of action. The state's role, in this stage, was never as powerful and dominant as argued by the typical state-centered thesis.

A model of theories of the welfare state for Hong Kong

From the above discussion, we can observe that, as others have argued, different factors played a different roles and different degrees of influence on the policy process. It is impossible to completely rule out the contribution of any one single factor, however minor, in the formulation of the welfare state. The overall policy direction was very much constrained by the capitalist structure and the values[12] that are embedded within it. Within this boundary, the interpretation of and reaction to social issues, needs and demands, and the selection of alternative policies, their timing and implementation were a product of the interplay between the state and the societal forces. The social action movements, and later the parties had relatively small effect on the overall policy direction but had more input on the operational level in the 1980s and the early 1990s. The scope of this influence was partly set by their internal weaknesses and partly, by their sharing of similar value orientations on the respective roles of the market, individual and the state.[13]

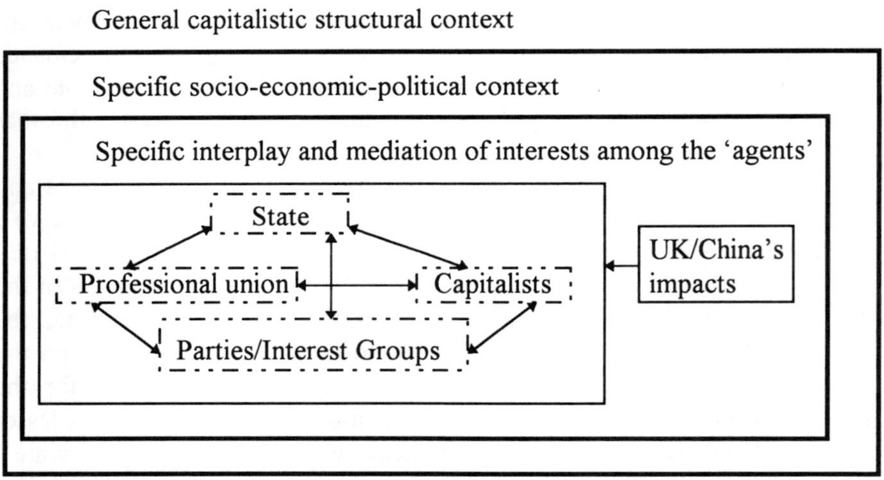

Figure 13.1 Relationship among capitalistic-structural, socio-economic-political and state-centered perspectives

In this sense, the wider capitalistic structure laid down a boundary to the types of intervention. But it was the political factors which could explain more details of the development of the welfare state. In the 1970s, the state's intentions served as a better explanation of the overall expansionist policy of the welfare state. However, from the mid-1980s, political conflict, either manifest or latent, among various groups and the state, better explained the details of the marketisation reforms. The participation of the business sector served to secure government policies in line with the economic structural needs and business interests and the parties' involvement in the process served to counteract their dominance and that of the state.

According to this construction, national differences and similarities may be explained by their differences in economic structure (the dominance of capitalist structure and interests), the specific policy context formed by social, economic and political factors and the power distribution and relationship and respective interests and orientation of those 'agents' involved in the policy making process. The two outer 'layers' serve as a policy context constrains or facilitates the adoption of different policy choices.

The differences between the Hong Kong and other welfare states concern the differential significance of the capitalist structure in Hong Kong, the power of its state, the administrative-led structure as a result of its colonial status and the lack of democracy, and the sharing of interests and value orientations towards capitalism, and the free market with the interdependence between the state and the opposition. In comparison with the Western welfare state regimes, while they are based on capitalistic structures, had a democratic policy process. Such democratic structures could help to reflect the peoples' demands and needs in the policy process and under such party-ruled democracies, the state has to respond to such demands.

However, the situations were totally different in Hong Kong. Not only did it lack any kind of real democratic structure but it lacked strong opposition forces, whether they be based on political parties, mass movements or social democratic organisations, in the policy process. This situation has only changed very recently but there have been no radical consequence of this so far, at least in terms of altering the fundamental nature of the policy process and the welfare regime.

Apart from such an explanation of the cross-national differences, the very definition of the welfare state adopted might also partly explain the variation noted above. As described in an earlier chapter, many studies of the welfare state have focused on social security and social insurance as dependent variables while the present study choose to ignore such variables.[14] Harloe has argued that income maintenance policies can be a fruitful area for examination but, 'there is no reason to believe ... that theories which have been developed to account for cross-national variations in one, albeit major, aspect of the welfare state will be equally applicable to other sectors, let alone to the overall 'regime'' (1995, p.535). Moreover, as argued above, the nature of the policy areas will attract the involvement of different interests. It was certainly true in Hong Kong that issues relating to labour welfare attracted greater interest from the trade unions and the business sector (for example, a long debate on the Central Provident Fund as a form of income maintenance policy). So the impact of the trade unions on welfare might been greater than we have envisaged here, if a wider definition of the welfare state had been adopted. This limited study cannot completely falsify any one of the theoretical perspectives. However, the model derived can provide a framework of explaining the forces behind he development of the welfare state in Hong Kong.

The model can also be used to throw light on the development of the welfare state in other industrialised societies in South East Asia. It is easily noticed that these newly-industrialised societies shared similar characteristics to Hong Kong in, 1) the primacy of economic growth and hence the boundary of capitalism set by this; 2) the relative dominance of the state's authority and hence its autonomy in the policy process and; 3) a developing but fragile democracy with relatively weak opposition.

The primacy of economic growth has given the economic interests a higher priority in the nation's development. This has also allowed the capitalists to have a relatively powerful position in influencing the policy process, either covertly or overtly. Lacking strong opposition forces, the state and the capitalists have formed governing alliance. This is not to say that the ruling groups design policies that are against the public's interests. However, whether the people's opinion can be incorporated or not is very much depends on the interpretation of the rulers. In fact, in these societies, opposition is always restricted to a token form of participation. In some situations, the international pressure can serve as a more effective means to influence the local policies, through diplomatic pressure or trading sanctions. However, with growing affluence and regional cooperation, such pressure from the West maybe reduced.

Future of the welfare state

The policy context of Hong Kong has, again, rapidly changed in these few years. The conflict between Patten and the China government has been intensified. Such conflict and mistrust has invited the China government to increase and speed up its intervention into local policies. The China government has set up the Preliminary Working Committee in the name of preparing the Preparatory Committee for the SAR government in mid-1993. This action was perceived as a strategy to establish the 'second stove'. This Committee has discussed thoroughly on the political, economic, as well as social policies and suggested policies for the future SAR government.

Apart from that, the China government also appointed a large number of Hong Kong Affairs Advisors and even larger number of District Affairs Advisors, and most of these were the current DB members and Councillors. In 1 January 1996, the Preparatory Committee was formally established and the concrete work of preparing the transition of sovereignty and selection of the first SAR Chief Executive. It is noticed that majority of the members of the Committee were with business background. It is also predicted that the coming committee responsible to select the Chief Executive will also be dominated by these groups of people. If this is the case, the Chief Executive has to be the one selected and supported by the business groups, though it has to be approved by the China government.

With the determination to terminate the current LegCo and to set up a provisional legislature from 1 July 1997, the Hong Kong government's authority has declined to a new level low. The situation can be reflected by the recent movement of the business sector, for the first time in Hong Kong history, has united to issue an open letter to condemn Patten's comment on them in destroying the democracy and well-being of Hong Kong.[15] The previous cooperation between the business sector and the state has been faded away. The Democratic Party has been repeatedly isolated by the China government and its supporters in Hong Kong. It is doubtful that whether they still have a significant role until June 1997 and more important, after July 1997.

Applying the model in analysing the future of the welfare state, it is almost certain that the boundary of capitalism and the business interests will be strongly protected. The business sector can, if they wish, directly control the politics and policy process, with the support from the professionals and middle class sharing similar orientations and most important, from the China government. As the China government has asserted that the administrative-led structure will not be changed, the power and authority of the officials will not be reduced, unless these officials are not supported by them. With the fading away of the opposition forces, the governing ideology will be formed by the ruling group formed by these groups of people. Of course, as in before, they still have to response to the specific socio-economic-political situations encountered in the future and the societal responses to the alternatives selected and also, their interests may not be totally different from the public and their opposition. It also depended on the SAR as well as China government's responses to the opposition forces and alternative proposals put forwarded. However, the policy alternatives will be very much defined and confined by the ideology and orientation of the governing groups.

Given the inherent scepticism of the powerful groups towards the 'welfare state', it is almost certain that further expansion of the welfare state are rather impossible but instead, the present efforts to re-define the role and scope of the welfare state, the implementation of marketisation reforms, provision of selective services, the promotion of the principle of 'users pay for it', home ownership etc., will be continued.

Notes

1 Though there are still some means-tests for those who apply for book grants, fee remissions and the student finance scheme for higher education, and those who are recipients of social security benefit could be waived hospital charge. But the services are primarily universal.

2 Of course, some services are still provided on a selective basis and through means-tested mechanisms (for example, see the note in above). In fact, there is need of certain mechanisms to choose those who need assistance.

3 Although MacLehose's speeches in LegCo have been interpreted as containing a few socialist values, i.e. an equal society and a caring community, he himself has denied to having the intention of building up a Western-type socialist welfare state. Such an interpretation was also denied by Lightbody and Williams. Data gathered from personal interviews.

4 Such status has also given Westerners and missionaries a special position in the colony and some of them have served as 'watchdog' monitoring the government especially in the earlier days of Hong Kong.

5 Therefore, in this thesis, the term state has been used with no reference to the meaning of a sovereign state. It is used interchangeably with the term 'government'.

6 Although Hong Kong did possess a strong armed force and police for maintaining peace and order and these forces were succeeded in dealing with the riots.

7 These could be explained by two reasons: 1) to maintain an impartial image of the state for their own sake; 2) to prevent any fraction within them to dominate the state and pursue a policy for its own interests. The primary concern of them is making money instead of involving too much in politics. This assumes that the capitalists were not a unified class. The same viewpoint was reflected by the early discussion over the requirement of the Chief Executive of the SAR by the Preparatory Committee for the Committee for the establishment of the SAR, such as Mr Ka-shing Li. However, the situation changed at a later time when people speculated about the candidates for the Chief Executive of SAR

government. The most frequent referred person is a businessman, and was guessed as nominated and supported by a group of businessman.

8 Such as investment from the United States, Japan and the South-East Asia countries.

9 Harloe argues that, in his comparative study of social housing that, 'a major expansion of such provision on a permanent basis would provide a radical challenge to core capitalist interests'. This explains why the role of social housing provision in the countries studied was 'extremely constrained' and social housing in a 'mass' form only happened when there were major social and economic conditions making it necessary (1995, p.538).

10 However, the distribution was not equal across groups.

11 This is not to say that in the 1970s, the societal preferences were always consensual but, as there were fewer groups putting forward different opinions, it was easier to arrive at a 'consensus' and conflicts were easily covered up.

12 Such as private ownership of resources and property, individual responsibility, cost-efficiency etc..

13 Though they stress more on the role of state than individual while the state argued for optimal intervention from the state and individual involvement in meeting the needs, they were still similar in the overall direction of expansion in the 1970s, improving efficiency, gaining value for money and better rationalisation of resources (hence fee charging) and home ownership in the 1980s.

14 The reasons are first, that was no comprehensive social insurance scheme in Hong Kong and second, that the expenditure and coverage, of the social security system was kept to a small proportion of the total welfare state (as defined in this study) expenditure.

15 The issue was stirred up by Patten's comment and interviews with press during his visit to North America in May 1996. In one of his interviews with 'Newsweek', it was reported that he condemned the business sector for damaging the well-being of Hong Kong (in the report, the word 'betraying Hong Kong' and 'choke off democracy' were used), especially its democratic development. Patten denied this report and he considered that the reporter had misinterpreted his meaning (the editor of Newsweek also clarified that the reporter chose to use such words). The 7 major Chambers of Commerce in Hong Kong had jointly issued an open letter to Patten and at the same time, to John Major, complaining about this comment.

Appendix 1
List of Interviewees

The author would like to express his sincere gratitude to the following person who has kindly consented to be interviewed and provide invaluable information for the study. Special thanks are also due to Lord MacLehose, Lord Wilson and Sir Ian Lightbody who have offered their generous help to introduce suitable interviewees for the research.

	Interviewee	Brief Biographical Note
1.	Sir David Akers-Jones	Former Chief Secretary, Acting Governor and Chairman of Hong Kong Housing Authority
2.	Mr Selwyn E Alleyne	Former Deputy Finance Secretary
3.	Dr Kay E Barker	Former Member of Education Commission
4.	Rev Joyce Mary Bennett	Former Unofficial of Legislative Council
5.	Mr Ron Bridge	Former Secretary of Education & Manpower
6.	Mr John Chambers	Former Secretary of Health & Welfare and Secretary General of Hospital Authority
7.	Mr Clement Cheung	Former Assistant Secretary of Health & Welfare (Hospital Service)
8.	Rev David Chi-kong Cheung	Former Unofficial of Legislative Council and Member of Education Commission
9.	Sir Sze-yuen Chung	Former Unofficial and Senior Member of Legislative Council & Executive Council and former Chairman of Hospital Authority
10.	Mrs Rita Fan	Former Unofficial of Legislative Council & Executive Council, and Chairman of Education Commission

11.	Mr Stephen Fisher	Former Assistant Secretary of Health & Welfare (Social Welfare)
12.	Mr Frederick K.K. Fung	Former Director of Hong Kong Peoples' Council on Public Housing Policy and, current Elected Member of Legislative Council, Member of Hong Kong Housing Authority and Chairman of Hong Kong Association for Democracy and People's Livelihood
13.	Mr Ho-lap Fung	Former Director of Society of Community Organisation
14.	Mr Tung Fung	Current Director of Housing
15.	Mr Man-ho Ha	Current Chairman of Education Action Group
16.	Mr Michael M.K. Ho	Current Elected Member (Health Constituency) of Legislative Council and Member of Hospital Authority, Member of Democratic Party
17.	Miss Virginia C.P. Ip	Current Director of Hong Kong Peoples' Council on Public Housing Policy
18.	Miss Kay Y.K. Ku	Current Deputy Director of Hong Kong Council of Social Service
19.	Mrs Shelley Lau	Former Deputy Secretary of Health & Welfare
20.	Lord Murray Crawford MacLehose of Beoch	Governor of Hong Kong, 1971-1982
21.	Mr Tom McNally	Former Advisor to Lord Callaghan
22.	Sir Ian Lightbody	Former Commissioner of Resettlement, Chairman of Hong Kong Housing Authority & Secretary of Housing
23.	Mrs Catherine Symons	Former Unofficial of Legislative Council & Executive Council
24.	Mr Wah Szeto	Former Chairman of Professional Teachers' Union, current Elected Member of Legislative Council, Member of Democratic Party
25.	Mr Kenneth W. J. Topley	Former Director & Secretary of Education
26.	Lord David Clive Wilson of Tillyorn	Governor of Hong Kong, 1987-1992
27.	Mr Bernard Williams	Former Director of Housing

Appendix 2
Interview Guidelines

The researcher has used face-to-face interview, following a semi-structured questionnaire to collect data. A brief interview guide would be prepared for each interview. Several common questions would be asked to collect the respondents' general comment. However, as each interviewee has unique and in-depth knowledge in respective policy areas, special questions related to their unique experience would also be prepared for that purpose.

The following is the general structure of an interview:

Part 1 Background Information

Interviewees were probed to disclose their involvement in the policy process and in different policy areas. Information such as their position occupied in the administration, in the Councils and in other committees will be collected. These information also served to help the interviewers to verify the information on hand and fine tune the focus of the interview.

Part 2 Specific Policy Areas -- historical development and policy dynamics

The part is further divided into two general part:

2.1 The interviewees were asked to review the details of the development of the policy areas and particular policy case that they have in-depth understanding;

2.2 The interviewees were asked to evaluate the respective influence and role of different parties/groups in the policy process:

a. officials (Governors, Financial Secretary, Chief Secretary, other Secretaries and government officials etc.)

b. Councillors (LegCo & ExCo)
c. business sector
d. pressure groups, interests groups and political parties
e. unions (trade unions & professional unions)
f. United Kingdom & China governments
g. other possible parties/groups as mentioned in the interview

Part 3 General Policy Areas -- historical development and policy dynamics

If the interviewees processed information and comments on other social services or on the overall policy dynamics, the interviewer would probe into these additional topics. The general structure is similar to the one of Part 2.

Part 4 Others

The interviewees were given room to elaborate on the topics, fields and issues that they have considered to be relevant.

Bibliography

Journals / books

Almond, Gabriel A and Verba, Sidney (1963), *The Civic Culture*, Princeton University Press: New Jersey.

Aaron, Henry J. (1967), 'Social Security: International Comparisons', in Eckstein, O (ed.), *Studies in the Economics of Income Maintenance*, The Brookings Institution: Washington, pp.13-48.

Adams, Paul (1988), 'Social Democracy, War and the Welfare State', *Journal of Sociology and Social Welfare*, Vol.15, No.2, pp.27-45.

Alber, Jens, Esping-Andersen, Gosta and Rainwater, Lee (1987), 'Studying the Welfare State: issues and queries', in Dierkes, M. et al (eds), *Comparative Policy Research: learning from experience*, Gower: Alderhsot.

Albrow, Martin (1970), *Bureaucracy*, MacMillan: MacMillan.

Alford, Robert R and Friedland, Roger (1985), *Powers of Theory -- Capitalism, the State, and Democracy*, Cambridge University Press: Cambridge.

Allan, Granham and Skinner, Chris (eds) (1991), *Handbook for Research Students in the Social Sciences*, Falmer Press: London.

Association for a Better Hong Kong (1991), *A Manual for Hong Kong Political Structure and Election*, Association for a Better Hong Kong: Hong Kong.

Babbie, Earl (1986), *The Practice of Social Research* (4th ed.), Wadsworth Publishing Company: California.

Baldwin, Peter (1989), 'The Scandinavian Origins of the Social Interpretation of the Welfare State', *Comparative Studies in Society and History*, Vol.31, No.1, pp.3-24.

Baldwin, Peter (1990), *The Politics of Social Solidarity*, Cambridge University Press: Cambridge.
Barrs, Nicholas A. and Hills, John (eds) (1990), *The State of Welfare:the welfare state in Britain since 1974*, Oxford University Press: Oxford
Barry, Norman (1990), *Welfare*, Open University Press: Milton Keynes
Bendix, Richard; Bendix, John and Furniss, Norman (1987), 'Reflections on Modern Western States and Civil Societies', *Research in Political Sociology*, Vol.3, pp.1-38.
Block, Fred (1977), 'The Ruling Class does not Rule: Notes on the Marxist Theory of the State', *Socialist Revolution*, Vol.33, pp.6-28.
Brannen, Julia (1992), 'Combining Qualitative and Quantitative Approaches: an overview', in Brannen, J (ed.), *Mixing Methods: Qualitative and Quantitative Research*, Avebury: Aldershot.
Bryson, Lois (1992), *Welfare and State:Who Benefit?*, Macmillan: London.
Cameron, D. (1978), 'The Expansion of the Public Economy: A Comparative Analysis', *American Political Science Review*, Vol.4, pp.1243-1261.
Carrier, John and Kendall, Ian (1973), 'Social Policy and Social Change: explanations of the social policy', *Journal of Social Policy*, Vol.2, No.3, pp.209-224.
Castells, Manuel (1986), *The Shek Kei Mei Syndrome:Public Housing and Economic Development in Hong Kong*, University of Hong Kong Centre for Urban Studies and Urban Planning: Hong Kong.
Castles, Francis G. (1978), *The Social Democratic Image of Society: A Study of the Achievements and Origins of Scandinavian Social Democracy in Comparative Perspective*, RKP: London.
Castles, Francis G. (1982), 'The Impact of Parties on Public Expenditure', in Castles, F.G. (ed.), *The Impact of Parties: Politics and Policies in Democratic Capitalist States*, Sage: London.
Castles, Francis G and Mitchell, Deborah (1992), *Three Worlds of Welfare Capitalism: Three or Four?*, Australian National University Graduate Programme in Public Policy Discussion Paper No.21, Australian National University: Canberra.
Cawson, Alan (1982), *Corporatism and Welfare: Social Policy and State Intervention in Britain*, Heinemann: London.
Chan, Rosanna (1982), *An Anatomy of the Failure of the Hong Kong Government's Announced 10 Years Public Housing Plan in 1972*, Research and Resource Service: Hong Kong.
Chan, Kam Wah (1985), 'Privatisation of Public Housing in Hong Kong', unpublished MA Social Service Planning dissertation, Department of Sociology, University of Essex: Colchester.

Chan, David K.K. (1987), 'Social Policy and Citizenship', in Ngan, Raymond M H et al (eds). *A Resonance to Social Policy in Hong Kong*. Writers and Publishers Cooperative: Hong Kong.

Chan, Raymond K.H. (1989), 'Privatisation and the Role of State: a case study of Hong Kong Housing Policy', unpublished MA Social Service Planning dissertation, Department of Sociology, Essex University: Colchester.

Chan, Wai Kwan (1991), *The Making of Hong Kong Society*, Clarendon Press: Oxford

Cheng, Kai Ming (1982), 'A Review of Education in the Past 11 Years', *Hong Kong Economic Journal*, Vol.6 No.3, pp.11-16.

Cheng, Kai Ming (1992), 'Educational Policymaking in Hong Kong: The Changing Legitimacy', in Postiglione, G.A. (ed.), *Education and Society in Hong Kong: Toward One Country Two Systems,* Hong Kong University Press: Hong Kong.

Cheng, Joseph Y.S. (1979), 'Goals of Government Expenditure in a Laissez-faire Political Economy: Hong Kong in the 1970s', *Asian Survey*, Vol.19, pp.695-706.

Cheng, Joseph Y.S. (1982), 'From Being Responsive to Being Responsible', in Cheng, Joseph Y.S. (ed.), *Hong Kong in the 1980s*, Summerson: Hong Kong.

Cheng, Joseph Y.S. (1984a), 'Pressure Groups and Hong Kong Politics', in Cheng, Joseph Y.S. (ed.), *A Collected Comments on Hong Kong's Economy, Politics and Society*, Tsun Shin Cultural Affairs Company: Hong Kong.

Cheng, Joseph Y.S. (1984b), 'The Trend of Citizens Rights Protest in Hong Kong', in Cheng, Joseph Y.S. (ed.), *A Collected Comments on Hong Kong's Economy, Politics and Society*, Tsun Shin Cultural Affairs Company: Hong Kong.

Cheung, Anthony B.L. (1987), 'Retrenchment of Social Policy? -- The Future of Social Policy from a Political Perspective', *Ming Pao Monthly Magazine*, December 1987, pp.56-57.

Cheung, Anthony B.L. (1988a), 'A Ruling Approaching Legitimacy Crisis', *Ming Pao Monthly Magazine*, December 1988, pp.28-31.

Cheung, Anthony B.L. (1988b), 'The Realistic Consideration and Political Implication of Privatisation -- the Establishment of Authority', *Ming Pao Monthly Magazine*, February 1988, pp.37-43.

Cheung, Anthony B.L. (1989), 'The Trend and Political Implication of Public Sector Reform in Hong Kong', *Ming Pao Monthly Magazine*, August 1989, pp.45-48.

Cheung, Anthony B.L. (1991), 'The Consideration and Future of Public Sector Reform in Hong Kong', paper presented in the conference

'Comparison of Guangtung and Hong Kong's Public Sector Administrative Reform' organised by The Chinese University of Hong Kong Institute of Asia-Pacific Studies, November 19th., 1991, mimeograph.

Cheung, Anthony B.L. and Louie, K.S. (1991), *Social Conflicts in Hong Kong, 1975-1986: Trends and Implications*, Institute of Asia-Pacific Studies, The Chinese University of Hong Kong: Hong Kong.

Cheung, Anthony B.L.; Lui, T. L.; Chan, M.H. and Wong, W. P. (1988), *Class Analysis in Hong Kong*, Ching Man Bookshop: Hong Kong

Chiu, Sammy W.S. (1985), 'The Myth of Economic Success and Hong Kong's Social Policy', in Wong, W. et al (eds), *The Challenge of Social Work in Hong Kong (3rd ed.)*, Writers and Publishers Cooperative: Hong Kong.

Chiu, Sammy W.S. (1987), 'Fabian-Reformism and Social Welfare', in Ngan, Raymond M.H. et al (eds), *A Resonance to Social Policy in Hong Kong*, Writers and Publishers Cooperative: Hong Kong.

Chiu, Sammy W.S. (1988), 'Discussion and Insight -- Privatisation of Social Service', *Social Welfare Quarterly*, No.104, pp.1-5.

Chouinard, Vera and Fincher, Ruth (1987), 'State Formation in Capitalist Societies:A Conjunctural Approach', *Antipode*, Vol.19, No.3, pp.329-353.

Chow, Nelson W.S. (1979), 'Economic Uncertainty and the Development of Social Policy in Hong Kong', *Hong Kong Journal of Social Work*, Vol.13, No.2, pp.1-8.

Chow, Nelson W.S. (1980), *The Development of Social Welfare Policy in Hong Kong*, University Press Company: Hong Kong.

Chow, Nelson W.S. (1982), 'The Reasons for Abundance of Social Insurance in Hong Kong', *Ming Pao Monthly Magazine*, No.193, pp.25-27.

Chow, Nelson W.S. (1983), 'The Chinese Family and Support of the Elderly in Hong Kong', *Gerontologist*, Vol.23, No.6, pp.584-588.

Chow, Nelson W.S. (1984a), 'An Examination of the Fuure of Hong Kong's Social Services from a Comparative Perspective', in Cheng, Joseph Y.S. (ed.), *The future of Hong Kong*, Cosmos: Hong Kong.

Chow, Nelson W.S. (1984b), *An Appraisal of Hong Kong Social Welfare Policy*, Cosmos: Hong Kong.

Chow, Nelson W.S. (1985a), 'Socio-Political-Economic Changes and its Impacts on Future Development of Social Welfare in Hong Kong', in Wong, W. et al (eds), *The Challenge of Social Work in Hong Kong (3rd ed.)*, Writers and Publishers Cooperative: Hong Kong, pp.9-18.

Chow, Nelson W.S. (1985b), 'The Development, Achievement and Defects of Social Services during MacLehose's Office', in Cheng, Joseph Y.S.

(ed.), *Hong Kong in the Mid-80s*, University Press Company: Hong Kong, pp.139-154.
Chow, Nelson W.S. (1985c), 'Welfare Development in Hong Kong -- the politics of social choice', in Jao, Y.C. et al (eds), *Hong Kong and 1997 -- Strategies for the Future*, University of Hong Kong Centre of Asian Studies: Hong Kong.
Chow, Nelson W.S. (1987), 'Western and Chinese Ideas of Social Welfare', *International Social Work*, Vol.30, pp.31-41.
Chow, Nelson W.S. (1988), 'The Social and Political Impacts of Privatisation of Social Services', *Social Welfare Quarterly*, No.104, pp.6-9.
Chow, Nelson W.S. (1990), *The Ideology and Structure of Social Welfare*, Chung Hwa Bookshop: Hong Kong.
Collier, David and Messick, Richard E. (1975), 'Prerequisites versus Diffusion: testing alternative explanations of security adoption', *The American Political Science Review*, Vol.69, pp.1299-1315.
Cook, Paul and Kirkpatrick, Colin (eds) (1988), *Privatisation in Less Developed Countries*, Wheatsheaf: Brighton.
Cuthbert, Alexander R. (1991), 'A Fistful of Dollars: Legitimation, Production and Debate in Hong Kong', *International Journal of Urban and Regional Research*, Vol.15, No.2, pp.234-249.
Cutright, Phillips (1965), 'Political Structure, Economic Development, and National Social Security Programs', *American Journal of Sociology*, Vol.70, pp.537-550.
Cutright, Phillips (1967), 'Income Distribution: A Cross National Analysis', *Social Forces*, Vol.46, pp.180-190.
Davies, S.N.G. (1977), 'One Brand of Politics Rekindled', *Hong Kong Law Journal*, Vol.7, No.1, pp.44-81.
Denzin, Norman (1989a), *Interpretative Interactionism*, Sage: London.
Denzin, Norman (1989b), *The Research Art -- A Theoretical Introduction to Sociological Methods (3rd ed.)*, Butterworth: London.
DeViney, S. (1983), 'Characteristics of the State and the Expansion of Public Social Expenditure', in Tomasson, R.F. (ed.), *Comparative Social Research: The Welfare State, 1883-1983*, JAI Press: Conneticut.
Donahue, John D. (1989), *The Privatization Decision:Public Ends, Private Means*, Basic Books: New York.
Durkheim, Emile (1964), *The Division of Labor in Society*, Free Press: New York.
Eckstein, Harry (1960), *Pressure Group Politics: The Case of the British Medical Association*, Allen and Unwin: London.
England, Joe and Rear, John (1981), *Industrial Relations and Law in Hong Kong*, Oxford University Press: Hong Kong.

Esping-Andersen, Gosta (1982), 'After the Welfare State', *Working Papers for a New Society*, Vol.9, No.3, pp.36-41.

Esping-Andersen, Gosta (1989), 'The Three Political Economy of the Welfare State', *Canadian Review of Sociology and Anthropology*, Vol.26, No.1, pp.10-36.

Esping-Andersen, Gosta (1990), *The Three Worlds of Welfare Capitalism*, Polity: Cambridge.

Esping-Andersen, Gosta and van Kersbergen, Kees (1992), 'Contemporary Research on Social Democracy', *Annual Review of Sociology*, Vol.18, pp.187-208.

Evans, P.; Rueschemeyer, D. and Skocpol, T. (1992), 'On the Roads Towards a More Adequate Understanding of the State', in Evans, P.; Rueschemeyer, D. and Skocpol, T. (eds), *Bringing the State Back In*, Cambridge University Press: New York, pp.347-366.

Flora, Peter and Alber, Jens (1981), 'Modernization, Democratization, and the Development of the Welfare States in Western Europe', in Flora, P. and Heidenheimer, A.J. (eds), *The Development of Welfare States in Europe and America*, Transaction Books: Princeton, pp.37-80.

Flora, Peter and Heidenheimer, Arnold J. (1981), 'The Historical Core and Changing Boundaries of the Welfare State', in Flora, P. and Heidenheimer, A.J. (eds), *The Development of Welfare States in Europe and America*, Transaction Books: New Jersey, pp.17-34.

Fong, Peter K.W. (1986), *Housing Policy and the Public Housing Programme in Hong Kong*, Centre of Urban Studies and Urban Planning, University of Hong Kong: Hong Kong.

Furniss, Norman and Tilton, Timothy (1977), *The Case for the Welfare State: from Social Security to Equality*, Indiana University Press: Bloomington.

Giddens, Anthony (1992), *Sociology*, Polity: Cambridge.

Ginsburg, Norman (1992), *Divisions of Welfare: A Critical Introduction to Comparative Social Policy*, Sage: London.

Gold, David A.; Ho, Clarence Y.H. and Wright, Erik Olin (1975a), 'Recent Developments in Marxist Theories of the Capitalist State (Part 1)', *Monthly Review*, Vol.25, No.5, pp.29-43.

Gold, David A.; Ho, Clarence Y.H. and Wright, Erik Olin (1975b), 'Recent Developments in Marxist Theories of the Capitalist State (Part 2)', *Monthly Review*, Vol.25, No.6, pp.36-51.

Gough, Ian (1979), *The Political Economy of the Welfare State*, Macmillan: London.

Gould, Derek B. (1992), 'Policymaking Style in the Transistional Period in Hong Kong', *Hong Kong Public Administration*, Vol.1, No.1, pp.120-140.

Gourevitch, Peter (1986), *Politics in Hard Times -- Comparative Responses to International Economic Crisis*, Cornell University Press: Ithaca.
Ham, Christopher and Hill, Michael (1987), *The Policy Process in Modern Capitalist State*, Wheatsheaf: Brighton.
Haralambos, Michael and Holborn, Martin (1990), *Sociology: themes and perspectives (3rd ed.)*, Unwin Hyman: London.
Harloe, Michael (1981), 'The Recommodification of Housing', in Harloe, M. and Lebas, E. (eds), *City, Class and Capital*, Edward Arnold: London.
Harloe, Michael (1995), *The People's Home? -- Social Rented Housing in Europe and America*, Blackwell: Oxford.
Harris, Peter (1978), *A Study in Bureaucratic Politics*, Heinemann: Hong Kong.
Heald, David and Thomas, David (1986), 'Privatisation as Theology', *Public Policy and Administration*, Vol.1, No.2, pp.49-65.
Heclo, Hugh (1974), *Modern Social Politics in Britain and Sweden*, Yale University Press: New Haven.
Henderson, Jeffrey (1991), 'Urbanization in the Hong Kong -- South China Region: An Introduction to Dynamics and Dilemmas', *International Journal of Urban and Regional Research*, Vol.15, No.2, pp.169-179.
Henig, Jeffrey R.; Hamnett, Chris and Feigenbaum, Harvey B. (1988), 'The Politics of Privatization:A Comparative Perspective', *Governance:An International Journal of Policy and Administration*, Vol.1, No.4, pp.442-468.
Hewitt, Christopher (1977), 'The Effect of Political Democracy and Social Democracy on Equality in Industrial Societies: A Cross-National Comparison', *American Sociological Review*, Vol.42, pp.450-464.
Ho, Harold (1980), 'Social Welfare Development in Hong Kong in the 1970s -- a cursory review', *Hong Kong Journal of Social Work*, Vol.14, No.1, pp.13-17.
Ho, Kam Fai (1978), 'Extension of Fee Charging for Social Welfare Services', *Hong Kong Journal of Social Work*, Vol.12, No.2, pp.2-9.
Ho, Yue Min (1986), 'Who's Power can compete with the businessmen?', *Pai-Sing Semi-Monthly Magazine*, No.132, pp.16-17.
Hoadley, Stephen (1970), 'Hong Kong is the Lifeboat: Notes on Political Culture and Socilaization', *Journal of Oriental Studies*, Vol.8, pp.206-218.
Hoadley, Stephen (1973), 'Political Participation of Hong Kong Chinese: Patterns and Trends', *Asian Survey*, Vol.13, No.6, pp.604-616.
Hodge, Peter (1973), 'Social Policy: An Historical Perspective as Seen in Colonial Policy', *Journal of Oriental Studies*, Vol.11, No.2, pp.207-219.
Hodge, Peter (1976), 'The Poor and People of Quality: Social Policy in Hong Kong', *Hong Kong Journal of Social Work*, Vol.10, No.2, pp.2-17.

Hodge, Peter (1981), 'The Politics of Welfare', in Jones, J.F. (ed.), *The Common Welfare: Hong Kong's Social Services*, Chinese University Press: Hong Kong, pp.1-20.

ICSW Hong Kong Committee (1970), 'Social Change and New Needs for Social Welfare', *Welfare Quarterly*, No.35, pp.12-16.

Johnson, Norman (1987), *The Welfare State in Transition:the theory and practice of welfare pluralism*, Wheatsheaf: Brighton.

Jao, Y.C.; Levin, David A.; Ng, Sek Hong and Sinn, Elizabeth (eds) (1988), *Labour Movement in a Changing Society: the experience of Hong Kong*, Centre of Asian Studies, University of Hong Kong: Hong Kong.

Jones, Catherine (1985a), *Patterns of Social Policy*, Tavistock: London.

Jones, Catherine (1985b), 'From Bureaucratic to Populist Social Policy? Prospects to 1997', *Hong Kong Journal of Social Work*, Vol.19, No.2, pp.1-9.

Jones, Catherine (1990), *Promoting Prosperity -- The Hong Kong Way of Social Policy*, Chinese University Press: Hong Kong.

Kasinitz, Philip (1983), 'Neo-Marxist Views of the State', *Dissent*, Vol.30, No.3, pp.337-346.

Kemans, Hans (1990), 'Social Democracy and the Politics of Welfare Statism', *Netherlands Journal of Social Sciences*, Vol.26, No.1, pp.17-34.

Kerr, C.; Dunlop, J,; Harbison, F. and Myers, C. (1973), *Industrialism and Industrial Man*, Penguin: Harmonsworth.

King, Ambrose Y.C. (1972), *The Political Culture of Kwun Tong: a Chinese Community in Hong Kong*, Social Research Centre, The Chinese University of Hong Kong: Hong Kong

King, Ambrose Y.C. (1975), 'Administrative Absorption of Politics in Hong Kong: emphasis on the grassroots level', *Asian Survey*, Vol.20, No.8, pp.422-439.

King, Ambrose Y.C. (1992), 'Paradigm and the Development of Sociology', in Lee, M.K. and Wong, S.L. (eds), *New Introduction of Sociology*, Commercial Press Company: Hong Kong, pp.13-36.

King, Desmond S. (1987a), *The New Right: Politics, Markets and Citizenship*, Macmillan: London.

King, Desmond S. (1987b), 'The State and the Social Structures of Welfare in Advanced Industrial Democracies', *Theory and Society*, Vol.16, No.6, pp.841-868.

King, Roger, 1986:*The State in Modern Society:new directions in political sociology*, Macmillan: London.

Kolderie, Ted (1986), 'The Two Different Concepts of Privatization', *Public administration Review*, Vol.46, No.4, pp.285-291.

Kolderie, Ted (1987), 'What do we mean by "Privatization"?', *Society*, Vol.24, No.6, pp.46-51.

Korpi, Walter (1983), *Democratic Class Struggle*, Routledge and Kegan Paul: London.

Korpi, Walter (1989), 'Power, Politics, and State Autonomy in the Development of Social Citizenship: Social Rights During Sickness in Eighteen OECD Countries Since 1930', *American Sociological Review*, Vol.54, pp.309-328.

Kuhnle, Stein (1981), 'The Growth of Social Insurance Programs in Scandinavia: Outside Influences and Internal Forces', in Flora, P. and Heidenheimer, A.J. (eds), *The Development of Welfare States in Europe and America*, Transaction Books: New Brunswick, pp.125-150.

Lam, Jermain T.M. and Lee, Jane C.Y. (1993), *The Dynamic Political Actors in Hong Kong Transition*, Writers' and Publishers' Cooperative: Hong Kong.

Lau, Siu Kai (1981), 'The Government, Intermediate Organizations, and Grass-roots Politics in Hong Kong', *Asian Survey*, Vol.21, No.8, pp.865-884.

Lau, Siu Kai (1982), *Society and Politics in Hong Kong*, Chinese University Press: Hong Kong.

Lau, Siu Kai (1985), 'Political Reform and Political Development in Hong Kong: Dilemmas and Choices', in Jao, Y.C. et al (eds), *Hong Kong and 1997 -- Strategies for the Future*, Centre of Asian Studies, University of Hong Kong: Hong Kong, pp.23-49.

Lau, Siu Kai (1991), 'The Trend of Sharing Power between China and Britain', *Wide Angle Monthly Magazine*, March 1991, pp.50-66.

Lau, Siu Kai and Kuan, Hsin Chi (1988), *The Ethos of the Hong Kong Chinese*, The Chinese University Press: Hong Kong.

Lau, Siu Kai; Lee, Ming Kwan; Wan, Po Shan and Wong, Siu Lun (eds) (1991), *Indicators of Social Development: Hong Kong 1988*, Institue of Asia-Pacific Studies, The Chinese University of Hong Kong: Hong Kong.

Lau, Siu Kai; Lee, Ming Kwan; Wan, Po Shan and Wong, Siu Lun (eds) (1992), *Indicators of Social Development: Hong Kong 1990*, Institute of Asia-Pacific Studies, The Chinese University of Hong Kong: Hong Kong.

Law, C.K. (1982), 'A Partial Analysis of the Public Housing Policy of Hong Kong', in Cheng, Joseph Y.S., *Hong Kong in the 1980s*, Summerson: Hong Kong, pp.109-117.

Layder, Derek (1993), *New Strategies in Social Research*, Polity: Cambridge.

Leat, Diana (1986), 'Privatization and Voluntarization', *The Quarterly Journal of Social Affairs*, Vol.2, No.3, pp.285-320.

Lee, Chi Fai (1987), 'An Analysis of Hong Kong Medical and Health Policies', in Ngan, R.M.H. et al (eds), *A Resonance to Hong Kong Social Policy*, Writers and Publishers Cooperative: Hong Kong, pp.209-229.

Lee, James K.C. (1987), 'Social Policy Approaching 1997', in Ngan, R.M.H. et al (eds), *A Resonance to Social Policy*, Writers and Publishers Cooperative: Hong Kong, pp.259-271.

Lee, James K.C. (1988), 'An Interpretation of Privatisation of Social Services', *Social Welfare Quarterly*, No.104, pp.14-18.

Lee, Ming Kwan (1984a), 'Social and Political Conscious of Hong Kong People', in Cheng, Joseph Y.S. (ed.), *A Collected Comments on Hong Kong's Economy, Politics and Society*, Tsun Shin Cultural Affairs Company: Hong Kong, pp.219-222.

Lee, Ming Kwan (1984b), 'The Power Structure and Pressure Group in Hong Kong', in Cheng, Joseph Y.S. (ed.), *A Collected Comments on Hong Kong's Economy, Politics and Society*, Tsun Shin Cultural Affairs Company: Hong Kong, pp.235-242.

Lee, Rance P.L. (1992), 'Sociological Research Methodology', in Lee, M.K. and Wong, S.L. (eds), *New Introduction of Sociology*, Commercial Press Company: Hong Kong, pp.57-84.

Leung, Benjamin K.P. (1990), 'Power and Politics: A Critical Analysis', in Leung, B.K.P. (ed.), *Social Issues in Hong Kong*, Oxford University Press: Hong Kong, pp.13-26.

Leung, Joe C.B. (1990), 'Problems and Changes in Community Politics', in Leung, B.K.P. (ed.), *Social Issues in Hong Kong*, Oxford University Press: Hong Kong, pp.43-66.

Lightman, Ernie and Irving, Allan (1991), 'Restructuring Canada's Welfare State', *Journal of Social Policy*, Vol.20, No.1, pp.65-86.

Lin, Yu Tang (1938), *My Country and My People*, Heinemann: London.

Lin, Wen I (1994), *Welfare State -- A Historical Comparative Analysis*, Jui Li Books Company: Taipei.

Lo, Shui Hing (1988), 'Decolonization and Political Development in Hong Kong', *Asian Survey*, Vol.28, No.6, pp.613-629.

Louie, K.S. and Sham, K.C. (eds) (1995), *A Summary of Hong Kong Elections, 1982 - 1994*, Institute of Asia-Pacific Studies, The Chinese University of Hong Kong: Hong Kong.

Lui, Tai Lok and Wong, Thomas W.P. (1992), *From One Brand of Politics to One Brand of Political Culture*, Institute of Asia-Pacific Studies, The Chinese University of Hong Kong: Hong Kong.

Lukes, Steven (1981), *Power: A Radical View*, Macmillan: London.

Lundqvist, Lennart J. (1986), *The Concept of Privatization:A Preliminary Analysis*, The National Swedish Institute for Building Research: Sweden.

MacPherson, Stewart (1985), *Social Policy in the Third World*, Wheatsheaf: Brighton.

March, James G. and Olsen, Johan P. (1984), 'A New Perspective on New Institutionalism', *American Political Science Review*, Vol.78, No.3, pp.734-749.

Marsh, David (ed.) (1983), *Pressure Politics*, Junction Books: London.

Marshall, T.H. (1963), *Class, Citizenship and Social Development*, Allen and Unwin: London.

Marshall, Catherine and Rossman, Gretchen B. (1989), *Designing Qualitative Research*, Sage: London.

McLaughlin, Eugene (1993), 'Hong Kong: a residual welfare regime', in Cochrane, A. and Clarke, J. (eds), *Comparing Welfare States*, Sage: London

Merton, Robert K. (1968), *Social Theory and Social Structure*, Free Press: New York.

Miliband, Ralph (1969), *The State in Capitalist Society*, Weidenfeld and Nicolson: London.

Miliband, Ralph (1973), 'The Capitalist State: Reply to Nicos Poulantzas', in Urry, John and Wakeford, John (eds), *Power in Britain -- Sociological Readings*, Heinemann: London.

Miliband, Ralph (1977), *Marxism and Politics*, Oxford University Press: Oxford.

Miliband, Ralph (1983), *Class Power and State Power*, Verso: London.

Millard, Frances (ed.) (1988), *Social Welfare and the Market*, Suntory-Toyota International Centre for Economics and Related Disciplines, London School of Economics and Political Science : London.

Mills, C Wright (1956), *The Power Elite*, Oxford University Press: New York.

Miners, Norman J. (1975), 'Hong Kong: a case study in political stability', *Journal of Commonwealth and Comparative Politics*, Vol.13, pp.26-39.

Miners, Norman J. (1989), *The Government and Politics of Hong Kong (4th ed.)*, Oxford University Press: Hong Kong.

Miners, Norman J. (1991), *The Government and Politics of Hong Kong (5th ed..)*, Oxford University Press: Hong Kong.

Mishra, Ramesh (1986), *The Welfare State in Crisis:social thought and social change*, Wheatsheaf: Brighton.

Mishra, Ramesh (1987), *Society and Social Policy:theories and practice of welfare*, Macmillan: London.

Mishra, Ramesh (1990), *The Welfare State in Capitalist Society*, Harverster and Wheatsheaf: Hemel Hemstead

Mok, Henry T.K. (1993), *Poverty in Hong Kong and Social Security*, Chung Hwa Bookshop: Hong Kong.

Mok, Hoi (1993), *The Development and Structural Change of Hong Kong Economy*, Joint Publishing: Hong Kong.

Nachimas, David and Nachimas, Chava (1981), *Research Methods in the Social Science (2nd ed.)*, St. Martin's Press: New York.

Namkoong, Keun (1990), 'A Cross-National Study on Public Health Program and Policy', unpublished doctoral dissertation, Michigan University: Michigan.

Ngan, Raymond M.H. (1987), 'Welfare Ideology of Marxism and Post-Marxism', in Ngan, Raymond M.H. et al (eds), *A Resonance to Social Policy in Hong Kong*, Writers and Publishers Cooperative: Hong Kong, pp.17-30.

Nordlinger, Eric A. (1981), *On the Autonomy of the Democratic State*, Harvard University Press: Cambridge, MA.

O'Connor, Julia (1988), 'Convergence or Divergence? Change in Welfare Effort in OECD Countries 1960-1980', *European Journal of Political Research*, Vol.16, pp.277-299.

Offe, Claus (1982), 'Some Contradictions of the Modern Welfare State', *Critical Social Policy*, Vol.2, No.2, pp.7-16.

Offe, Claus (1987), *Contradictions of the Welfare State,* Hutchinson: London.

Orloff, Ann S. and Skocpol, Theda (1984), 'Why Not Equal Protection? Explaining the Politics of Public Social Spending in Britain, 1900-1911, and the United States, 1880s-1920', *American Sociological Review*, Vol.49, pp.726-750.

Palme, Joakim (1990), *Pension Rights in Welfare Capitalism: The Development of Old-Age Pension in 18 OECD Countries, 1930 to 1985*, Swedish Institute for Social Research, Stockholm University: Stockholm

Pampel, Fred C. and Williamson, John B. (1989), *Age, Class, Politics, and the Welfare State*, Cambridge University Press: New York.

Parry, Geraint (1985), 'Welfare State and Welfare Society', *Government and Opposition*, Vol.20, No.3, pp.287-296.

Parsons, Talcott (1966), *Societies*, Prentice Hall: Englewood Cliffs.

Parsons, Talcott (1968), *The Structure of Social Action*, Free Press: New York.

Peterson, Wallace C. (1985), 'The US Welfare State and the Conservative Counterrevolution', *Journal of Economic Issues*, Vol.19, No.3, pp.601-641.

Poulantzas, Nicos (1973a), 'The Problem of the Capitalist State', in Urry, John and Wakeford, John (eds), *Power in Britain -- Sociological Readings*, Heinemann: London.

Poulantzas, Nicos (973b), *Political Power and Social Classes*, New Left Books: London.

Poulantzas, Nicos (1976), 'The Capitalist State: A Reply to Miliband and Laclau', *New Left Review*, Vol.65, No.1, pp.63-83.

Poulantzas, Nicos (1987), 'On Social Classes', in Giddens, A. and Held, D. (eds), *Classes, Power, and Conflict: Classical and Contemporary Debates*, Macmillan: London, pp.101-111.
Pryor, Frederick (1968), *Public Expenditure in Capitalist and Communist Nations*, Irwin: Homewood.
Pulkingham, Jane (1989), 'From Public Provision to Privatisation: The Crisis in Welfare Reassessed', *Sociology*, Vol.23, No.3, pp.387-407
Quadagno, Jill (1987), 'Theories of the Welfare State', *Annual Review of Sociology*, Vol.13, pp.109-128.
Rabushka, Alvin (1975), *Value for Money -- The Hong Kong Budgetary Process*, Hoover Institute Press: Stanford.
Richardson, J.J. and Jordan, G. (1979), *Governing Under Pressure*, Martin Robertson: Oxford.
Robertson, Alex (1988), 'Welfare State and Welfare Society', *Social Policy and Administration*, Vol.22, No.3, pp.222-234.
Rimlinger, Gaston V. (1971), *Welfare Policy and Industrialism in Europe, America and Russia*, Wiley: New York.
Rose, Richard (1983), *Getting by in the Three Economies:The Resources of the Official, Unofficial and Domestic Economies*, University of Strathclyde: Glasgow.
Salamon, Lester M. (1993), 'The Marketization of Welfare: Changing Nonprofit and For-profit Roles in the American Welfare State', *Social Service Review*, Vol.67, No.1, pp.16-39.
Samson, Colin (1994), 'The Three Faces of Privatisation', *Sociology*, Vol.28, No.1, pp.79-97.
Sankey, Colin (1993), 'Public Sector Reform in Hong Kong -- Recent Trends', *Hong Kong Public Administration*, Vol.2, No.1, pp.71-93.
Saunders, Peter (1979), *Urban Politics -- a sociological interpretation*, Penguin: Middlesex.
Saunders, Peter and Harris, Colin (1990), 'Privatization and the Consumer', *Sociology*, Vol.24, No.1, pp.57-75.
Schiffer, Jonathan R. (1991), 'State Policy and Economic Growth:a note on the Hong Kong Model', *International Journal of Urban and Regional Research*, Vol.15, No.2, pp.180-196.
Scott, Ian (1986), 'Policy-making in a Turbulent Environment: the case of Hong Kong', *International Review of Administrative Sciences*, Vol.52, No.4, pp.447-469.
Scott, Ian (1989), *Political Change and the Crisis of Legitimacy in Hong Kong*, Hurst and Company: London.
Scott, Ian and Cheek-Milby, Kathleen (1986), 'An Overview of Hong Kong's Social Policy Making Process', *Asian Journal of Public Administration*, Vol.8, No.2, pp.166-176.

Shalev, Michael (1983), 'The Social Democratic Model and Beyond: Two 'Generations' of Comparative Research on the Welfare State', *Comparative Social Research*, Vol.6, pp.315-351.

Silverman, David (1993), *Interpreting Qualitative Data -- Methods of Analysing Talk, Text and Interaction*, Sage: London.

Skocpol, Theda (1979), *States and Social Revolution:a comparative analysis of France, Russia and China*, Cambridge University Press: Cambirdge.

Skocpol, Theda (1980), 'Political Responses to Capitalist Crisis:Neo-Marxist Theories of the State and the Case of the New Deal', *Politics and Society*, Vol.10, No.2, pp.155-201.

Skocpol, Theda (1985), 'What is Happening to Western Welfare States?', *Contemporary Sociology*, Vol.14, No.3, pp.307-311.

Skocpol, Theda (1992), 'Bringing the State Back In: Strategies of Analysis in Current Research', in Evans, P.; Rueschemeyer, D. and Skocpol, T. (eds), *Bringing the State Back In*, Cambridge University Press: New York, pp. 3-43.

Skocpol, Theda and Amenta, Edwin (1986), 'State and Social Politics', *Annual Review of Sociology*, Vol.12, pp.131-157.

Skocpol, Theda and Ikenberry, John (1983), 'The Political Formation of the American Welfare State in Historical and Comparative Perspective', *Comparative Social Research*, Vol.6, pp.87-148.

Smelser, Neil J. (1964), 'Toward a Theory of Modernisation', in Etzioni, A. and Etzioni, E. (eds), *Social Change*, Basic Books: New York.

Starr, Paul (1987), 'The Limits of Privatization', in Henke, Steve (ed.), *Prospects for Privatization*, Academy of Political Science: Washington DC.

Starr, Paul (1989), 'The Meaning of Privatization', in Kahn, A.J. and Karmamen, S. (eds), *Privatization and the Welfare State*, Princeton University Press: New Jersey, pp.15-48.

Stephens, John D. (1979), *The Transition from Capitalism to Socialism*, University of Illinois Press: Urbana.

Strauss, Anselm and Corbin, Juliet (1990), *Basic of Qualitative Research: Grounded Theory Procedures and Techniques*, Sage: London.

Sung, Yan Wing (1984), 'Hong Kong's Economy is on the Door-step of Affluence', in Cheng, J.Y.S. (ed.), *A Collected Comments on Hong Kong's Economy, Politics and Society*, Tsun Shin Cultural Affairs Company: Hong Kong, pp. 3-8.

Taira, Koji and Kilby, Peter (1969), 'Differences in Social Security Development in Selected Countries', *International Social Security Review*, Vol.22, No.2, pp.139-153.

Tam, Y.Y.W. (1989), 'The Politics of the New Middle Class:a case study of this class in Hong Kong in relation to the democratic movement', unpublished MA Sociology dissertation, Department of Sociology, University of Essex: Colchester.

Tang, Shu Hung (1990), 'The Fiscal Policy of Hong Kong Government and the Development of Social Welfare', *Ming Pao Monthly Magazine*, May 1990, pp.10-15.

Tang, Shu Hung (1992), *Hong Kong Public Finance in Late Transistional Period*, Joint Publishing Company: Hong Kong.

Therborn, Goran (1978), *What does the ruling class do when it rules?*, New Left Books: London.

Therborn, Goran (1983), 'When, How and Why does a State become a Welfare State?', paper presented in the European Consortium of Political Research Workshop on 'Comparative Study of Distribution and Social Policy in Advanced Industrial Nations', Freiburg, Germany, March 20-25, 1983.

Therborn, Goran (1984a), 'Classes and States: welfare state developments, 1881-1981', *Studies in Political Economy*, Vol.14, pp.7-41.

Therborn, Goran (1984b), 'The Prospects of Labour and the Transformation of Advanced Capitalism', *New Left Review*, No.145.

Therborn, Goran (1986), 'Karl Marx Returning:The Welfare State and Neo-Marxist, Corporatist and Statist Theories', *International Political Science Review*, Vol.7, No.2, pp.131-164.

Therborn, Goran (1987), 'Welfare States and Capitalist Markets', *Acta Sociologica*, Vol.30, No.3 and 4, pp.237-254.

Thomas, George M. and Lauderdale, Pat (1987), 'World Polity Sources of National Welfare and Land Reform', in Thomas, G.M. et al, *Institutional Structures: constituting state, society, and the individual*, Sage: London.

Thomas, George M. and Lauderdale, Pat (1988), 'State Autonomy and National Welfare Programmes in the World System Context', *Sociological Forum*, Vol.3, No.3, pp.383-399.

Titmuss, Richard M. (1968), *Commitment to Welfare*, George Allen and Unwin: London.

Turner, H.A. (1980), *The Last Colony:But Whose? A Study of the Labour Movement, Labour Market and Labour Relations in Hong Kong*, Cambridge University Press: Cambridge.

United Nations (1991), *Compendium of Social Statistics and Indicators*, United Nations: New York.

Uusitalo, Hannu (1984), 'Comparative Research on the Determinants of the Welfare State: the State of the Art', *European Journal of Political Research*, Vol.12, pp.403-422.

Veljanovski, Cento (1988), *Selling the State: Privatisation in Britain*, Weidenfeld and Nicholson: London.

Vettenranta, Jari (1986), 'Restructuring Welfare Policy by Means of Privatization', *Acta Sociologica*, Vol.29, No.3, pp.255-264.

Vickers, John and Wright, Vincent (eds) (1989), *The Politics of Industrial Privatisation in Western Europe*, Frank Cass: London.

Walker, Alan (1983), 'Social Policy, Social Administration and the Social Construction of Welfare', in Loney, M.; Boswell, D. and Clarke, J. (eds), *Social Policy and Social Welfare*, Open University Press: Milton Keynes, pp.127-150.

Walker, Alan (1984), 'Political Economy of Privatization', in Le Grand, J. and Robinson, R. (eds), *Privatisation and the Welfare State*, George Allen and Unwin: London.

Walker, Alan (1987), 'The Future of the British Welfare State:Privatisation or Socialisation?', in Evers, A.; Nowotny, H. and Wintersberger, H. (eds), *The Changing Face of Welfare*, Gower: Cambridge.

Waters, Malcolm (1994), *Modern Sociological Theory*, Sage: London.

Weed, Frank J. (1979), 'Industrialization and Welfare System: a critique of the convergence hypothesis', *International Journal of Comparative Sociology*, Vol.20, No.3-4, pp.282-292.

Weir, Margaret and Skocpol, Theda (1983), 'State Structures and Social Keynesianism -- responses to the Great Depression in Sweden and the United States', *International Journal of Comparative Sociology*, Vol.24, No.1-2, pp.4-29.

Wetherly, Paul (1988), 'Class Struggle and the Welfare State: Some Theoretical Problems Considered', *Critical Social Policy*, Vol.8, No.1, pp.24-40.

Wilensky, Harold L. (1975), *The Welfare State and Equality:structural and ideological roots of public expenditures*, University of California Press: Berkeley.

Wilensky, Harold L. (1981), 'Leftism, Catholicism, and Democratic Corporatism: The Role of Political Parties in Recent Welfare State Development', in Flora, P. and Heidenheimer, A.J. (eds), *The Development of Welfare States in Europe and America,* Transaction Books: Princeton, pp.345-382.

Wilensky, Harold L. and Lebeaux, Charles N. (1958), *Industrial Society and Social Welfare*, Free Press: New York.

Wilensky, Harold L.; Luebbert, Gregory M.; Hahn, Susan R. and Jamieson, Adrienne M. (1987), 'Comparative Social Policy: theories, methods, findings', in Dierkes, M. et al (eds), *Comparative Policy Research: learning from experience*, Gower: Alderhsot.

Wong, Chack Kie (1989), *Social Action and Hong Kong*, Ching Man Bookshop: Hong Kong.

Wong, Cheong Wing (1992), *Towards a Recommodification of Medical Care: The Case of Hong Kong*, Department of Social Work, Hong Kong Baptist College: Hong Kong.

Wong Chong Hei (1982), 'Who are influencing Hong Kong Education Policy?', in Hong Kong Federation of Students and Chinese University of Hong Kong Students Union (eds), *Seeing Through Education in Hong Kong*, Wide-Angle Publisher: Hong Kong, pp.281-286.

Wong, Siu Lun (1992), 'Emigration and Stability in Hong Kong', *Asian Survey*, Vol.32, No.10, pp.918-933.

Yeung, Wai Tsang (1985), 'To Speed Up the Redistribution Process to Achieve a Justice Society', in Wong, W et al (eds), *The Challenge of Social Work in Hong Kong (3rd ed.)*, Writers and Publishers Cooperative: Hong Kong, pp.81-94.

Yeung, Wai Tsang (1987), 'Approaching to a Fair Social Policy', in Ngan, Raymond M.H. et al (eds), *A Resonance to Social Policy in Hong Kong*, Writers and Publishers Cooperative: Hong Kong, pp.49-65.

Yeung, Sum (1987), 'An Analysis of Education Policy', in Ngan, Raymond M.H. et al (eds), *A Resonance to Hong Kong Social Policy*, Writers and Publishers Cooperative: Hong Kong, pp.193-207.

Yin, R.K. (1984), *Case Study Research: Design and Methods*, Sage: London.

Youngson, A.J. (1982), *Hong Kong:Economic Growth and Policy*, Oxford University Press: Hong Kong.

Government documents / publications

Census and Statistics Department (1978), *Hong Kong Annual Digest of Statistics*, Hong Kong Government Printer: Hong Kong.

Census and Statistics Department (1981), *Hong Kong Annual Digest of Statistics*, Hong Kong Government Printer: Hong Kong.

Census and Statistics Department (1983), *Hong Kong Annual Digest of Statistics*, Hong Kong Government Printer: Hong Kong.

Census and Statistics Department (1985), *Hong Kong Social and Economic Trends, 1974 - 1984*, Hong Kong Government Printer: Hong Kong.

Census and Statistics Department (1986), *Hong Kong Annual Digest of Statistics*, Hong Kong Government Printer: Hong Kong.

Census and Statistics Department (1987), *Hong Kong Social and Economic Trends, 1976 - 1986*, Hong Kong Government Printer: Hong Kong.

Census and Statistics Department (1989), *Hong Kong Social and Economic Trends, 1978 - 1988*, Hong Kong Government Printer: Hong Kong.
Census and Statistics Department (1991), *Hong Kong Social and Economic Trends, 1980 - 1990*, Hong Kong Government Printer: Hong Kong.
Census and Statistics Department (1992a), *Hong Kong Monthly Digest of Statistics (Nov 1992)*, Hong Kong Government Printer: Hong Kong.
Census and Statistics Department (1992b), *Hong Kong Annual Digest of Statistics (1992 Edition)*, Hong Kong Government Printer: Hong Kong.
Census and Statistics Department (1993), *Hong Kong Social and Economic Trends, 1982 - 1992*, Hong Kong Government Printer: Hong Kong.
Education Department (1971), *Departmental Annual Report, 1970/71*, Hong Kong Government Printer: Hong Kong.
Home Affairs Branch (1980), Information Paper for Chief Secretary Committee Monitoring of Pressure Group Activities, mimeograph, April 11, 1980.
Hong Kong Government, *Hong Kong Annual Report*, Hong Kong Government Printer: Hong Kong, various year.
Hong Kong Government (1965), *Education Policy*, Hong Kong Government Printer: Hong Kong.
Hong Kong Government (1967a), *Kowloon Disturbances 1966, Report of Commissin of Inquiry*, Hong Kong Government Printer: Hong Kong.
Hong Kong Government (1967b), *Report of the Working Party on Local Administration*, Hong Kong Government Printer: Hong Kong.
Hong Kong Government (1967c), *A Report by the Inter-Department Working Party to Consider Certain Aspects of Scoial Security*, Hong Kong Government Printer: Hong Kong.
Hong Kong Government (1973a), *Social Welfare: the Way Ahead*, Hong Kong Government Printer: Hong Kong.
Hong Kong Government (1973b), *Care in the Community: The Right Basis for Services to the Elderly*, Hong Kong Government Printer: Hong Kong.
Hong Kong Government (1973c), *Report of the Board of Education on the Proposed Expansion of Secondary Education -- Green Paper*, Hong Kong Government Printer: Hong Kong.
Hong Kong Government (1974a), *Future Development of Medical and Health Services in Hong Kong -- White Paper*, Hong Kong Government Printer: Hong Kong.
Hong Kong Government (1974b), *Secondary Education in Hong Kong Over the Next Decade -- White Paper*, Hong Kong Government Printer: Hong Kong.
Hong Kong Government (1977a), *Services for the Elderly, a Green Paper*, Hong Kong Government Printer: Hong Kong.

Hong Kong Government (1977b), *Integrating the Disabled into the Community: A United Effort*, Hong Kong Government Printer: Hong Kong.
Hong Kong Government (1979), *Social Welfare into the 1980s, a White Paper*, Hong Kong Government Printer: Hong Kong.
Hong Kong Government (1981), *White Paper -- District Administration in Hong Kong*, Hong Kong Government Printer: Hong Kong.
Hong Kong Government (1982), *A Perspective on Education of Hong Kong (Llewellyn Report)*, Hong Kong Government Printer: Hong Kong
Hong Kong Government (1984a), *Green Paper -- The Future Development of Representative Government in Hong Kong*, Hong Kong Government Printer: Hong Kong.
Hong Kong Government (1984b), *White Paper -- Development of Representative Government*, Hong Kong Government Printer: Hong Kong.
Hong Kong Government (1987a), *Long Term Housing Strategy -- a policy statement*, Hong Kong Government Printer: Hong Kong.
Hong Kong Government (1987b), *Review of the Long Term Housing Strategy*, Hong Kong Government Printer: Hong Kong.
Hong Kong Government (1989), *Public Sector Reform*, Hong Kong Government: Hong Kong.
Hong Kong Government (1991a), *Social Welfare into the 1990s and Beyond*, Hong Kong Government Printer: Hong Kong.
Hong Kong Government (1991b), *The Five Year Plan for Social Welfare Development in Hong Kong -- Review 1991*, Hong Kong Government Printer: Hong Kong.
Hong Kong Government (1992), *Green Paper by the Working Party on Rehabilitation Policies and Services on Equal Opportunities and Full Participation: a better tomorrow for all*, Hong Kong Government Printer: Hong Kong.
Hong Kong Government (1993), *Towards Better Health -- a consultative document*, Hong Kong Government Printer: Hong Kong.
Hong Kong Housing Authority (1984), *Public Housing Allocation Policy Review: consultative document*, Hong Kong Housing Authority: Hong Kong.
Hong Kong Housing Authority (1985), *Green Paper: Housing Subsidy to Tenants of Public Housing*, Hong Kong Housing Authority: Hong Kong.
Hong Kong Housing Authority (1986), *Report of the Domestic Rent Policy Review Committee*, Hong Kong Housing Authority: Hong Kong.
Hong Kong Housing Authority (1990), *Report of the Ad Hoc Committee on Sale of Flats to Sitting Tenants*, Hong Kong Housing Authority: Hong Kong.

Hong Kong Housing Authority (1992), *Committee on Review of the Subsidy Policy for Public Housing Tenants -- consultative document*, Hong Kong Housing Authority: Hong Kong.
Hong Kong Housing Authority, *Annual Reports,* Hong Kong Housing Authority: Hong Kong, various years.
Provisional Hospital Authority (1989), *Report of the Provisional Hospital Authority*, Hong Kong Government Printer: Hong Kong.
W.D. Scott Pty. Company (1985), *The Delivery of Medical Services in Hospitals*, Hong Kong Government Printer: Hong Kong.

Newspaper

Hong Kong Economic Journal
Ming Pao
Sing Tao Jih Pao (*Sing Tao Daily News*)
South China Morning Post
Star

Magazine

Far East Economic Review
Hong Kong Economic Journal (Monthly Magazine)
Ming Pao Monthly Magazine
Pao Shing Semi-Monthly Magazine
Wide-Angle Monthly Magazine